FROMMER'S

ATHENS

JOHN MACNEILL

D0638923

□

1989–1990

Published by Prentice Hall Trade Division
A Division of Simon & Schuster, Inc.
Gulf + Western Building
One Gulf + Western Plaza
New York, NY 10023

ISBN 0-13-047606-4
ISSN 0899-2924

Manufactured in the United States of America

Text Design: Levavi & Levavi, Inc.

CONTENTS

MAPS

INFLATION ALERT. It is hardly a secret that a wave of inflation has battered the countries of Europe, and Greece has not escaped. The author of this book has made every effort to ensure the accuracy of prices appearing in this guide. As we go to press, we believe we have obtained the most reliable data possible as of summer 1988. However, we cannot offer guarantees for the tariffs quoted, and so in the lifetime of this edition—especially its second year, 1990—the wise traveler will add 15% to 20% to the prices quoted.

THE DOLLAR AND THE DRACHMA. Where currency conversions from drachmas to dollars appear in parentheses on these pages, they were prepared on the basis of 130 drachmas = $1, generally rounded off to the nearest dollar. That rate may not be accurate by the time you travel, as it varies from day to day, depending on the relative values of both currencies on world markets. Use these currency conversions, therefore, only as a gauge for what you'll be spending and check with a banker before you leave for Greece to determine what the actual rate of exchange is at that time.

CHAPTER I

THE GREEK IN ALL OF US

□ □ □

Greece is the cradle of civilization, the origin of the West, the birthplace of democracy . . . etcetera, etcetera. That gets the clichés out of the way. Nevertheless, it's hard to imagine what civilized life would be like today without the influence of Ancient Greece. The Greeks invented drama, and amphitheaters to perform it in. They invented the Olympic Games. Euclid and Pythagoras formulated the theories geometry students slave over to this day. And there isn't a computer programmer who hasn't studied the logic of Aristotle. Ancient Greece created a style of architecture that was the model for the White House, the Lincoln Memorial, and state capitols all across the land. Doctors still take the Hippocratic Oath, named for the father of medicine—a Greek, of course. Children learn about the ant and the grasshopper and other characters from the fables of Aesop. And Greek myths have become so interwoven with our civilized consciousness that we sometimes forget where they came from. Oedipus, after all, was a Greek, not a character living in Freud's Vienna.

And then there's the Greek language. It doesn't exactly sound like poetry when spoken in the streets of Athens, but what a debt we owe it! Sophisticated, metropolitan, aristocratic, philanthropy, gymnastics, pornographic—are all from the Greek. Even a "modern" word like ecology comes from the Greek words *oikos,* meaning house, and *logos,* meaning word or thought.

The mighty Romans, conquerors of almost the entire ancient world, were so awed by the accomplishments of Ancient Greece that they copied its art, its architecture, and in general acted as if they had been conquered by the Greeks rather than the other way around. Perhaps in a way they were. Perhaps in a way we *all* were.

CHAPTER II

A REFRESHER COURSE IN GREEK HISTORY

□ □ □

Ancient Greece, rather than modern Greece, is what brings most visitors to Athens (the Greek islands are something else again), and since you're going to be looking at quite a lot of ruins you might as well take a quick refresher course in Minoans, Mycenaeans, and Macedonians. After all, the more you remember, the more you'll enjoy.

THE BULL DANCERS: Around 3000 B.C., the most ancient civilization of Greece began to flourish. The **Minoan** civilization of Crete is one of the oldest civilizations in Greek history, and this civilization, with Crete at its center, lasted almost 2,000 years.

The Minoans were generally peace-loving people. They lived in cities without protective walls, and they were never invaded. They were an artistic people, but didn't develop a script until some time around 1700 B.C. Their art, which you can still see in some of the ruins at Knossos in Crete, was colorful and sunny—red columns and sky-blue temple walls.

One of their favorite pastimes was bull jumping (the bull dancers would grab the bull's horns and flip themselves over its back, etc.), a sport that makes today's bullfighting look like a sheepdog trial. Bulls, in fact, were a key part of the culture, and were worshipped by the Minoans. The most famous bull of all, the Minotaur, was a creature with a bull's head and a human body, the mythological offspring of a bull sent from the sea as a sign to prove

King Minos's right to the throne of Crete. Unfortunately, when the king refused to sacrifice the bull to the god Poseidon, his queen was cursed with a passion for it. Her child, the Minotaur, was then imprisoned by King Minos in the center of the Labyrinth, a maze so convoluted no one could reach the center to kill it and thus free the people from the influence of the monster. Except the great Theseus, of course, but even he couldn't kill the Minotaur without the help of Minos's daughter, Ariadne. We'll come back to Theseus in a minute.

THE FAMILY THAT SLAYS TOGETHER . . . : On mainland Greece the first civilization you have to contend with is the **Mycenaean,** which started to make its presence felt about 1400 B.C. It was focused on the city of Mycenae, about 25 miles from Corinth in the region known as the Peloponnese. Mycenae was the home of that happy family headed by Agamemnon, who was put to death by his wife, Clytemnestra, and her lover, who in turn were wiped out by her son, Orestes, at the instigation of her daughter, Electra. The Trojan War was launched from here.

Then about 1100 B.C., a people called the Dorians invaded Mycenae and other cities of Greece and crushed them. Almost overnight, the great "palace bureaucracies" disappeared, and the Greeks were reduced to small, illiterate communities. This was the Dark Age of Greece.

THE YARN SPINNERS: Throughout history the Greeks have been nothing if not hardy, and at this time they began to develop the *polis* that was to become the central political unit in the upcoming classical period. The polis was a cluster of houses around a "palace" that stood on a safe hill, called an *akropolis,* and its inhabitants usually had a common family relationship. Apart from that, they had nothing—no culture, no literature, only memories of past glories. So they got together on their akropolis and consoled themselves by singing songs and reciting poetry extolling the heroism of their ancestors. Two of these songs were the *Iliad* and the *Odyssey.* No one knows for sure in what form Homer learned the legends he wrote about in the *Iliad,* but no matter how he received them he handed the legends along in a great new art form that excites scholars to this day.

Around this time, 800 B.C., the Greeks came into contact with the Phoenicians, who did have an alphabet and knew how to put things in writing; so the Greeks adapted it, just in time for Homer to polish up his spoken poetry and get it down on stone.

THE SPARTANS: Slowly, aristocracy began replacing monarchy (except in Sparta and Macedonia); trade was flourishing, slavery increasing, and coined money was introduced to simplify trading throughout the entire Mediterranean. Revolutionaries came along, roused the slaves, and overthrew governments—except in Sparta, where two kings ruled, and reared their people to live frugally (hence the word "spartan") and to cultivate physical discipline. From the age of seven, Spartan youths were given military training. All men of military age lived in barracks and were not allowed to live with their wives until they were 30. Thus, when any revolutionary tried to start anything in Sparta, he was quickly put down by the militaristic establishment.

THESEUS RIDES AGAIN: The scene now shifts to Attica, which is the part of mainland Greece where Athens, and several other small independent cities, were located. These city-states were being united by King Theseus (this is the same Theseus who penetrated the Labyrinth and killed the Minotaur—the Minoan civilization was still there all this time). No sooner had Theseus finished with the Minotaur than he was off battling the Centaurs. Somewhere along the way he became king of Athens, married an Amazon, conquered Thebes, and united Attica.

Sometime around 621 B.C. a legislator named Draco appeared on the Athenian scene and codified laws that substituted public justice for personal revenge, and thus outlawed the feuds that were a popular Greek pastime. His laws were so severe that the legislator has been immortalized by the word "draconian." The laws were said to be written in blood rather than ink, because he rewarded many types of crime (such as stealing a cabbage!) with the death penalty. These laws held for only a quarter of a century until Solon, who came to be called the founder of Athenian democracy, abolished the death penalty for everything but murder. Solon also instituted constitutional reforms that set up free elections and brought all classes (except slaves) into the process of government. And so democracy began.

MARATHON AND SALAMIS: A hundred years later democracy and everything else Greece had built up were threatened by Persia. The first of Persia's expeditions took place in 490 B.C., when its army arrived at Marathon. This was the event where a Greek soldier ran the 26 miles back to Athens, managed to gasp "We have won," then collapsed and died. In their second expedition the Persians were matched by the genius of Themistocles, an Athenian leader who made his people nervous by going out and building a huge fleet rather than an army. However, he turned out to be right: the Persians were blasted off the sea at the battle of Salamis. When the Greeks and their Spartan allies turned to the attack on land at the pass of Thermopylae, they trapped the Persians for four days. But the Persians eventually gained the upper hand, and rather than retreat, the Spartans remained and died to the last man. A Greek poet composed one of history's most famous epitaphs for them: "Stranger, go tell the Spartans that here we lie in obedience to their wishes."

THE GOLDEN AGE: Athens, now a naval power, was headed for its golden age. Its ruler at this time (the middle of the 5th century B.C.) was **Pericles,** the most dazzling orator in a city of dazzling orators. He practiced democracy at home, imperialism abroad. One of his wisest decisions was to pay jurors, so that even the poorest citizens could sit on juries. One of his not-so-smart decisions was to restrict Athenian citizenship to people whose mother and father were both Athenians. This would have been fine if he hadn't at that time fallen under the spell of Aspasia. Aspasia had been born in Mileta but had migrated to Athens because that was where the action was in those days; she quickly established herself as a beautiful and intelligent courtesan, who taught rhetoric on the side. One of her students was Socrates, and another was Pericles. Pericles took her as his mistress and promptly divorced his wife, but he couldn't marry Aspasia because of the new law he himself had brought into being. So they lived together. Aspasia became the uncrowned queen of Athens, and their son was later honored with citizenship by a special act of the Athenians. Aspasia was later condemned to death for impiety, a trumped-up charge, and Pericles had to muster all his dazzling oratory to save her. It was Pericles who built the Parthenon, the Propylaea, the long walls to Piraeus, and many of the temples you'll see on your strolls around town. This was quite a time in Athens. Aspasia was right—Athens was *the* place. While Pericles was building his Parthenon, Aeschylus, Sophocles, and Euripides were writing their plays, and Socrates and Plato were teaching. But Sparta was smoldering with jealousy and became increasingly worried about Athens's imperialistic policies.

Now we get involved with another series of wars. Or rather one long, lingering, 27-year war—the **Peloponnesian War.** Pericles led Athens, avoiding battles on land, attacking the Peloponnese from the sea, because Athens ruled the waves. Pericles, unfortunately, saw only two years of the war—he died of a plague which struck Athens in 429 B.C. A host of demagogues and lesser leaders followed, who eventually brought Athens to defeat in 404

B.C. But victorious Sparta's influence lasted only 30 years after; it was then superseded by Macedonia, a kingdom in the north of Greece.

THE PRINCE AND THE HORSE: Philip of Macedon's ambition was to unify all of Greece, restore Greek culture to Macedon, and eliminate Persia as a lingering threat. But before he could do that, he too divorced his wife, who thereupon hatched a plot and had him assassinated because she was jealous of his new consort. His nephew was next in line to the throne, but the crown went instead to his first wife's son, **Alexander.** One of the first legends about Alexander began when he fulfilled an oracle's prediction by succeeding in mounting a high-spirited horse named Bucephalus. Philip had intended to destroy this horse because he was unmountable, but the clever Alexander noticed that the problem with Bucephalus was that he was literally afraid of his own shadow; so Alexander turned the horse's eyes into the sun and mounted. At the age of 20, Alexander became king, and Bucephalus would soon carry him across an empire.

ALEXANDER THE GREAT: Alexander, as you know, conquered Greece, united it against Persia, then marched his armies across continents, conquering Asia Minor, Syria, Egypt, Babylon, Susa, Persepolis. He was on his way to conquer India when his troops finally became so exhausted they compelled him to return to Macedon. He was a humane man (he had studied under Aristotle), who maintained the civil liberties of all the peoples he conquered, honored their gods and their customs. He even went so far as to adopt one Oriental custom for himself, and married several Eastern princesses. In 323 B.C. Alexander the Great caught a fever and died. He had lived an extraordinary life, and died when only in his early 30s.

Alexander's death marked the end of the great classical period of Greece—in literature, philosophy, and art. The city-states withered, the upper classes took over, and there was constant bickering and battling until 146 B.C. when Greece was conquered by the powerful and indomitable armies of Rome.

CENTURIONS AND CHRISTIANS: Although the Romans, as we noted earlier, admired the art and culture of Greece, they had no respect at all for its countryside. Rather than fight all their battles on Roman soil, they tended to move them to neutral territory. Mark Antony and Octavius fought it out with Brutus and Cassius in Greece, at Philippi; Octavian then routed Antony and turned back Cleopatra's ships in Greek waters.

For 500 years, right through the early era of Christianity, Greece was subject to the power of Rome. It also became a stronghold of Christianity. Saint Paul preached in Greek, and his famous epistles were written to the Greek communities of Corinth, Thessaloniki, and Ephesus.

For most practical purposes the history of classical Greece ends at this point. Tourists come to Greece mainly to see the remains of the classical ruins, and to relive the days of glory of Pericles and the Athenians. That's what Greece is all about. Obviously, though, its history continues, and there are many people who want to see the country's examples of Byzantine art and culture (which you'll read about next)—but that's not the essential Greece. From the time of Saint Paul and the Apostles, the history of Greece is a chronicle of sieges, battles, and struggles to regain independence. The struggle was heroic enough but it lacked the grandeur of Ancient Greece. Or maybe they just didn't have a Homer to glorify it.

BYZANTIUM: In A.D. 330 the Roman emperor Constantine chose a fishing village on the Bosporus, the channel leading to the Black Sea, to be his eastern capital. He named it Constantinople. Eventually it became the capital of its own empire, the Byzantine, and managed to resist invasions and maintain its hold on the Balkan Peninsula, Asia Minor, Cyprus, the Middle East, and Egypt. Rome at the time was slowly succumbing to invasions of barbarians. Greece was a mere province.

For many hundreds of years, Byzantium was the only civilized part of Europe. Art, especially religious art, flourished, and churches, monasteries, and palaces were going up everywhere. Then the Eastern and Western churches separated; Venetians, Franks, and soldiers from other countries in Western Europe formed their crusades and pillaged Constantinople. The city eventually fell to the Ottoman Turks, Greece was reduced to an even more insignificant province, and Athens became a small town. The Parthenon was turned into a Turkish mosque.

For the next 400 years Greece remained under Turkish rule. In the early 1600s Venice tried to move in, without success (although you can still see the Venetian influence in places like Corfu). In the early 1800s the Greeks started to muster groups of revolutionaries, and in March 1821 they formally began their struggle for independence when an archbishop raised a new blue-and-white flag at a monastery near Patras. (The date, March 25, is now Greek Independence Day.)

This was the period when Lord Byron and other volunteers rallied to the Greek cause. Byron died at Missolonghi in 1824, but

A READY REFERENCE FOR ANCIENT GREEK HISTORY

Period	Approx. dates	Key events and people
Minoan	3000 to 1400 B.C.	Knossos (Crete) King Minos The Minotaur Theseus
Mycenaean	1400 to 1150 B.C.	Agamemnon Jason and the Argonauts Achilles Troy
Dark Age	1200 to 1100 B.C.	
Aristocratic Age	800 to 600 B.C.	Athens unites with towns of Attica Draco proclaims severe laws Solon reforms constitution Homer composes the *Iliad* and the *Odyssey*
Persian Wars	520 to 480 B.C.	Themistocles fortifies Piraeus Greeks win at Marathon and Salamis Aeschylus wins Athens drama festival
Classical Age	480 to 430 B.C.	Parthenon built Pericles in power Aeschylus, Sophocles, and Euripides at work
Peloponnesian War	430 to 400 B.C.	Naval battle of Syracuse Erechtheum on Acropolis completed Aristophanes writes comedies Pericles dies Socrates drinks hemlock Sparta triumphs
Macedonian Age	360 B.C. to 300 B.C.	Alexander the Great conquers Aristotle founds school
Roman	200 B.C. to A.D. 300	Rome sacks Corinth
Byzantine	A.D. 300 to 1200	Constantine builds Constantinople Crusaders build forts, sack Constantinople

in the end, with the help of Britain, Russia, and France, Greece finally defeated the Turks in a spectacular sea battle off the Bay of Navarino—spectacular and extraordinary because the Turks lost 53 ships with 6,000 men on board but the allied fleet didn't lose a single vessel.

INDEPENDENCE, DEFEAT, INDEPENDENCE: In 1829 the "protecting powers" declared Greece an independent nation. Unfortunately, they couldn't agree among themselves on territorial and legal conditions (some of these problems remain undecided to this day). A year later Greece became a kingdom; a 17-year-old Bavarian prince was named to the throne, Prince Otto (or Othon). He lasted until 1862, when he was replaced by the Danish ruling house. Thessaly, Macedonia, and Thrace meantime remained under Ottoman rule, but after the Balkan War of 1912–1913 they became part of Greece, leaving Turkey with only the eastern half of Thrace, including Constantinople (which was then renamed Istanbul). We can leave Greek history there, at least until October 28, 1940, when an emissary from Mussolini demanded that the Greek-Albanian border be opened to Italian troops. The Greek patriot, General Metaxas, replied "Ohi," or no, and thereby brought Greece into World War II. (October 28 is now celebrated as Ohi Day.) Greece was invaded by the Nazis, freed by its own Resistance and the Allies, and settled down once more to the intramural squabbles characterizing the period. Greece is now a republic, with a democratically elected parliament, prime minister, and president; it is a full-fledged, albeit sometimes cantankerous, member of the North Atlantic Treaty Organization and the European Common Market.

Regimes may come and regimes may flounder, but the glory that was Greece remains. Or as Pericles once said, "Future ages will wonder at us, as the present age wonders at us now."

CHAPTER III

MOUNTAINS, ISLANDS, AND RUINS

□ □ □

An Outline of Modern Greece

On a map, Greece looks almost like an inkblot that landed in one large glob and burst into a score of splotches. The glob is the mainland, the splotches the islands. The total land area of Greece is 51,182 square miles—roughly the size of Louisiana. One-quarter of this area is islands, the remainder is mountains. The island quarter I leave to later chapters in this guide; right now let's examine the three-quarters that make up the land mass.

It's a complicated land, so let's begin by dividing it, like Gaul, into three parts: the Olympian north, central Greece, and the Peloponnese.

THE OLYMPIAN NORTH: This region includes Epirus, Thessaly, Macedonia, and Thrace. Mount Olympus, the dwelling place of the gods, is up there; so is Mount Athos, with its famous monastery. Thessaly is considered the breadbasket of Greece, supplying most of its wheat, corn, barley, and cotton.

CENTRAL GREECE: This region can be subdivided into six areas—Aetolia, Acarnania, Phthiotis, Phocis, Boeotia, and Attica. The first four names you can forget for the moment, but Attica is the land around Athens (you'll probably be seeing quite a bit of it), and Boeotia is where you'll find Delphi of oracle fame.

THE PELOPONNESE: To the southwest is a peninsula known as the Peloponnese, which can almost be considered an island since the completion of the Corinth canal which separates it from central Greece. The canal, incidentally, was begun by Nero, way back then, but not completed in its present form until 1893. It's a spectacular tourist sight in its own right.

The Peloponnese is where you find such haunts of the ancient Greeks as Corinth, Mycenae, Epidaurus, Olympia, and Sparta, 4,000 years of history, and mountains rising to almost 8,000 feet.

THE COUNTRYSIDE: Greece is a land of bleached limestone ridges, brown hills, olive groves, and an incredible collection of bays and coves lapped by green and turquoise seas. In the north, Greece is cut off from Albania, Yugoslavia, and Bulgaria by mountains; in the west, she's isolated by the Ionian Sea; in the south, by the Mediterranean; and in the east, by the Aegean. Because of the mountains and valleys, communities have historically been cut off from each other and have tended to retain their own individual characteristics, and Greeks still tend to identify themselves as Cretans, Athenians, Rhodians, and so forth. This individuality has helped make the country's folk art and folklore so varied and fascinating.

All the groups still retain their rivalries, as you'll find out if you go to a taverna and the singer announces a song from beautiful Thessaloniki (cheers!), then a song from beautiful Rhodes (hurrahs!), and a song from Macedonia (whistles!). The most reliable, charming, tolerant, intelligent of these groups is the one you happen to be talking to at a particular time.

GREEK HOSPITALITY: Over all, however, the Greeks are a lively, friendly, fun-loving, sometimes exuberant, people. And Greek is the only language in the world in which the word for stranger is also the word for guest—*xenos*. They take a great delight in the fact that so many tourists appreciate their country, and a great pride in their country, its heritage, and its ruined symbols of glory.

Hospitality has always been an admirable Greek trait. From the fishing families who open their homes to tourists on the islands (it's more than that they can use the money) to the hotel clerk who acts like he's always known you, the Greek actually seems to like visitors.

Perhaps it's because Herodotus, one of the first world travelers, was so tolerant of other races, and because for centuries Greeks have roamed the world and come back home to settle with a less

GREECE, THE ISLANDS, AND AEGEAN TURKEY

insular view of things than many other nations. (In almost every small village there's a local Greek-American—an older man who spent his youth in the U.S., made his "fortune," and came back to settle and be the ultimate arbiter of all arguments about that country and its doings. Sometimes he's living on monthly Social Security checks.)

But perhaps it's nothing more than the innate native sense of drama—the opportunity to take the stage at somebody else's prompting. To any Greek all the world's a stage, just as it always has been—especially the marketplace, the main square, or the cafés along the harbor.

Stop and ask for directions in the street and everybody gathers around and puts in their two-bits' worth. At last, weary of making yourself understood or getting any uniformity out of the replies, you walk away and leave the discussion. When you look back, they're still arguing.

Friendliness, in short, is a characteristic, and you'll often encounter the all-purpose greeting *Yiasu!* (good health) spoken by people you don't know. *Kalimera* (good morning) and *kalispera* (good evening) are useful greetings to sprinkle around too.

The Greek government also is trying to be friendly, and has launched an all-out drive to attract tourists. It's done a lot to make them welcome. Overseas, it has opened new offices to tell people about Greece, and has stocked the offices with lavishly enticing brochures. In Greece, it has streamlined arrival and Customs facilities, put up hotels where they were needed, built new highways to get you to the new hotels. The tourists responded. By 1985, seven million visitors a year (almost half a million of them Americans) were trudging through the archeological sites or cruising through the islands. But because of troubles (primarily fear of terrorism) largely beyond the control of hoteliers and tour operators, visits by Americans took a nose-dive in 1986. Three of the city's long-established hotels closed, cruise ships sailed off from the Aegean Sea to the climatically chillier but politically warmer seas off Alaska. The Europeans, the Japanese, and the Australians, however, kept coming to view the antiquities, and by 1988 things were more or less back to normal. The cruise ships returned—and *some* good came out of the slump. For one thing, owners of some of the moderately priced hotels got out their paint brushes and hammers and fixed up their hotels (a task they had somehow overlooked when the going was good); and the unaccustomed need to *woo* visitors instead of just catering to them may be goading owners and managers into improving service and facilities.

This trend to better service had better continue for a few more years or Greece may find itself in trouble again: membership in the European Common Market has led to a steady increase in prices, and inflation is now a real problem (the government claims it's 14%, the gossip in the cafés has it nearer to 30%). While Athens is still less expensive than Paris or London, it's no longer the delectable bargain it was only a few years ago; and while a mediocre taverna meal is probably acceptable when it costs only a few bucks, when the prices get up around $10 and $12, visitors are going to want more than slapdash service and food.

Regardless of the outcome of inflation, political ineptness, or whatever, there is no question that the Acropolis and Delphi, Epidaurus and Mycenae, Corfu and Crete will continue to exert their mystical pull on the rest of the world. And in a world where tourists constantly have to worry about mayhem and muggings, Greece is refreshing because it's a country where you rarely have to worry about crime. Maybe a little fiddling with a bill now and again, or an improperly adjusted taxi meter, but nothing that's going to cause you to waste half your vacation sitting in the American consulate's office or a police station.

CHAPTER IV

THE ACROPOLIS— AND THE CITY AT ITS FEET

□ □ □

Getting to Know Athens

Everyone's image of Athens is a white, rocky hill with a ruined, but glorious, temple on top. Or maybe a soldier in a skirt with pompoms on his shoes. But your first impression of Athens will be nothing like that.

Your introduction to Athens is a marble parthenon of the 20th century—a gleaming, elegant airport terminal that puts you in the atmosphere of a big, modern, successful city.

On your ride in from the airport you pass through disheveled suburbs of two-story white houses, past women dressed in black, and despite the alien but unmistakable injunction to drink Coca-Cola you're left with no doubt that you're now in a Mediterranean country.

When you get to your hotel in the heart of the city, you're in a sophisticated European city of avenues, jewelry shops, spacious squares, and terrace cafés.

Step a few streets from this chic city and you're treading in the marbled steps of Aristotle, Pericles, and Sophocles.

In other words, there's no point in trying to put Athens into any kind of category. It's unique. It's a city where you brush shoulders with Ancient Greece, Rome, Sparta, Macedonia, Byzantium, the East, the West, Venice, Germany, France, Italy, America. They've all left their imprint, and what you're treated to is a fascinating, intriguing, unbelievably historic, but not particularly beautiful city.

Let's pinpoint it. Athens is roughly on the same latitude as Louisville (Kentucky), San Francisco, and Tokyo. Its climate is considered mild, and probably is except when you're trudging around town looking for a hotel at high noon in August. Rainfall is a skimpy 15 inches a year, most of it in short showers in winter (if it rains in summer before the last week of August, it's news). June, July, August, and September are hot, but bearable because the air is so dry. On the other hand, don't try to fit in half a dozen temples between noon and 2 p.m.; try to confine your sightseeing to the early morning or late afternoon. In winter, specifically January and February, things can get a little chilly. The cafés and tavernas move indoors, and occasionally you may have to hold on tight for fear of being blown off the Acropolis.

ATHENS: AVERAGE MONTHLY TEMPERATURES (Fahrenheit)

	Low	High		Low	High
January	45.0	56.3	July	73.6	90.1
February	44.6	57.7	August	73.8	90.1
March	47.7	61.9	September	68.0	83.8
April	53.4	68.7	October	60.6	75.4
May	60.8	75.9	November	52.0	66.6
June	68.5	84.2	December	48.2	59.5

But all the statistics in the weather bureau will never do justice to the Athenian evenings. The air is soft, scented, seductive, scintillating—even alliteration doesn't do it justice, although, to be frank, in recent years it has become less seductive with the increasing hours of *nefos,* or smog, a frequent topic of discussion in the cafés these days.

GETTING THERE

BY AIR: TWA and Olympic Airways, the Greek national carrier, fly daily nonstops to Athens from New York's JFK. In addition, TWA flies direct (that is, without change of plane but not necessarily nonstop) flights from several other cities in the USA. From Canada, there are direct flights from Montreal and Toronto. Pan

Am also flies to Athens from various U.S. cities, with a change of aircraft in Frankfurt; and during the peak months several non-scheduled airlines can get you to Athens either nonstop or, more likely, with intermediate stops along the way. (These services are, of course, subject to change, so be sure to check with your travel agent in plenty of time to come up with alternative plans.)

From other cities in the U.S. the obvious plan would seem to be to fly to New York or one of the above-listed and connect with the Athens flights, but check with your travel agent and you may find that this is not necessarily the most efficient, most convenient, or fastest routing. For example, your connecting flight to New York might take you to LaGuardia Airport rather than JFK, leaving you the task of getting from one to the other in time for boarding. Your travel agent may discover from the computers that it's smarter to fly from Atlanta, Chicago, Houston, or Los Angeles with a European carrier like KLM Royal Dutch Airlines or Lufthansa, and make your connection at Amsterdam's Schiphol Airport or Frankfurt Airport. It may sound crazy, but in fact both are one-terminal airports and more efficient than JFK, and your travel time will probably work out about the same—maybe even faster. The fares will be identical. And for a small additional charge you will have the option of stopping off for a few days in, say, Amsterdam, thus adding a whole new dimension to your trip. However, the fare situation is so complicated at the time of writing, I suggest you talk to your travel agent about detailed, up-to-the minute promotion fares.

BY SEA: Once in Europe, you can get to Greece by boat or train. The usual route is to take the train (or your car) from Rome to Brindisi, where you catch a ferryboat to Corfu or Patras, in the Western Peloponnese. At Patras there are special bus services to take you to Athens, a four-hour trip. However, you may not want to head directly to Athens, since many of the sights you may have come to Greece to visit are along the way or nearby—Olympia, Corinth, Nafplion, Mycenae, Epidaurus. You can rent a car in Patras, or take local buses stage by stage to Athens.

BY TRAIN: It's a long haul, to be sure, but if you're using a Eurailpass and you're planning to see other parts of Europe along the way, you have a bargain—and the longer you travel, the better the bargain. In 1988, the Eurailpass brings you 15 days of unlimited first-class travel for just $298, or 21 days for $370.

The passes are valid also on ferryboat services between Brindisi, Italy and Patras, Greece, but from June through September you may have to pay a surcharge for those segments. Several trains go to Greece, either direct from or with connections from major cities like Amsterdam, Paris, Frankfurt, and Vienna. If you plan to go by train all the way, you can estimate traveling time from, say, Munich will be about 36 hours.

PLANNING AHEAD

WHAT TO WEAR: Since what you wear in Athens relates to the climate more than anything else, I'll deal with it right now. In summer, wear your lightest clothes. Wear comfortable, *sturdy* shoes for scrambling over all those marble ruins. Men rarely need a jacket, except in the evening for the smarter restaurants or night-clubs. Women should bring along a sweater or jacket (you can buy one there inexpensively) for evenings, cruises, or the mountains. But, generally, how you dress is up to you. The Greeks dress casually. Shorts or short skirts are now acceptable, although sometimes startling to the peasants in the countryside. You're expected to dress in a respectable manner when you enter a cathedral or church, but there are no hard-and-fast rules.

WHEN TO COME: As soon as you can get away—now, if you can. From the point of view of things to see and do, any time of the year is fine. For dogged sightseeing, in fact, winter might even be best. On the whole, the best times are April, May, June, September, October, November. Those are the months when the weather is gentlest and the ruins are not swamped (not only by Americans, remember, but also by Germans, British, Dutch, Scandinavians, French, Japanese, and the Greeks themselves). You'll have a better choice of hotels then, also. Avoid the Greek Easter unless you want to stay in Athens: it's a week-long celebration, and everyone heads for the countryside and islands; the airport is a mob scene of people trying to get on overbooked flights. (Remember that I'm talking here only about Athens; some of the islands, particularly Crete and Rhodes, are almost as busy in winter as in summer.) If you're on a tight budget, you'll find at least one advantage in coming in winter: many hotels lower their rates then.

THE LAYOUT OF ATHENS

Let's begin where Athens began—with the **Acropolis.** From the summit of the hill you get the second-best view of the city. Around the base of the Acropolis is the **Plaka,** built on the ancient city (you'll be reading more about it later), with some of the most notable archeological finds—the Agora and the Temple of The-seus. To the northeast is the **Hill of Lycabettus;** and beyond that the spreading suburbs and the ring of mountains separating

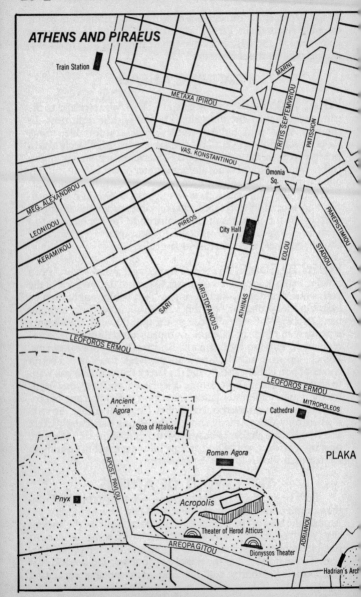

ATHENS AND PIRAEUS

Train Station

MARNI

METAXA IPIROU

TRITIS SEPTEMVRIOU

PATISSION

VAS. KONSTANTINOU

Omonia
Sq.

PANEPISTIMIOU

MEG. ALEXANDROU

LEONIDOU

KERAMIKOU

PIREOS

City Hall

EOLOU

STADIOU

SARI

ARISTOFANOUS

ATHINAS

LEOFOROS ERMOU

LEOFOROS ERMOU

MITROPOLEOS

Ancient
Agora

Cathedral

Stoa of Attalos

Roman Agora

PLAKA

APOST. PAVLOU

Pnyx

Acropolis

ADRIANOU

Theater of Herod Atticus

AREOPAGITOU

Dionyssos Theater

Hadrian's Arch

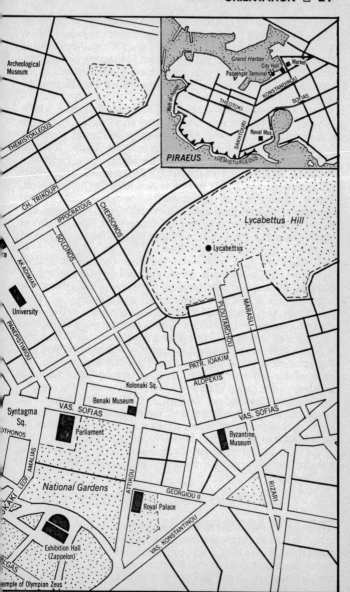

Athens from the rest of Attica. Between Lycabettus and the Acropolis is the heart of the city, distinguished from this height (about 450 feet) mainly by the green patch of the National Gardens and the hint of broad avenues radiating from **Syntagma,** or Constitution Square. To the other side, the west and south, the avenues and suburbs lead off to the coast and the Saronic Gulf, with Piraeus hidden behind a couple of hills.

At street level, the focal point of Athens is Syntagma (which, as you've just read, is also called Constitution Square, but if you want to ask directions of an Athenian, call it Syntagma). Syntagma is a large square, sloping in the direction of the Acropolis. At the upper end is the neoclassical shuttered façade of the Parliament Building, which used to be the Royal Palace. The other three sides are surrounded by hotels and office buildings (including several airline offices and travel agencies). The great attraction of Syntagma, however, is its cafés. There are cafés on three sides and in the middle. In fact, it has been estimated that there are almost 3,000 chairs here (and most of them really are chairs, upholstered and with arm rests).

There are three streets running from the bottom end of Syntagma, all laden with shops and hotels: **Karageorgi tis Servias, Ermou,** and **Mitropoleos.** Mitropoleos leads you to the cathedral, the Agora, the Temple of Theseus, and the Temple of the Winds; and if you make a left turn when you get to the cathedral, you go up into the Plaka, and from there up to the Acropolis.

Back to Syntagma. The broad avenue running off from the top-left corner of the square is variously known as **Venizelou** and **Panepistimou;** it takes you past the magnificent neoclassical façade of the university to the helter-skelter bustle of **Omonia Square,** another swirl of greenery, with a fountain in the middle, but without the elegance of Syntagma. Omonia Square is to Syntagma what Times Square is to, say, Rockefeller Center. From Omonia Square you can follow the avenue known as **October 28** or **Patission** to the National Archeological Museum.

I've just touched on the major landmarks of Athens in this chapter, and will get back to them in detail later on in the sightseeing chapter.

GETTING AROUND ATHENS

TROLLEYS AND BUSES: The trolley bus and bus routes crisscross the city, and you can get to all the main tourist haunts for no more than 30 drs (25¢), exact change necessary. Some of the main routes from Syntagma, for example, are the nos. 3, 5, 9, and 12 trolley buses, which will take you to Omonia Square and the National Archeological Museum; the no. 230 blue bus goes to the Acropolis, the Pnyx, Philopappos Hill; the no. 1 trolley bus to Omonia Square and the Larissis railroad station; no. 161 bus to Faleron; and the no. 40 green bus from Filleninon Street to Piraeus.

If you're in any doubt about which route to take and where to get off, ask your hotel receptionist to write out the number and the stop in Greek and simply show this to the conductor, or one of the passengers (unless you're traveling at the peak hours, when everyone's too busy trying to stay upright to have much time to help a stranger).

TAXIS: Still incredibly cheap. Even the ride from the airport is less than you'd pay in most cities for the fare on the airline bus. The ride to the next town, Piraeus, is around 500 drs ($4), to the night-clubs along the shore about 600 drs ($5). If you're sharing with another couple, taking a taxi in Athens is like taking a bus back home. You don't have to tip the drivers, although they've gotten into the habit of expecting to keep the small change at least; and a few of them seem to have trouble counting out your change in the hope that you may just tell them to forget it. The drivers are, on the whole, honest—but erratic. Shut your eyes and don't look. They also have a tendency to have conversations with other cab drivers as they ride along, since many of them can't converse with their foreign passengers. If you're setting off for a night on the town, it's wise to have the doorman or receptionist at your hotel write down the address in Greek for the benefit of your driver. And, of course, like cab drivers everywhere they disappear at rush hours.

In order to cut down the exhaust fumes that are threatening to tumble down the Acropolis, the Greek government enacted new antipollution measures. Taxis and automobiles may only circulate through central Athens on an alternate-day, even-numbered, odd-numbered license plan. Therefore, a taxi driver, if it's not his day, may not be able to take you where you want to go.

The law allows drivers to pick up additional passengers going in the same direction; conversely, you can now try to flag down a taxi that's already taken. This is a very practical idea intended to save gasoline and space; but the problem is defining "same direction," and you may find yourself making a few unscheduled detours that add minutes (though *not* drachmas) to your trip. If you concur in sharing your taxi, try somehow, stumblingly but politely, to insist that you get to your destination first.

Although taxi fares are still inexpensive, they have gone up yet again. The meter now starts at 25 drs (20¢), but ticks over at the rate of 20 drs (17¢) a kilometer; there's an additional charge between midnight and 7 a.m., 100 drs (75¢); for boarding at an airport or station 100 drs also; each piece of luggage is an additional 50 drs (40¢), and there's a *minimum* fare of 170 drs ($1.30). Most drivers are honest, but always check that the meter is on Tariff 1 as you set off.

THE SUBWAY: It goes in a straight line—from Omonia Square to Piraeus and from Omonia Square to the hill town of Kifissia (30 drs, or approximately 25¢, in each direction). You probably won't have too many occasions to use it, unless you're staying around Omonia Square and you want to get to Piraeus to catch a ferryboat or cruise ship, in which case it's the fastest and cheapest way to get there.

RENTING A CAR: You could, of course, rent a car, but even a small European runaround won't free you from the frustrations of one-way streets, blue zones, and parking places. While you're sightseeing in the city, forget about a car; if you're planning to do some trips out into the country or along the coast, then a car makes more sense. That's a subject I'll come to in the chapter "Touring the Hinterlands."

GREEK MONEY

One **drachma** is currently worth roughly .77¢ U.S., which means that the dollar is worth 129.87 drs, or thereabouts. For all practical purposes 130 drs equals $1. Check rates and prices in advance. Use the figures in these pages *as a guide only.*

The drachma is made up of 100 **leptas.** There are copper coins for 50 leptas (now almost obsolete), and for 1, 2, 5, 10, and 20 drachmas. Bills are worth 50 drachmas (blue), 100 drachmas (red), 500 drachmas (green), 1,000 drachmas (brown), and 5,000 drachmas (blue).

Some coins may seem to be worth peanuts, but you'll need them for tipping, telephones, and trolleys.

Note: In the following pages, the dollar equivalents have been rounded off to the nearest dollar for the sake of simplicity.

Regardless of the color of the currency, prices have a habit of changing. I've tried to be as accurate about prices as possible. I've checked and double-checked, and to the best of my knowledge, all these prices were accurate at press time (fall 1988). Rumors are that the authorities will try to hold hotel and restaurant prices to an increase of 15% to 20%, but I can't guarantee it. *So please: Check all prices in advance.*

CHAPTER V

WHERE TO STAY IN ATHENS

□ □ □

What's the hotel situation in Athens? Most people visiting Athens for the first time naturally have this question on their minds. After all, Athens is a very, very old city—does it have very old hotels? Do they have private baths? And since summers are hot in Athens, do the hotels have air conditioning?

Well, here's the surprise—most hotels in Athens seem to have been built in the past decade, and those that weren't have been renovated and modernized in the past 20 years. Most of them (except in Class D and E) have private bathrooms; most of them have air conditioning.

Nevertheless, the outstanding attraction of hotels in Athens is their relatively low rates. Where else in Europe can you get a room with private bath, air conditioning, room service, and roof-top pool smack in the center of a capital city, in peak season, for under $35 a night?

If you're seeing Europe on a tight budget, you can probably get a better room, dollar for dollar, in Athens.

If you're traveling on a shoestring, you can survive longer in Athens.

But you'd better hurry: a few years ago the best rooms in the city were going for $54, and you could get simple but comfortable rooms for as little as $8 a night. Now the really deluxe doubles are $138 and up, the more comfortable budget rooms $25 and up. In addition, the quality of hotel services seems to be declining, and staffs are eager to get their tips despite the fact that a service charge is already included in the bill.

Before going on to individual hotels, here are some general notes on the hotel situation in Athens today.

CATEGORIES: All hotels in Greece are classified by the Greek government. There are six official categories—beginning with L, or Deluxe, running through Class A and ending with E. In this guide I will confine the reviews to the first four categories, with a quick look at some hotels, guesthouses, and hostels in the lowest price ranges. The factors the government uses in judging hotels are the number of bathrooms and restaurants and the quality of service. According to the official government hotel book, "in the new hotels, all the rooms have private bathrooms and showers. In the majority of old hotels down to category 'C,' most rooms have private bathrooms; these seldom exist in 'D' and 'E.' But in some cases the designations are a holdover from seasons long gone; consequently, some Class C hotels are better than some Class B hotels, and the Class B Athens Gate Hotel, for example, is a better value than, say, the Class A Astir Hotel. Again, the relatively new Electra Palace Hotel offers more comfortable rooms than most of the accommodations in the "deluxe" Acropole Palace. In the following pages you'll read about a few hotels that seem to offer outstanding values.

RATES: The government also establishes and enforces the rates for each category. The minimum price and what it includes must be posted in each room—service, taxes, handling of luggage, central heating, air conditioning, meals, and so on. Usually these signs are in English as well as Greek. However, this does not mean you will not encounter misunderstandings here and there, because hotel keepers are allowed to tack on a few extras: "an increase of 10% may be added to room rates if the stay is two days or less"; "the room rates of hotels located in summer holiday areas, or spas, may be increased by 20% during the period July 1st to September 15th". Throw in a slight language problem and there could be a minor international incident. You can avoid any misunderstandings if you reserve your room in advance (preferably through a travel agent) and have a written confirmation *with rates* in your hand.

TAX AND SERVICE CHARGE: As of this writing, the government tacks on a 6% VAT tax to all hotel rates; there's also a 4.5% *city* tax and a *stamp* tax of 1.2% on the total bill. In addition, hotels are allowed to add a 15% service charge to the bill. Most hotels, however, quote rates that include both service charge and

AN IMPORTANT NOTE ON HOTEL RATES. With all these rules and controls you might think that getting accurate, up-to-date hotel rates would be a simple matter. It isn't. When this guidebook was being updated (spring 1988), neither the Greek National Organization for Tourism nor the Hellenic Chamber of Hotels had established the official room rates for 1989.

Because of all these imponderables, therefore, the rates quoted throughout this guide are *the rates in effect in the summer of 1988*. For an estimate of 1989 and 1990 rates, add 15% to 20%.

tax. *All the estimated rates quoted in these pages include the government and city taxes and the 15% service charge.*

BREAKFAST: Some hotels also quote a rate that includes service charge, tax, *and* breakfast. That is—continental breakfast, which consists simply of coffee with rolls or toast and butter with marmalade or jam. Recently the government instructed hoteliers to add fresh fruit or fruit juice. If breakfast is served in your room, you may have to pay a few extra drachmas. When a hotel quotes "English breakfast," this means eggs and bacon with your coffee and rolls. If you're on a very tight budget, you may prefer a rate that does *not* include breakfast, since you can probably walk around the corner to a neighborhood café and have the same thing for half the price.

HALF BOARD, FULL BOARD: The government also controls the prices of meals served in hotels, and one way a hotel keeper will try to boost his income is to insist that guests pay a rate that includes meals—*half board,* with breakfast and lunch or dinner (the equivalent of Modified American Plan, and sometimes also known as demi-pension), or *full board,* with breakfast, lunch, and dinner (the equivalent of American Plan). This may be an advantage if you're staying in a hotel where you can dine in their roof garden; in most hotels it will probably be a drawback. On the one hand the tourist organization advertises tempting waterfront tavernas; on the other the hotel keepers force you to dine where *they* want you to dine. Whenever possible, resist half-board and full-board rates and leave yourself the option of dining out.

SEASONS: There are basically two seasons for hotels in Athens: the off-season usually runs from November 1 through March 31, but in some cases it may begin on October 1 and in others end on May 31; some hotels add "shoulder" seasons in spring and fall, while a few hotels no longer distinguish between the seasons, so steady is the stream of visitors, business and vacation, to the city. Get your travel agent to look closely into precise dates, because this may save you several dollars. But please note: *except where specified, all the rates that follow are for the peak summer season.*

CHOOSING A HOTEL IN ATHENS: Once you've determined what price you want to pay, the situation is fairly simple. Most of the hotels are in one of two clusters in the center of town —either around Syntagma (Constitution Square) or around Omonia Square. A few, like the Hilton, Inter-Continental, and Marriott, are a few blocks farther away, but still convenient to the center of town. Most hotels in Athens are within walking distance of almost everything you want to see, and in any case, taxis are so cheap that getting around the city is not much of an expense—if you can find a taxi in the first place.

COMPARE BEFORE BUYING: If you come in the off-season, when the choice of rooms is greater, it's a perfectly acceptable practice to inspect rooms before taking one. If you give yourself half an hour or an hour, you can walk from hotel to hotel, looking at locations, checking out facilities and the view from the balconies or roofs. Even in the hotel you finally decide on, check out the room, because the standards in some of the older hotels vary considerably from one room to another.

THE VIEW FROM THE TOP: The Acropolis is one of the most stunning sights in the world. Every corner you turn in Athens brings you another glimpse of this sacred hill. You'll probably want to sit on your balcony at sunset and watch the Parthenon turn a glowing honey color. You may even want to sit on your balcony in the morning and watch the Parthenon's columns loom through the morning light. There's nothing like it, so try to get a room with a view, even if you have to give up luxury or space or a private bathroom.

RESERVATIONS: During the peak season, don't go near Athens without a reservation. You may end up like the Parthenon— without a roof over your head. In the end you'll very likely find a place to stay, but you may spend half your day finding it. Make a reservation in advance. And if you want a room with a view, be sure to specify. In recent years, with more and more visitors flocking to the city, it's wise to make reservations well in advance even during the off-season, if you want to be sure of staying in the hotel of your choice. (This is true not only of Athens but also of places out in the countryside like Delphi and Nafplion.)

LONGER STAYS: Because hotel rates in Athens are so reasonable, you may be tempted to linger a while in that city. If you do, consider renting an apartment rather than staying in a hotel room. Apartments are usually cheaper, well equipped, and they give you a chance to live a more truly Athenian life. It's a particularly economical idea if you have a family. The **Delice Hotel Apartments** and **Riva Hotel Apartments** both offer one-bedroom and two-bedroom suites with fully equipped kitchenettes and air conditioning, 24-hour reception, and telephone service; the Riva also has bar and restaurant service. The Delice is at 3 Vassileos Alexandrou St., the Riva at 114 Michalakopoulou St., both near the Hilton hotel. Double rates are in the region of 5,590 drs ($43) to 6,890 drs ($53) per night for stays of a month or longer.

SERVICE CHARGE AND TIPPING: A service charge of 15% is included in your hotel bill. The theory behind a service charge was to avoid the confusion resulting from having to tip different members of the hotel staff; the service charge would be added to the bill and that would take care of all tipping. Except that it doesn't. The staff still expects tips. Don't encourage this. Tip only for small *extra* services like shining shoes and fetching cabs.

Here are some tips on tipping in hotels: according to the sign in your room, luggage handling is included in the service charge built into the room rate. So you're not obliged to tip any more, but if you feel like it, offer 100 drs (75¢) a bag (the same rate for porters at airports and stations). In a deluxe hotel you may want to double that. You're also expected to tip the waiter who brings you breakfast in bed, 100 drs (75¢) to 200 drs ($1.50), say, depending on the type of hotel. (But remember—there is probably an additional service charge already added to the room service bill.) Doormen who hail your cab also get 100 drs (75¢) to 200 drs ($1.50).

THE ROOMS: Greeks are traditionally people who like to get out into the open air. And why not, with a climate as balmy as theirs? They'd rather spend a summer evening sitting beneath an olive tree discussing politics or soccer than being cooped up at home watching the TV. Since they spend so much time outdoors, they don't bother about spending a bundle furnishing their homes. By American standards, Greek homes are bare. Ditto Greek hotels, especially the older ones. The lobbies may be like marble palaces, but upstairs the corridors may be spartan, and the rooms furnished only with the essentials. No frills. So don't come to Athens expecting all the trimmings you'd normally find in an American hotel (except in places like the Ledra Marriott or the Inter-Continental, and the reliable Athens Hilton). The rooms will be spotlessly clean and comfortable, but in many cases they won't have wall-to-wall carpeting, armchairs, radios, and writing desks. You may be discouraged at first, but you'll soon discover that it doesn't matter, because you, too, will soon prefer to spend your evenings beneath an olive tree.

AIR CONDITIONING: The majority of Athens hotels now have air conditioning, at least in the *L, A,* and *B* categories. Hotels in other categories probably have air conditioning in *some* of the rooms, and you will have to request one of these rooms—and pay an additional charge. Temperatures in Athens in midsummer go up into the 90s by day, and linger in the 70s at night. If you're accustomed to air conditioning back home, you'll probably want it in Athens also, at least in July and August. Moreover, Athens is really a rather noisy city, so you may want to switch on the air conditioning and leave windows and shutters closed to keep out the hubbub.

BATHS AND SHOWERS: There are two types of bathtubs in Athens—the regular kind and the sit-in kind. The sit-in type is about three feet by three feet. It's fine for feet that have trudged all the way up the Acropolis and back, but inadequate for weary shoulders that have carried camera bags and shoulder purses. If you want a real bath, tell the reception clerk when you're checking in. Most hotels have both types. Most baths of either dimension also have hand-held showers, which have one advantage—when you're in your bath you can also switch on the shower *underwater* and use it for a whirlpool bath, or to massage your weary thighs. If you do get an overhead shower, you may not get a shower curtain. The technique is to let the water splash onto the floor, which has been angled to drain off the surplus. It makes sense—but just remember not to leave your slippers or bathrobe on the floor.

RADIO: Many hotels don't have a radio in the room. Unless the radio has three channels and one of them picks up the American Armed Forces Network or the BBC, all you'll get from your "radio" is a steady stream of taped music.

TELEVISION: Don't expect TV in your room, except at deluxe hotels, which probably also have in-house movies. Greece has had television transmission for less than 25 years, and it's still not the big thing it is in the U.S., and hardly worth paying extra for. (Many new hotels have TV sets in the lobby or the lounge—but that's it.)

SWIMMING POOLS: You'll find few hotels with pools in Athens. Of the ones listed in this guide, only the Athens Hilton, Caravel, Inter-Continental Athenaeum, Ledra Marriott, Royal Olympic, St. George Lycabettus, Chandris, President, Stanley, Electra Palace, Dorian Inn, Athens Center, Holiday Inn, Divani-Zafolia Palace, and Novotel Mirayia have pools. Many hotels have sundecks on the roof. But, generally speaking, people come to Athens for sightseeing rather than a tan. If you do want to get in some swimming and sun, stay at one of the nearby resorts—like Glyfada and Vouliagmeni. They're both close enough for jaunts into town for sightseeing and dining.

DELUXE "L" HOTELS
(FROM $96 TO $281 DOUBLE,
PEAK SEASON)

The **Athens Hilton,** Vassilissis Sophias Avenue (tel. 7220-201), is not so much a hotel as a city. On weekends its lobby is filled with wide-eyed Athenians who can't afford a trip to New York but want to see what America is like. There's plenty for them to see—but it's not America. Not with all that marble. There's probably enough marble in the Athens Hilton to have built a second Parthenon—30,000 square yards of it, of 11 types, from Arta, Timos, Pendeli, Yannina, and Salamis. You arrive at the hotel beneath a great curving portico with brown-and-white marble (a work of art which later centuries may dig up and prize as highly as we prize fragments from Knossos). You walk through newly restyled hallways with marble floors and marble pillars, down marble steps to a lounge with dozens of plush armchairs, then down a few more marble steps to another, wider, furnished lounge where you can have afternoon tea and look out on the marble pathways leading to the swimming pool and the poolside café.

Just inside the hotel entrance are two courtyards (the traditional Greek atrium), 200-year-old olive trees in the middle, and boutiques and shops around the sides—fashion shops, an antique store, a bank, an optician, beauty salon, barbershop, photo shop, florist, drugstore, travel agencies, airline office, Avis Rent-a-Car office. Without ever leaving the Hilton you can buy designer clothes, records, jewelry, flowers, books, souvenirs, handcrafts, copperware, rugs, bags, cigars.

One of the favorite spots (especially for brunch or weekends) for the Athenian sightseer is the Byzantine Café, where Greeks sample American coffee, American hamburgers, and American apple pie; two others are the downstairs restaurants: Ta Nissia and the Kellari (see Chapter VI, "Dining Out in Athens").

On the Hilton roof, 12 floors above the city, you'll find the Galaxy Bar with dancing to a live band. No ordinary nightspot this. When you step off the elevator you'll see why. Ahead of you, through floor-to-ceiling windows, lies one of the most spellbinding views in Europe—the black, star-speckled mass of the Mediterranean sky, the twinkling lights of the city, and, smack in center stage, the floodlit Acropolis and Parthenon. In summer, of course, you can sit outside on the terrace itself and soak in the view and the soft Athenian air.

All the guest rooms at the Hilton have views of either the Acropolis or Mount Pentelicon, and a few have views of both the Acropolis and Lycabettus Hill. Spacious and comfortable, as you've come to expect of Hilton hotels everywhere, the guest rooms feature five-channel radio, seven-channel satellite TV with in-house movies, direct-dial telephone, mini-bar, wall-to-wall carpeting, and, of course, sliding glass doors opening onto spacious balconies. The bathrooms (more marble, this time gray) have American-style shower-baths. The Hilton's maids fix your room twice a day, and turn down the sheets while you're up on the roof dancing. Recent refinements and innovations include remodeled front desks, computerized check-in, computerized cards in place of room keys, sleek computerized "Elevonic" elevators; the top two floors are now given over to the Executive Club, with its own hostesses and exclusive lounge; and the three presidential-style suites have been completely redesigned with Jacuzzis, custom-designed Greek embroideries, Murano glass—even the doorknobs are works of art.

Other Hilton facilities include the swimming pool, sauna, massage, executive services, and spacious garage. Located in a smart residential district among the embassies, the Hilton is still only a 15-minute walk or a five-minute ride on the hotel's shuttle bus to Syntagma (Constitution) Square. There's also airport shuttle service.

The Athens Hilton is one of the most expensive hotels in town: singles run from 16,770 drs ($129) to 25,610 drs ($197); doubles, 20,540 drs ($158) to 29,380 drs ($226). Executive-floor rates are from 32,240 drs ($248) to 138,710 drs ($1,067).

The **Hotel Grande Bretagne,** Syntagma (tel. 3230-251), is the Dowager Duchess of Athens's hotels. It was built in 1862 as a 30-room annex to the royal family's summer palace across the street (now the Houses of Parliament), and put in the care of Eustace Lampsa, chef to the royal household who knew all the preferences of the royal visitors who'd be staying there. It's still a family-run hotel, with long-serving staff (its two classic concierges recently retired after 50 years of service apiece), but the original three-story building is now seven stories with a total of 450 rooms. Generations of distinguished guests have created a unique atmosphere at the GB (no one refers to it as the Grande Bretagne). Its doors have been whisked open by uniformed attendants for princes, czars, tycoons, and millionaires, for composer Richard Strauss, the Grand Duchess Helen, and more recently, Sir Laurence Olivier and Paul Newman. During World War II, the GB was Nazi headquarters; at the end of the war, Sir Winston Churchill stayed here for a few nights and narrowly escaped an assassination attempt which involved using the labyrinthine sewers of the hotel. Today the GB is virtually a "reviewing stand" for state occasions at the Parliament Building and the Tomb of the Unknown Soldier across the street.

The lobby of the GB is one of those monumental Athenian halls of marble—marble floors, green marble walls, marble pillars, Oriental carpets, and plushly upholstered sofas and fauteuils; beyond it is an equally comfortable and spacious lounge with a decorative glass ceiling, and beyond that the dignified, classical dining room. Two contemporary touches are the intime, dimly lit cocktail lounge in one corner, and the GB Corner café-restaurant in the other. If you simply want to sample the opulence of the GB's public quarters, drop into the lobby for a coffee; it costs a few drachmas more than it would cost in one of the cafés in the square, but it comes to you in a silver pot, on a silver tray, with a silver milk jug and silver sugar bowl—plus a wine glass of chilled water, served with great dignity by a waiter in immaculate white uniform.

The GB is one of *the* grand hotels in Europe, and although it may have been overtaken by others in terms of sheer plushness (decor and furniture date from more elegant days), it is constantly being upgraded: latest innovations include direct-dial telephones (with bathroom extensions), mini-bars, air conditioning, and color TV with in-house movies, in a custom cabinet that matches the individual room decor. The prize rooms are those facing the square (especially those on the sixth floor), all now with double french doors and windows to block out traffic noise; but the huge inner courtyard has been restored in its neoclassical style, complete with window boxes and fragrant flowers, and these rooms will be welcomed by people who like to sleep with their windows open—no traffic sounds here. Rates are 14,124 drs ($109) to 21,632 drs ($166) single, 18,089 drs ($139) to 26,924 drs ($207) double; suites are 38,711 drs ($298) to 196,900 drs ($1,515) and up.

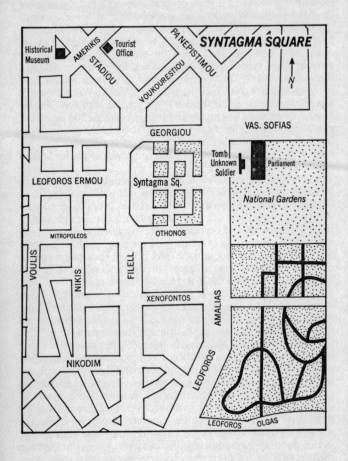

The largest, most expensive, most extravagant of the city's top-flight deluxe hotels is the **Athenaeum Inter-Continental**, 89-93 Syngrou (tel. 9023-666). Completed in 1982, it rises ten floors above the main avenue from the city center to the sea, its white U-shaped, stepped-back façade dominating the not-too-inspired surroundings. About half of the Athenaeum's 597 guest rooms have views of the Acropolis or Lycabettus Hill (you pay more for the Acropolis view, but it's worth it, especially at sunset —although you should get a discount from the Rothman cigarette people to compensate for their garish and gigantic neon-lit billboard, as good a reason as any for giving up smoking).

The guest rooms are among the plushest and most tasteful in town: each with separate sitting area (marble floor, flokati rug, desk, sofa, armchair), carpeted bedroom, marble-clad bathroom (with wall-mounted hairdryer and bathrobes). In addition, all 50 suites come with a pantry and dining nook; but if you opt for one of the new "golf" suites or "health" suites, you also get a private putting green or a mini-health club, respectively—right there in your room! All rooms and suites come with individual air conditioning, direct-dial telephone with message light and bathroom extension, color TV with bedside controls and video channels, radio, and stocked mini-bar.

For the remainder, the Athenaeum is self-contained and handsomely accoutered, its multilevel atrium lobby ringed by shopping arcades (jewelry, high fashion, coins, stamps, drugstore) and the hotel's private collection of works by leading contemporary Greek artists in an array of techniques—kinetic/magnetic, neon assemblage, fiberglass bas-relief, trompe l'oeil, and wood sculptures.

The Athenaeum's dining facilities include everything from crêpes to Chateaubriands to Asian barbecues, served in a coffeeshop opening onto the patio pool; lobby tearoom, rooftop buffet, and classy rôtisserie serving classic cuisine. Other Athenaeum services include 24-hour room service, a free shuttle bus running to three locations in downtown Athens, health club, disco, hairdressing salon, business center with Telex and fax machines, a garage for 170 cars.

Room rates are 9,930 drs ($76) to 19,861 drs ($153) single, 16,701 drs ($128) to 22,118 drs ($170) double; suites run 25,278 drs ($195) to 162,500 drs ($1,250).

Marriott's 258 room entry in Athens, the **Ledra Marriott,** 117 Syngrou (tel. 9347-711), is a near neighbor of the Athenaeum, with a balconied façade of white marble separated from the avenue by a service road and driveway. The hit of the Ledra is, surprisingly, the city's first Polynesian/Japanese restaurant, the lavishly waterfalled and batiked Kona Kai, which is *the* smart place for Athenians to be seen and entertained. Other restaurants include a small, stylish Grill Room (which from October to June serves 75 different dishes from around the world) and the wicker-and-lattice Zephyros coffeeshop, featuring a popular Sunday buffet lunch for 2,600 drs ($20) or thereabouts—including champagne and orange juice on the house.

The Marriott's guest accommodations come in four categories, including sumptuous suites where people like Liz Taylor and Malcolm Forbes are apt to check in. But even the most "modest" rooms are above average with elegant designer decor (soft tans, ecrus, and browns), cool, all-marble bathroom with built-in hair dryer and sun lamp, individual air conditioning, mini-bar, radio (with extension speaker in the bathroom), armchair and sofa, and extravagant closet space—with drawers and sliding doors that positively glide. A whole *extra* set of double-glazing has been added to the windows on the lower floors, which let in the light and the views, but keep out the sounds of Syngrou. Only one-third of the Ledra's rooms have views of the Parthenon, but in nice democratic fashion, every guest (and only hotel guests, by the way, no "local memberships" allowed) can lounge on the rooftop deck, plunge into a big pool, or soak in a hydrotherapy pool while admiring the Parthenon. There's also a rooftop bar and in summer, nightly "Panorama Buffets," with Greek music, that are quite popular and a delightful way to enjoy the view, enjoy the local cuisine —and maybe make a few new friends in the bargain!

Ledra guests may also relax in the Crystal Lounge piano bar, in the lobby, underneath a huge, 1,000-crystal chandelier.

Overall you'll find the Ledra staff young, enthusiastic, and efficient; the hotel has something or someone to take care of all your needs, right down to the shuttle bus that leaves for Syntagma several times a day. Rates: singles, 17,800 drs ($137) to 19,600 drs ($150); doubles, 19,800 ($152) to 21,600 drs ($166); suites, from 42,300 drs ($325).

The Astir chain of palace hotels has dominated leading Greek resorts for many years, but the new ten-story, glass-sheathed **Astir Palace Athens Hotel** on Syntagma (tel. 3643-112) is the first time the AH logo has decorated an Athens hotel. The location is ideal, at least in terms of convenience: at the junction of Panepistimiou and Sofias Avenues, facing the Parliament Building on one side, the Hotel Grande Bretagne on the other. Prime real estate indeed, but since the Astir properties are owned by the National Bank of Greece, money seems to be little object. In Athens they've lavished some $100 million on just 79 rooms, two restaurants, and a bar. Even the inner stairwell is lined with white Pendeli marble and decorated with ceramic tile murals.

Extra-large guest rooms feature spacious sitting areas furnished with sofa, armchair, glass-and-marble coffee table, and desk. Other facilities include mini-bar, four-channel radio (and an extension speaker in the bathroom), color TV, direct-dial telephone. Each room sports projecting floor-to-ceiling tinted windows with extra-thick glass not quite thick enough on the lower floors to eliminate completely the rumble of traffic, but it's not a major drawback).

The Astir's main dining room, Apokalypsis, hides out on the lower level, an unusual setting of bronze and crystal beneath a reflective ceiling, facing a wall of glass shielding a backdrop that is no less than a section of the 2,000-year-old city wall, revealed for the first time when the hotel foundations were being excavated. The Apokalypsis menu is Greek and international on an ambitious scale—budget 10,400 drs ($80) for two for dinner—but you can dine more simply in the Astir Coffee Shop, one floor above the lobby.

Rates are for singles 10,400 drs ($80), 13,700 drs ($105) for doubles; suites run from 19,670 drs ($152).

The striking gray façade of the **Holiday Inn** rises eight stories above Michalakopoulou, a broad avenue just beyond the Hilton, a short walk from the American Embassy. Indoors, it makes most other Holiday Inns look like country cousins, with its lobby in dazzling "disco" decor, a glass-paneled shopping arcade, a contemporary bar/lounge and 12-lane bowling alley. Other attractions are underground parking, hairdresser, coffeeshop (open to 2 a.m.), bistro-restaurant, disco, and outdoor swimming pool. Guest rooms, in cool soothing colors, sport radio/TV, air conditioning, direct-dial telephone, two double beds, and an efficient bathroom. Rooms on the top two floors have balconies; of the 190 rooms, only 35 are singles, so solo visitors may be offered a double room at a special rate (one reason, perhaps, why 60% of the hotel's guests are business people). The Holiday Inn, owned and operated by a local company, is located at 50 Michalakopoulou Ave. (tel. 7248-322). Rates are 11,640 drs ($90) single, 12,480 drs ($96) to 16,640 drs ($128) double.

France's Meridien chain, too, now has a toehold in Athens—and what a toehold! The **NJV-Meridien Hotel** is right on Syntagma (tel. 3255-300), sharing the same block as the GB and the former King George hotels, and boasting a sleek efficiency the older hotels might envy. Soundproofing has been built in from the beginning, the central air conditioning is unobtrusive, and all rooms come equipped with satellite TV (including a video channel), radio, automatic alarm clock, mini-bar, direct-dial telephone;

bathrooms have thermostatic control, double vanities, and telephone extensions. The Meridien's 182 rooms include half a dozen singles on each floor, most of them at the rear; upper-floor doubles have balconies overlooking the square, some with views of the Acropolis. On the mezzanine floor, guests can settle into a comfy bar upholstered, paneled, and pillared with leather, and dine off nouvelle cuisine prepared by a French chef in the hotel's spacious restaurant. Meridien rates range from 17,400 drs ($134) for singles, from 21,600 drs ($166) to 36,590 drs ($281) for doubles.

OTHER DELUXE "L" HOTELS (FROM $45 TO $143 DOUBLE, PEAK SEASON)

The hotels listed above are truly deluxe; the following selection is officially in the category but in terms of facilities and furnishings they are really only a cut above first class. Fortunately, their rates are considerably lower than the group above.

Two longtime favorites in this category, the **King George** on Constitution (Syntagma) Square and the **Athenée Palace** around the corner on Kolokotroni Square, already prey to stiff competition from newcomers, suffered the coup-de-grâce of the terrorist-related troubles of '85 and '86 and closed their shutters for good.

St. George Lycabettus Hotel, 2 Kleomenou St. (tel. 7290-711), with 150 rooms, and as many balconies, is located on a residential street in the foothills of Lycabettus. Glass doors open to cool, spacious elegance, gleaming black marble floors are highlighted with upholstered chairs and couches in blends of caramel, pumpkin, and gold, and smoky-glass tables with brass accents. Tony's Bar is down a few steps to the left. One floor below that, going down the hill, there's a pâtisserie/coffeeshop. Crowning it all is a rooftop pool and restaurant, eye-to-eye with the pine groves of Lycabettus; and most guests will probably opt for this rooftop restaurant—white chairs among potted oleanders in the summer, indoors in the Grill Room in winter; with dancing to a combo all year round. The 30-foot-long pool is surrounded by "astroturf"-style matting, with comfortable chaises and poolside showers.

The accommodations are trim and contemporary—light blue wall-to-wall carpeting, pale blue upholstery, wood paneling, furniture with brass trim, a luxurious bathroom with tile walls and marble floors, radio, and direct-dial telephone, and now most of them also have mini-bar (but TV is available only upon request).

The plushest rooms are the corner suites, especially those on the fourth and fifth floors which have balconies on two sides, breathtaking views, two rooms, two bathrooms, and a sense of spaciousness that you might miss in the basic rooms. The St. George Lycabettus (don't get it confused with the plain Lycabettus Class B hotel farther down the hill) is popular with visitors (especially business people) who want modern facilities and comfort in a quieter location with Syntagma, a seven-minute walk downhill and a 170 drs ($2) cab ride back up. Other facilities include TV, garage, beauty parlor, barbershop, and bank. Rates: singles run 8,000 drs ($62) to 10,000 drs ($77),doubles, 11,000 drs ($85) to 14,000 drs ($108); 20% less during the off-season.

The balconied façade of the **Amalia Hotel** at 10 Amalias Ave. (tel. 3237-301) is known to thousands of visitors who have never stayed there—it's simply the place where airport buses and hotel shuttles begin and end their downtown trips. Apt choice: the Amalia is conveniently located just around the corner from Syntagma and across the avenue from the National Garden (about one-third of the hotel's rooms have balconies overlooking the foliage).

For 1988, the Amalia emerged from a long-awaited, top-to-bottom renovation, the gloomy wooden walls of its lobby giving way to acres of glass and coral-pink paneling, the prim furniture replaced by upholstered armchairs. New facilities include a "streetside" but air-conditioned coffeeshop in the lobby, and a spacious restaurant and TV lounge one floor up. The 100 guest rooms have been restyled—new color schemes, new beds, new drapes (but still no television—you have to watch that in the lounge).

Peak season doubles go for 9,800 drs ($76), including breakfast. And, of course, if you're bound for the international airport (Hellenikon East), you couldn't be in a handier spot.

The **Royal Olympic Hotel,** 28 Diakou (tel. 9226-411), is just ten blocks from Constitution (Syntagma) Square. But what a location! If you have a room facing the front, you can throw back the drapes, open the sliding windows, step out onto your balcony, and there in live wide-screen Cinemascope is the entire Temple of Olympian Zeus spread out in front of you. And right behind it, almost growing out of the temple's cluster of columns, is the hill of Lycabettus, with the greenery of the National Garden filling the gap between. It's a breathtaking sight. And well worth the ten blocks between you and Constitution Square. Into the bargain, this hotel is handsomely furnished—bedrooms as well as the public rooms.

The steps up to the lobby, the floors, and the pillars are inevitably of marble. The bar separates the lobby from the square swimming pool at the back of the hotel, and on the left of the lobby there's an elegant dining room decorated with engravings of old Athens. One of the most attractive of the public rooms is the lounge, up a few marble steps, to raise it above the level of the traffic so that you can get an undisturbed view of the temple. (Even if you're not staying at the Royal Olympic, remember this grandstand lounge is a place to drop into for morning coffee or afternoon tea.)

The Royal Olympic's guest rooms are roomy and modern. There are carpets on the floor, computerized direct-dial telephone, radio, air conditioning, balcony, sliding doors of double-glazed glass, amply fitted closets, chairs, coffee tables, a well-equipped bathroom complete down to a second phone, and big towels. The hotel's corner suites can keep an entire family in comfort, with even an icebox attractively disguised as a wood-grained cabinet. There are also suites with sliding screens to separate sleeping area from working area, and equipped with a full-size desk, studio couch, refrigerator, and coffee table. The choice rooms are on the sixth floor. They're a shade more "designed," and they have larger balconies—and of course, the higher you are the more stunning the view and the more muffled the sound of the traffic. But take a room on any floor as long as it's at the front.

There are now 310 rooms, including 15 suites, each with different decor, an enormous bed, carved inner doors, big oval bathtub, and large silk prints of recumbent maidens.

If you check into a room without a view you can always head for the lounge overlooking the temple. The dining room of the Royal Olympic is a spruce, chandelier-bright place, and there's also a specialty restaurant called the Templars' Grill, which you'll read about in the next chapter. Rates at the Royal Olympic are 9,000 drs ($69) single, 11,000 drs ($85) double.

Syngrou, the long straight avenue that links the city with the sea, is currently undergoing a major facelift, and one of the landmarks in this new-style Athens is the glistening 386-room **Athens Chandris Hotel,** 385 Leoforos Syngrou (tel. 9414-824), which opened its automatic doors in 1977. It's close to the sea, equidistant from downtown Athens, downtown Piraeus, and the airport, and facing the Ippodromo, or race track. The interior is a glistening art deco extravaganza of holiday colors, marble, and contrasting textures. The furniture, imported from Italy, is all Milan Modern—the bedside lamps are like giant ice cubes, the chrome trim of the headboards has a built-in radio, and the ultramodern suites (22 in all) must be among the smartest in Athens. All rooms now have mini-bar, and most of them have satellite TV with in-house video. On the roof, eight floors up, guests can cool off in a small pool, have lunch, snacks, and a buffet dinner, or just enjoy vast views of the city, the mountains, and the Saronic Bay; many guests also have a grandstand view of the races from their balconies. Other Chandris features include a trio of smart restaurants and a late-night coffeeshop. Room-only rates for summer range from 9,000 drs ($69) to 11,000 drs ($85) single, from 11,000 drs ($85) to 13,500 drs ($104) double, including full American buffet breakfast—some of the lowest deluxe rates in Athens. And there's also a free shuttle bus every half hour to the city center.

The **Acropole Palace,** 51 Patission (tel. 5223-851), probably has the most elegant façade of any hotel in Athens. It was built at the turn of the century, with some of the embellishments you'd find in a French hotel of that period—bay windows, tiny iron balconies, and a curved corner. However, the ambience here is *faded* elegance. Rooms are still furnished as they were originally, and there are antique items in some of the rooms—but the rooms and hallways are looking dowdy and threadbare, despite continuing efforts to renovate them, including double-glazed windows. The main lobby has a marble and wrought-iron stairway that sweeps gracefully up to the air-conditioned lounges and the circular, domed dining room. Downstairs there's the oddly named Sky Room Bar and the winter nightclub. In summer the dining room and the nightclub are on the Roof Garden, eight high-ceilinged floors up.

The Acropole Palace has many of the facilities you'd expect of a long-established, fine hotel—tea room, beauty parlor, barbershop, American bar, air conditioning. It's a quiet hotel in a convenient location—opposite the National Archeological Museum, about five minutes on foot from Omonia Square and seven minutes by cab from Constitution (Syntagma) Square, so if you don't want to be surrounded by tourists (other than groups of Japanese), souvenir shops, and cafés, the Acropole Palace might be the answer. But go forewarned: it's somber and not really much of a savings. Summer rates are 5,800 drs ($45) single, 8,900 drs ($69) double, both with breakfast.

The **Park Hotel,** 10 Leoforos Alexandras (tel. 883-2712), is smaller, more intimate, welcoming guests with a club-like lobby of wood paneling and leather decorated in muted colors. It's across the street from one of the city's most spacious parks, and many of the upper rooms have pleasant views overlooking the treetops. Pampering seems to be the philosophy here: bar/refrigerator in all the rooms (plus 24-hour room service), marble bathroom with direct-dial telephone, fingertip bedside controls for the gadgetry—message light, door lock, "Do Not Disturb" sign, heating and air conditioning, radio, and music channels.

In addition to a late-night coffeeshop, the Red Horse, the Park's Latina Restaurant offers Greek and international dishes. In summertime, the Blue Peacock bar on the roof garden gives you an even better view of the treetops and a refreshing breeze. The Park's 111 double rooms cost 13,028 drs ($100) to 18,592 drs ($143) with breakfast in summer.

The modern 520-room **Caravel Hotel**, 2 Vas. Alexandrou Ave. (tel. 7290-721), is a near neighbor of the Hilton. The two hotels seem to be competing on the spaciousness of their lobbies; both of them have late-night coffeeshops, lobby-level shopping galleries and beauty parlors. The Caravel's rooftop cocktail lounge, the Horizon, has a spectacular view of the Acropolis and Lycabettus Hill; likewise, the sunning terrace around the full-size heated pool, now enclosed in a glass dome for year-round use. Up here you'll also find, saunas, an indoor gymnasium (with windows to let you admire the view of the Acropolis when you come up for breath), and an active Muslim mosque. The Caravel's guest rooms are spacious, colorful, and tasteful, with small balconies, individual room controls for heating and air conditioning, marble bathrooms, and small refrigerator/bars (in addition to 24-hour room service). Summer rates are singles from 8,300 drs ($64), doubles from 10,900 drs ($84), and suites to almost 71,890 drs ($553).

Your main interest in Parnes is probably the Casino (discussed farther on), but I'll list a hotel here in case you want a change of pace at some point. The **Mount Parnes Hotel-Casino,** Parnes (tel. 2469-111), is located on the 3,000-foot mountain 22 miles from midtown Athens. It's comfortable and clean, the rooms have private baths and showers and central heating, and although it's officially classed as a first-class hotel there are no frills here. Except that view! All the rooms face Athens, and they all have big terraces (big enough to have a meal on) overlooking the valley and the city, Piraeus and the sea. You get an identical view from the pool terrace. The hotel has a restaurant, snackbar, nightclub, and of course the casino. Also a TV room, tennis, and gardens. What's the point of staying way up there? It's cooler, and it's by the casino. Otherwise the hotel is quite dull. The rates in summer are around 4,000 drs ($31) double.

CLASS A AND B HOTELS
(FROM $31 TO $80 DOUBLE,
PEAK SEASON)

Some of the best buys, and some of the most attractive accommodations, are to be found in these two categories, and for most travelers the following hotels are the ones most likely to match their tastes and budgets. Rates listed include continental breakfast and, of course, taxes, service charge, and air conditioning, unless otherwise mentioned. Remember, please, that the rates are for 1988 only, and subject to change for the reasons explained elsewhere in this guidebook.

First, I'll give details of a half dozen of the newer hotels in these categories, all of them at a slight remove from the clutter of Syntagma and Omonia. The first three are in the part of town known as **Makriyanni,** a predominantly residential area bounded by the Acropolis (the side opposite the Plaka), the Temple of Olympian Zeus, and Syngrou Avenue, which is rapidly becoming one of the main business and commercial centers of the city.

The **Hotel Herodion,** 4 Rovertou Galli St. (tel. 9236-832), is located on a quiet side street, but so close to the Theater of Herod Atticus it's especially popular with performers and culture buffs during the Athens Festival; since it's also just five minutes on foot from the Plaka and a five-minute bus ride from Syntagma, the Herodion is a good address at any time of the year. Its spacious marble lobby leads to a lounge and patio garden where you can have drinks and snacks beneath the trees; the dining room is taverna style, with ceramics and native rugs on white stucco walls. The Herodion's 90 guest rooms are tastefully decorated; many of them have a balcony, and in any case there's a solarium/roof terrace with a stunning view of the Acropolis. With the spic-and-span singles going for 7,940 drs ($61) and the doubles for 10,300 drs ($80), the Herodion is a good bet. You can get slightly lower rates at the nearby **Hotel Parthenon,** 6 Makri St. (tel. 9234-594), where a cavernous contemporary lobby of shiny marble leads to a lounge, bar, and restaurant; the 79 trim rooms all have private bath or shower and air conditioning. Singles cost 7,229 drs ($56); doubles, 9,584 drs ($74). A few blocks away, at the **Hotel Christina,** 15 Petmeza, at the corner of Kallirrois Avenue (tel. 9215-353), the cabin-size guest rooms rent for 4,900 drs ($38), with breakfast, single, 7,500 drs ($58) double; they're convenient to the Olympic downtown terminal.

The modern, immaculate **Divani-Zafolia Palace,** 19-25 Parthenonos St. (tel. 9222-945), is popular with tour groups from all over Europe, but the cool, marble lobby is almost spacious enough to accommodate everyone's luggage at one time. There's a

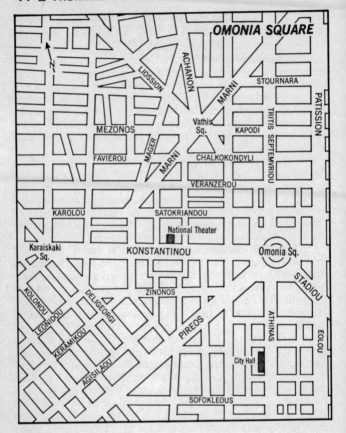

OMONIA SQUARE

pleasant dining room to the right of the lobby that offers a three-course lunch or dinner for 1,170 drs ($9), a lounge/bar on the left, and down a flight of steps a gift shop shares a foyer with a glass-enclosed expanse of the Wall of Themistocles, dating from 479 B.C. Guest rooms fill six floors, each with marble floors and trim-and-tidy decor in shades of brown, individual air conditioning, telephone, radio, and balcony. Parthenonos is a residential street in the shadow of the Acropolis, so street noise is not too much of a problem. Rooms at the front have angled views of the Parthenon, but those at the rear on the upper floors have unobstructed views of Philopappus Hill. This is an ideal location if you're planning to spend much time at the Athens Festival performances in the Herod Atticus Theater—a five-minute walk away. Rates are 8,400 drs ($65) single, 9,500 drs ($73) double.

Farther down Syngrou Avenue, the eight-story, Class B **Hotel Ilissos River,** 72 Kallirrois Ave. (tel. 9215-371), opened its doors in the spring of 1980. Its location is perhaps more suited to business travelers and groups than to tourists (it's ten minutes by taxi from Syntagma), but anyone would welcome the smart Class A comfort of its 96 rooms, twin-level dining room, and club-like, marble-floored lounge although the dining room lacks charm or character. The rooms (with bath/shower, air conditioning, radio, direct-dial telephone) are good value at 4,764 drs ($37) single, 6,726 drs ($52) double.

There's more good value in the opposite direction, four blocks beyond the Hilton and near the Holiday Inn, where 8,682 drs ($67) gets you a double room with breakfast at the **Golden Age Hotel,** 57 Michalakopoulou Ave. (tel. 7240-861). You're greeted by a multimarbled lobby with an unusual decorative frieze lining the mezzanine, a streetside café with desultory service, and a comfortable bar/lounge; downstairs, the attractive taverna doubles as a discothèque after dinner in winter. The 122 guest rooms are comfortable furnished (the singles have double beds), and rent for 6,807 drs ($53) single, 8,682 drs ($67) double.

At 25 Michalakopoulou, the Class B **Hotel Ilissia** (tel. 7244-051), now tucks 72 trim and tidy rooms (only 18 of them singles) into a corner site just around the corner from the Hilton, next door to the Flame Steak House. The friendly owners don't insist on half board (they don't have a restaurant, but they do serve light snacks from 7 p.m. to midnight), take in very few groups, and cater primarily to business travelers, many of them connected with the American Embassy. All rooms have air conditioning plus bath or shower; most of them have balconies. Singles cost 3,982 drs ($31) to 5,131 drs ($39); doubles, 5,971 drs ($46) to 7,818 drs ($60).

The high-rise, 513-room **President Hotel,** 43 Kifissias Ave. (tel. 692-4600), is one of Athen's biggest Class A establishments, although its stylishly modern lobby (acres of marble in earthy colors, concealed lighting, pop music) might lead you to believe you'd stepped into a deluxe hotel; bars, lounges, and dining facilities are equally spacious. The guest rooms, on the other hand, are dainty, although pretty to look at and fitted with direct-dial telephone, air conditioning, radio, and balcony. The 22nd floor is given over to a swimming pool, sun terrace, and discothèque, but the President's basement may be the best feature if you plan to do a lot of driving—it has space for 500 cars. Room rates are 6,455 drs ($50) double, and the fact that you don't have to take a half-board rate even in summer may compensate for its slightly inconvenient location. The President is located on one of the main avenues leading north from Athens (convenient for touring by car), but a 10- to 15-minute taxi ride from Syntagma.

NEAR SYNTAGMA: Still another relatively new hotel, still another American-style façade, the **Astor Hotel,** 16 Karageorgi tis Servias (tel. 3255-555), is right in the center of one of the busiest areas of town, with taxis and people constantly passing up and down Karageorgi tis Servias on their way from the Plaka to Constitution (Syntagma) Square. Once inside, however, you're not too conscious of noise. The hotel sits back from the street, with its entrance under an arcade that blocks out the traffic noises as well as the harsh sun.

The Astor has 11 air-conditioned floors, with the top floor given over to the Roof Garden. One of Athens's few year-round roof gardens, it sprawls over the terrace in summer, but in winter it's enclosed in glass that doesn't confine the view. And what a view! Look up from your table and there's the Acropolis looking as though it's across the street. Over on the right you can see Lycabettus Hill, and over on the left Mount Pentelicon. You can have lunch or dinner up here for 1,700 drs ($13).

The Astor has 133 rooms and suites, and most of the rooms above the sixth floor have views (except for the singles, which are all at the rear), and most of them also have balcony. The furniture is nothing to write home about and the place needs sprucing up, but again, you may be too busy looking at the view from your balcony to care much. Down in the basement there's a well-stocked souvenir shop and beauty parlor, and just off the lobby, a small, rather dreary bar. Summer rates are 4,898 drs ($38) single, 6,276 drs ($48) double, with breakfast.

The **Hotel Electra,** 5 Ermou St. (tel. 3223-223), is another of those modern hotels that look more like office buildings than hotels—especially at street level where the narrow glass door is surrounded by shops and cafés. Once you step through into the lobby, however, you're unmistakably in a grand hotel. The lobby, recently restyled, now has an island reception desk and a stylish bar with decorative tiles, oak counter top, and padded stools with backrests.

The corridors on the guest-room floors have olive carpets, dark-green ceilings, and gray floral wallpaper. The floral wallpaper overflows into some of the rooms, which all have polished parquet floors or spotless linoleum with scatter rugs, marble-floored bathroom with tiled walls, twin beds, a desk/dresser unit, armchair, phone, and individual air-conditioning control.

On the eighth floor there are four rooms with eight-foot-square terraces. The hotel is air-conditioned throughout, and all 110 rooms have massage units attached to the beds (25 drs per three-minute massage). The Electra insists on half board all year; in summer, singles are 9,560 drs ($74); doubles, 13,580 drs ($104).

Turn right into Filellinon Street from the Mitropoleos Street corner of Syntagma, and three blocks later you come to a small square with an old Byzantine church and tower and three palm trees. The **Olympic Palace Hotel,** 16 Filellinon (tel. 3237-611), is the modern building just across the street, with the neat square verandas on three sides. The lobby is the usual palace of glass and marble, leading into a larger lounge with almost enough armchairs to seat every guest in the hotel. There's also a small bar with comfy upholstered chairs, and, one floor up, a big bright dining room with lots of windows and flowers.

All the Olympic Palace's rooms, which should have been renovated by 1989, have private bath, music, telephones, air conditioning, modern furniture, and the bathrooms have marble floors and floral wallpaper. Most rooms have (albeit small) balconies. There are corner suites that sleep three. Despite its location close to Constitution Square, the Olympic Palace is a relatively quiet hotel; and despite the tempting photograph on its brochure, none of the rooms has a proper view of the Acropolis though some pleasantly overlook the church square. Rates are 5,500 drs ($42) single, 6,900 drs ($53) double.

Esperia Palace, 22 Stadiou St. (tel. 3238-001), is on one of the big thoroughfares that link Syntagma with Omonia Square, and 22 is closer to Syntagma than to Omonia. It's a convenient location, but it can get noisy at rush hours so ask for a room high up (there are nine floors) or at the rear. (There are balconies of sorts, but only for standing on, so they're not worth making a hassle over.) The Esperia is yet another of those Athenian palaces with acres of marbled space—a two-story lobby, with marble floors and columns, marble hallways on each floor—and the inevitable highly polished floors. The 185 newly renovated rooms have fresh wallpaper, prints or pictures to brighten them up, colorful bedspreads and curtains, carpeting and furniture that's a shade more substantial and comfortable than usual in Greece. Rooms on the sides have views of Lycabettus (from the sixth floor up), or the Acropolis (fourth floor up). There's also an attractive wood-paneled restaurant and café on the main floor and a big comfortable lounge at the

A SWIM WITH A VIEW. Imagine staying in a modern hotel five minutes from Syntagma, on the edge of the Plaka, in the shadow of the Acropolis, *and being able to have a swim in a rooftop pool before your siesta.* Then check into the **Electra Palace Hotel,** 18 Nicodimou St. (tel. 3241-401), and have your dreams come true. It is here that you may also find yourself sitting at sundown in a swinging, canvas love seat, sipping an ouzo and watching the light fade on the Parthenon. This roof garden, with its loungers, bamboo chairs, elevated pool, and bar, is reason enough for staying at the Electra Palace (opened in 1974), but it's by no means the only one. Even without its roof, this would be one of the best values in the city, a Class A hotel with more attractive rooms than many deluxe hotels. For a start, the 106 rooms are "warmer," less institutional than most of the city's hostelries—with brown-gold-red wall-to-wall carpeting, matching headboards, and twin beds, plus a sofa and armchair, occasional tables, desk/dresser, and fitted closets all in warm-hued wood. The tile-and-marble bathrooms have sophisticated fixtures and beautiful floral tiles; chambermaids and room waiters are announced by door chimes rather than a rat-ta-tat, and hallways are carpeted for soundproofing. All the rooms have air conditioning, radio, taped music, telephone, television, mini-bar, and lots of closet space; most of them also have balconies with sliding glass doors and sliding screens, and the suites on the upper floors have big terraces rather than balconies. Nikodimou Street is only one car wide, a trifle noisy at times, so ask for a high room. In any case, you have to be above the third floor to get the best view. But even if you can't have one of the upper rooms, stay there anyway—you can always spend your spare hours on the roof. The Electra Palace is owned by the same people who run the highly regarded Electra Hotel a few streets away, so the service is efficient, polite, and friendly. Other facilities include a sunken lounge in a spacious marble-and-mahogany lobby, a cozy bar, a large mezzanine dining room and lounge/card room, and adjoining garage. Summer rates are 6,640 drs ($51) single, 8,300 drs ($64) double for half board (which is obligatory year round).

top of the spiral staircase. High-season rates are 5,820 drs ($45) single, 7,750 drs ($60) double.

A Class B choice, **Hotel Lycabettus,** 6 Valaoritiou St. (tel. 3633-514), is a five-minute walk from Syntagma, on one of the quieter shopping streets now part of the pedestrians-only mall. All the rooms on its seven floors have telephones, radio, balconies, and air conditioning. The best of the bunch are on the upper floors (where the balconies are bigger). The Lycabettus is a friendly little place, with a TV bar, coffeeshop, and a breakfast room. Room rates here are 4,738 drs ($36) for a single, 7,072 drs ($54) for a double, including breakfast. It's not a steal, but good value considering the location and the coziness.

Athens Gate Hotel, 10 Syngrou Ave. (tel. 9238-302), is, on the other hand, one of Athens's top values. Location first: a five-minute walk from Syntagma and directly across the avenue from the Temple of Olympian Zeus and its attendant Hadrian's Gate. There's also a gleaming black-leather, chrome, and marble bar and lounge on the ground floor, but don't linger—head straight for the elevator and press the top button. The roof is eight stories up, a walk-around marble sundeck with a view! All the sights are there —Olympian Zeus and Hardrian's Gate just across the street, the Zappeion and Parliament to the left, Lycabettus in the distance, the Olympic Stadium, and the Royal Palace; then on the other side, the towering Acropolis, and away in the distance the Saronic Gulf.

Most of the 106 rooms come with balconies, and depending on location, you'll probably enjoy some part of this vista without leaving your room. Get your reservation in early, ask for a room on the seventh floor at the rear, and you'll get a large, plant-filled terracotta terrace rather than a balcony, with room for breakfasting or sunning while you look up at the looming Acropolis. The rooms themselves are livelier than the usual in Athens—with fresh razzle-dazzle wallpapers and drapes, carpeted floors, functional mahogany furniture (desk/dresser, armchair), radio, bedside lamps, modern tiled bathrooms, and a couple of features you don't normally find in Class B hotels—air conditioning and direct-dial telephones. Other facilities include room service until midnight, a cheery 100-seat restaurant on the second floor, and a new roof-garden restaurant with bar, barbecue, and breathtaking views of the Parthenon, Temple of Zeus, Lycabettus Hill, and Hadrian's Gate. There are also garage facilities available. High-season rates, all with breakfast, are 8,350 drs ($64) single, 10,450 drs ($80) double—and well worth every drachma.

Kolonaki is one of the most fashionable neighborhoods in Athens, much sought after by bankers and novelists, and now you can stay there in a quiet residential street, surrounded by high-rent apartments, for reasonable prices. The **Athenian Inn,** entered by a flower-decked entrance at 22 Haritos, just two blocks from

Kolonaki Square (tel. 7238-097), is owned by a Greek couple who've decorated it tastefully in "Greek village" style (dark beams, white stucco walls, tile floor). The lounge-breakfast-room-bar features an open fire, rustic furniture, and watercolors by local artists; the 28 guest rooms have wall-to-wall carpeting, quaint rustic-style wooden bed, radio, telephone, and bath or shower; 23 of the rooms have balcony, some with a view of Lycabettus Hill. Summer rates: 4,625 drs ($36) single, 6,728 drs ($52) double, including service charge, taxes, and breakfast in the pretty, rustic lounge.

While the outside of the **Hotel Arethusa,** corner of Mitropoleos and Nikis (tel. 3229-431), is gift-wrapped in what looks like Reynolds-Wrap aluminum foil, the interior decor is a lively blend of marble, polished hardwoods, and fabrics in once-sprightly colors. All 87 rooms in this attractive hostelry are decked out with contemporary furniture, wall-to-wall carpets, air conditioning (with individual controls), radio, telephone, big bathroom. Up top there's an indoor-outdoor roof garden (superb view, dinner for around 1,200 drs, or just over $9), and you can have an after-dinner drink in the modern bar (with TV), one hushed floor above busy Mitropoleos. The Arethusa is unusually handsome as Class B hotels go, and the rates are still reasonable— 4,500 drs ($35) single, 6,700 drs ($52) double, including breakfast and air conditioning.

You can't get a much more central location than the **Minerva Athens Hotel,** 3 Stadiou St. (tel. 3230-915)—the upper floors of the business center above the arcade that runs from Syntagma to Stadiou Street. The Minerva was transformed into a Class B hotel in 1960, 50 rooms on three floors (6, 7, 8), all with private tub or shower, room phone, and air conditioning. The rooms are clean but spare, with balconies; the first two floors pick up a lot of street noise. There's no restaurant, but a spiral staircase leads from the arcade-level lobby to a small lounge where you can sit down to the continental breakfast that's included in the room rate—3,540 drs ($27) single, 5,392 drs ($41) double, with air conditioning.

Appollonos Street is hotel row. It runs for half a dozen blocks from the Plaka to Constitution Square, and it's full of good budget hotels. The **Omiros Hotel,** 15 Apollonos St. (tel. 3235-486), is one of the newer and smaller ones. It has 37 rooms, all with pink or green tiled bathroom, telephone, radio, and air conditioning. It's a dapper little hotel. The lobby has handsome wood paneling with Ancient Greek ceramic decorations on the walls, and a coffee corner at the back. There's also a small but pleasant breakfast room. The rooms are equally compact, some with head-to-head beds along one wall, a small couch along the other. The rooms facing the street have a balcony overlooking the narrow, typically Athenian street, with balustrades, arcades, shutters, and pots of flowers. Some of the back rooms (ask for no. 504 or 505) have huge terraces. Most of the rooms have scatter rugs on linoleum floors, and the furnishings are standard: twin beds, desk, wardrobe. There's taped pop music everywhere at the Omiros—in the lobby, in the elevator, in the rooms, on the roof. The pride and joy of the Omiros is its Roof Garden, which has one of the most unobstructed views of the Acropolis in the entire city (it's amazing how a modest little hotel can take on a new dimension of majesty with a superb Roof Garden vista of that omnipresent sacred hill).

The Omiros's rates are 4,150 drs ($32) for a single, 5,750 drs ($44) for doubles.

NEAR OMONIA SQUARE: What the **Hotel Acropolis House** (tel. 3222-344) claims to offer its guests is "comfortable rooms and realistic prices at the gateway of the old city"—to be precise, doubles for 5,290 drs ($40), including breakfast and shower—at 6-8 Kodrou St. on the corner of Voulis Street, just seven minutes on foot from Syntagma (maybe 10 with a backpack or suitcase). This family-run, B-class pension fills a handsome 100-year-old villa with many of the original architectural devices preserved (decorative ceilings and friezes, intricate plasterwork and moldings, that sort of thing) and a newer 30-year-old wing. The breakfast room just to the left of the lobby is a high-ceilinged, old-style salon, and the owners, the Choudalakis family, are warm and welcoming. The 19 guest rooms come in various shapes and sizes, some with balcony, some with private shower, a few with Acropolis views.

A few paces up Kodrou and across the street, at No. 3, another B-class hotel, the **Adonis** (tel. 3249-737), is a complete contrast—modern, unadorned façade, 26 rooms with private shower and telephone. But what the Adonis has to show off about is a roof terrace for breakfast or evening snacks against a stunning backdrop of the looming Acropolis. Peak rates are 4,238 drs ($33) single, 5,040 drs ($39) double, with reductions for stays longer than two days.

In recent years, newcomers on the Athens hotel scene have all been in the deluxe category, but the only major opening in the past two "post-Libya" years is rated category A; however, with its smart lines, spacious ambience and stylish interiors, it's a better buy than many of the city's so-called deluxe hotels. The new **Novotel Mirayia Athens Hotel** at 4-8 Michail Voda St. (tel. 8627-053) is located about seven walking minutes from the National Archeological Museum in one direction, a few paces less from the railroad station in the other. The French hotel chain's first venture in Athens, the new Mirayia is a handsome eight-story structure of white stone, its first two floors set behind two-story windows, the top two floors stepped back behind balconies and verandas, the remainder trimmed with window boxes trailing geraniums. The shiny marble lobby leads to an inviting café/restaurant, Le Grill, designed as a sort of conservatory with arched glass ceilings and floor-to-ceiling walls overlooking a decorative courtyard with still more geraniums. But it's the Roof Garden that's the real stunner here: big tiled swimming pool surrounded by split-level sunning terraces, blue-and-white striped awnings for shade, terraced gardens at one end and behind them a panoramic view of the Acropolis and Lycabettus.

With the exception of five suites on the seventh floor, the Novotel's 190 rooms are identical except for location: with double-glazed windows and additional soundproofing throughout, traffic noise is unlikely to be a factor on the street side; and with the window boxes and decorative courtyard at the rear, rooms at the back are more appealing than usual. All rooms come with smart modern bathrooms (including speaker and phone extensions), direct-dial telephone, satellite TV, mini-bar, alarm clock, air conditioning, double beds, and sofa—all done in light soothing colors.

Additional public features include underground parking for 150 cars, room service, and business facilities. One rate applies for the entire year: 8,600 drs ($66) single and 10,500 drs ($81) double for the rooms, 16,500 drs ($127) single or double for the suites. Buffet breakfast in the conservatory restaurant is an additional 750 drs ($6).

The **King Minos Hotel,** 1 Piraeus St. (tel. 5231-111), is a Class A hotel, close to Omonia Square. It's only a few steps from the square, but its glass-and-grillwork façade is more reminiscent of the Caribbean. The hotel has a spacious lobby, with a marble frieze of King Minos's Palace in Knossos dominating one wall. Up on the mezzanine floor are acres of comfortable lounges, two desks with typewriters, an American bar, fountains, birds in a gilded cage, and a restaurant. There are seven floors of rooms (200 all together), and the King Minos was fully renovated in 1987, including repainting, installing double windows to block street noise and fitting the rooms with individual heating and air-conditioning units. The room furnishings are fresh and modern, with roomy closets, chairs and desks, and marble balconies. Bathrooms have full-size bathtub, marble floors, and walls, and piles of towels; studios have twin beds, arranged at right angles around a brace of chairs and a coffee table. If you feel cramped, you can always sit out on the balcony and watch the action in Omonia Square. Or go up to the roof to sunbathe. Peak-season rates are 6,500 drs ($50) single, 9,200 drs ($71) double, including breakfast.

Hotel Stanley, 1 Odysseos St. at Karaiskaki Square (tel. 5241-611), is another moderately priced Class B hotel with a pool on the roof. It's a slight distance from the center of town, but its roof is one of the coolest, breeziest places in town at high noon, with a great view as a bonus. The 400-room Stanley dominates the big square at the end of Aghiou Konstantinou Avenue, between Omonia Square and the Larissis railroad station.

It's a modern air-conditioned hotel, where every room has a bath or shower, balcony, and direct-dial telephone. The rooms are big and have been repainted and refurnished with new, dark wood beds, vanities, etc. The rooftop pool and garden are open from May through October. An attractive first-floor restaurant with Scandinavian decor and mottled marble floor is open year round (with three-course meals for 1,450 drs, or less than $11) and there's also an inexpensive cafeteria as well as a bar and TV lounge.

Despite its size, the Stanley is usually full, so if you don't have a reservation, call ahead first. It's a good value, with singles for 5,505 drs ($42) and doubles for 7,466 drs ($57).

Two of the best values in and around Omonia Square are relatively recent Class B Superior hotels—the Titania and the Dorian Inn, both opened in 1976.

A stylish tinted-glass façade rising eight floors above a street-level shopping arcade (look for the hotel sign *inside* the arcade) identifies the **Hotel Titania** at 52 Panepistimiou Ave. (tel. 3609-611). Up on the roof, the terrace and bar (sometimes with music) have impressive views of Lycabettus Hill and the Acropolis. The Titania's 400 rooms and a score of suites fill six floors with bright colors and trim design; all the rooms have telephone, individual heating/cooling controls, fitted wall cabinets, three-channel music, television (on request), and tiled bathroom with tub and hand-shower. Public facilities include a colorful coffeeshop (there's also room service from 7 a.m. to 11 p.m.), spacious restaurant, and lounge/writing room on the mezzanine. Summer rates are 7,470 drs ($57) single, 9,750 drs ($75) double, with breakfast. Good value in a convenient location, with parking for 400 cars (the traffic hurtling along Panepistimiou is not too intrusive with the windows closed, but if you want complete quiet, ask for a room at the rear).

The **Dorian Inn Hotel** is located on the far side of Omonia Square at 15-17 Piraeus St. (tel. 5239-782). Its 117 comfortable, carpeted rooms and 29 junior suites were all recently repainted and have direct-dial telephone, individual controls for heating and air cooling, and three-channel music; half of them have balcony.

There's room service from 7 a.m. to midnight, a restaurant, a bar-lounge with TV, and another bar/grill on the roof, 12 floors above the city, with an excellent view of the Acropolis and Lycabettus. But the Dorian's main attraction for many people will be the rooftop pools—one for adults, one for children. Peak-season rates are 4,500 ($35) single, 6,800 drs ($52) double, with buffet breakfast.

The Class B **Grand Hotel,** 19 Patission St. (tel. 5243-156), doesn't quite live up to its name—but then neither do its rates. The decor, if not very inspired, is crisp and fresh, newly renovated with brand-new interior spring mattresses, and tiled bathroom that are shiny clean (some have bath and shower, some shower only); several rooms have small balcony and Acropolis views. The mezzanine floor is given over to spacious lounges (with TV), bar, and dining room, and the high-ceilinged lobby has three elevators to speed you to your room. The 100 guest rooms come with air conditioning, telephone, two channels of music, and balcony. The Grand is located in a bustling part of town, just off Omonia Square, a few blocks from the National Archeological Museum; if you want complete silence, check into one of the viewless rooms at the rear, but with windows and shutters closed, the rooms over-looking the traffic are tolerable. Doubles cost 7,748 drs ($60); singles 5,535 drs ($43).

At first glance, the **Hotel Ionis,** 41 Halkokondyli (tel. 5232-311), looks like yet another modern office building on a street of undistinguished office buildings, but once you step through the smoked-glass doors you enter an oasis of style. Gleaming gray marble, polished wood, and brightly colored ceramics create a welcoming lobby; a marble stairway winds up to a mezzanine restaurant, spacious lounge with TV, and a bar with ceramic friezes depicting willowy nymphs. Corridors are carpeted, windows are double glazed, cheerful curtains and bedspreads are color coordinated, and each recently refurbished room has air conditioning, telephone, and two-channel radio. Rooms on the street side have balcony (on the upper floors, terraces rather than balconies). Although Halkokondyli is not the "smartest" street in town it has some advantages: it's quiet in the evening when all the office workers have gone home; it's only five minutes on foot from Omonia Square and 15 to 20 minutes to the National Archeological Museum; and rooms cost less than they would on more fashionable thoroughfares. For 5,400 drs ($41) single and 7,400 drs ($57) double (both with breakfast), you probably won't find smarter rooms in Athens.

If you enjoy browsing around markets, the **Athens Center Hotel,** 26 Sofokleouus St. at Klisthenous (tel. 5248-511), puts you within walking distance of the central meat, fish, vegetable, and fruit markets, and close enough to the flea markets at Monastiriki. This may not be the most congenial corner of the city for women traveling alone, but the hotel itself is bustling with small tour groups and there's an amiable atmosphere around the lounge/piano bar and rooftop terrace, now with bar and a brand-new swimming pool to add to the fun. All 136 good-sized rooms have private bath or shower, carpeting, and air conditioning; a few have balcony (ask for an eighth-floor room, with a huge terrace and stunning views). Other amenities include a convivial snackbar, restaurant, and parking garage for 25 cars. Rates, including breakfast, are 5,294 drs ($41) single, 7,485 drs ($58) double.

CLASS C AND D HOTELS
(FROM $17 TO $52 DOUBLE,
PEAK SEASON)

Good news for budget travelers: the official hotel guide to Athens includes more names in categories C and D than in all the others put together. In all, there are well over 100 hotels in Athens offering rooms between $13 and $36 a night for doubles in peak season. This guide can't possibly review all of them, but in the following pages you'll find a selection of some of the best budget hotels in the city.

NEAR SYNTAGMA: The 14-year-old **Hermes Hotel,** 19 Appollonos St. (tel. 3235-514), has an entrance like an airline terminal, but its severe façade is softened somewhat by hints of shrubbery draping over the balconies. It's a small hotel—only 45 rooms—all with balcony, air conditioning, phone, and bath or shower. The rooms at the rear look out on a school playground; the upper floors have views of the city, and in some cases the Acropolis. Room rates are 4,050 drs ($31) for a single, 5,500 drs ($42) for a double—all the rooms are actually double-size.

The **Imperial Hotel,** 46 Mitropoleos (tel. 3227-617), has a slightly Germanic façade—square cut with small windows. It doesn't have a lobby at the entrance, but when you go up one flight you'll find a pleasant sitting room, and the manager, G. Klissouris, who speaks English, is anxious to please, and enjoys meeting all the Americans who stay in his hotel. The Imperial's rooms are simple, clean, and large, and all but two have shower or bath. All have a telephone, balcony, and central heating (but no air conditioning). The singles have double beds and tend to be roomier than most singles in this price range. There's free parking in the square across the street. Most of its balconies look toward the cathedral and

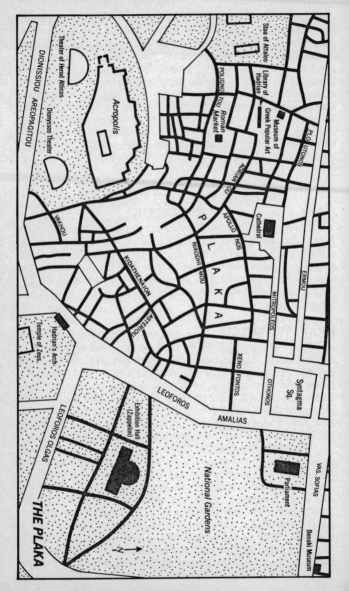

THE PLAKA

Acropolis. There are 21 rooms on five floors; rates are 3,200 drs ($25) single, 3,840 drs ($29) double.

Kolokotroni is the street that begins at the National Historical Museum and runs more or less parallel to Ermou and Mitropoleos. The **Hotel Carolina** is about halfway down at 55 Kolokotroni (tel. 3220-837), easily identified by its freshly painted façade. It's one of those places you walk into and instantly feel at home. The Carolina is family owned and run by the affable Athanasios Papayiannoulas and his brother, George. Every room faces the front or side, most have balcony, and they share eight spanking-clean bathrooms (some private baths available). The best rooms are on the top floor and the corner rooms have Acropolis views, but since this is the kind of hotel where you'll be constantly meeting new friends and dashing off to a favorite taverna in the Plaka, the view probably doesn't matter much. There's a small snackbar on the first floor, a few steps up from the lobby. You can also store your luggage here if you're planning short stays away from Athens. The single rates are 2,658 ($20) without bath, 3,323 drs ($26) with bath; doubles are 3,766 drs ($29) without, 4,320 drs ($33) with. The rooms are quiet. The fun is free.

For people who want to be in the heart of things, you can't be much closer to the heart of old Athens than the intersection of Iperidou and Asteriou Streets in the Plaka. Here the 14-year-old **Hotel Nefeli,** at 16a Iperidou St. (tel. 3228-044), squeezes 18 spic-and-span rooms into a three-story wedge, each of its chambers equipped with modern tiled bathroom, room phone, trim furniture, and windows that open on to cheery geranium planters. Nothing fancy, but comfortable and functional. The spacious, cool lobby is dominated by an orange plastic phone bubble, and there's a pleasant breakfast room-lounge right on the corner. It's obviously not the quietest spot in the city, and when the Plaka wakes up so will you, but here are modern rooms in a central location for only 4,000 drs ($31) single, 5,200 drs ($40) double, including room, breakfast, and taxes. First choice in this category.

Walk into the lobby of the **Hotel Phoebus** at 12 Peta St. (tel. 3220-142) and you're likely to hear strains of Strauss—Johann *and* Richard. This pleasant little Class C hotel on a quiet Plaka street off Filellinon is family owned and operated by the friendly, helpful Drina Papadopoulou (she grew up in the house) and her gracious, multilingual husband, Marcos Bournelakis. All but four or five of the 23 big, comfortable rooms have balcony; on the top floor they turn into huge terraces with terrific Acropolis views. The high-ceilinged rooms were recently repainted and are plainly furnished: single bed, sturdy wardrobe, a few chairs, but antique floral prints and big, blossomy window boxes cheer things up. The private bathrooms are small, with hand-held shower. Downstairs, there's a cozy breakfast room/living room with fresh flowers, a tiled fireplace, borrowers' library, writing desk, and comfy, oversize chairs. Rates are reasonable: 3,300 drs ($25) single, 4,400 drs ($34) double. Reservations are suggested since many guests book return visits in advance.

A GOOD VALUE FIND. Here's a real little find, opened in 1983—the **Hotel Hera,** 9 Falirou St. (tel. 9236-682), facing a small square in a residential section between the Acropolis and Syngrou Avenue, a five-minute walk from the Plaka. The stylish façade, like a miniature Ledra Marriott, fronts a spic-and-span split-level lobby that opens onto a lounge with TV and a coffeeshop with marble-topped tables, which in turn leads to a quiet, sunny patio café. The 49 guest rooms, on five floors, are compact to be sure, but sensibly designed (plenty of storage space for suitcases or backpacks), each with air conditioning, direct-dial telephone, radio, twin cot-size beds covered with brightly colored spreads, skimpy drapes covering sliding windows that shut out most neighborhood noise. The tiled bathrooms (showers only) are spotless. For Acropolis views you have to head for the rooftop terrace. It's a good value at 4,500 drs ($35) single and 6,700 drs ($52) double.

The **Philippos Hotel,** 3 Mitseon (tel. 9223-611), is something of an oddity—it's on the *other* side of the Acropolis, the side with the classic picture-postcard view. This is a residential district, except during the Athens Festival when it becomes a funnel for the crowds heading up the road to the Pnyx for the Son-et-Lumière show. If you're staying at the Philippos, you don't have to join the crowd, you simply step out onto your balcony and there's the whole show, right there.

The Philippos is a simple little hotel, that has been completely redecorated in recent years. You go up a few stairs to the tiny lobby and TV-fitted bar, where there always seem to be American college girls sitting around reading Aeschylus. The Philippos is another of those cozy, communal, everybody's-a-buddy places. Rooms on the upper floors can sleep five. The other rooms are plainly furnished, slightly cramped, but if you're in the first flush of Aeschylus you probably won't notice. The bathrooms are clean, tiled, and fitted with hand-shower. There is a balcony in every room, and on the upper floor they're as large as terraces and face up toward the Acropolis. And a surprise for a small budget hotel, you can phone down for sandwiches, snacks, or omelets 24 hours a day. You can sunbathe on the hotel's roof, and if you want to go sightseeing, you can catch the bus two blocks away and take it to Constitution Square and Omonia Square. Rates with breakfast are 3,722 drs ($29) single, 5,678 drs ($44) double in summer.

The location of the **Phaedre Hotel,** 16 Cherefontos St. (tel. 3238-461), belies the ominous overtones of its legendary namesake—on a quiet little square facing the palm-filled courtyard of St. Katherine's Church, surrounded by neighborhood tavernas and narrow streets, one block from Filellinon Street, near the Monument to Lysicrates. The rooms are relatively big and some have a small terrace, but none of them has a private bathroom, just washbasin, with three toilets to every floor—but then consider the rate: 3,127 drs, or just $24, double.

NEAR OMONIA SQUARE:
One of the best buys in the Omonia district is the three-year-old, Category C **Hotel La Mirage,** adjacent to the Omonia Hotel and right in the square although its official address is 3 Marikas Kotopouli St. (tel. 5234-071). It rises seven stories above the square, its 208 rooms blocking out the sounds with double-glazing, and each with tiled bathroom (shower only), radio, reading lamps, desk, telephone, and air conditioning. The second floor is given over to spacious lounges (with TV), a bar and restaurant, all with widescreen windows overlooking the square and the fountain—and worth keeping in mind for a moderately priced lunch or dinner (you can have an omelet for 280 drs, about $3, although the meat dishes are more expensive than in Plaka tavernas). The service is pleasant and you're only a few steps from the Metro. Single rates are 4,030 drs ($31), doubles 5,130 drs ($39).

The **Omonia Hotel,** right on Omonia Square (tel. 5237-211), has ten floors and 275 rooms, each of which has an iron balcony and picture windows which give the building an airy appearance. The lobby, one floor up above the entrance to the subway, is surrounded by a bar-café facing the square, with a restaurant at the rear. There's always plenty of activity around this friendly, spotless hotel; all rooms have private bath and shower, phone, and comfortable furniture, and they're particularly spacious, especially the singles—good value at 2,215 drs ($17) single, 2,880 drs ($22) double.

The **Asty Hotel,** 2 Pireos (tel. 5230-424), is a slightly younger hotel than its competitor on the next block—the Omonia. Its 128 rooms, most with balcony, half of them facing the square with its fountains and greenery, are clean and comfortable but rather "institutional." The Asty's restaurant, on the mezzanine overlooking the square is, incidentally, one of the more popular eating places in the neighborhood. Rates: doubles with bath cost 5,843 drs ($45); singles, 3,974 drs ($31).

The **Hotel Pythagorian,** 28 Aghiou Konstantinou (tel. 5242-811), is another of those good-guy Class C hotels with a very friendly staff, in the region of Omonia Square. The attractive entrance with square marble columns and vinyl "wood" paneling leads to a lobby and dining room with a white spiral stairway that goes up to a mezzanine lounge with green marble floor and overstuffed chairs. The 56 rooms, spread over seven floors and topped with a roof garden, all have tiled bathroom with bath and bidet, rooms with typical lino-floor-plain-modern-furniture decor. Rooms at the front have balcony. 1989 rates are 4,600 drs ($35) single, 5,600 drs ($43) double, with breakfast.

The street that runs from Omonia to Ermou is called Athinas, and halfway down it crosses Evripidou. Aghiou Demetriou is where the two streets meet (round the corner, off Evripidou). Okay? The **Hotel Kronos,** 18 Aghiou Demetriou (tel. 3211-601), is actually in a convenient location for either the hustle and bustle of Omonia or the hustle and bustle of the Plaka. It's a small modern hotel with a very small sign, across from a small square with a church, trees, and grass. Most of the rooms (comfortable, big, and spotless) have private tiled bath. Rooms with bath are 2,105 drs ($16) single and 2,215 drs ($17) double. (*Note:* A sister hotel, **Neon Kronos,** a few blocks away at 12 Assomaton St., is also good value at roughly the same rates.)

Theater Square, unfortunately, no longer has a theater—it's now backstage Athens, a beehive of importers and exporters by day, and quiet as a church by night (but probably not for single women). The 18-year old **Hotel Alkistis,** 18 Platia Theatrou (tel. 3219-811), has a sleek ten-story façade of glass, steel, and marble, and 128 rooms and eight suites with motel-modern decor, private bath and shower, and telephone. Some 128 of the rooms have balcony, and if you pick the right one, you'll have a fine view of the Acropolis. All the rooms and hallways are spotless and freshly painted; the comfortable, spacious lounge has TV and a bar and the roof garden boasts a panoramic view (there are tables and chairs, but no bar service so you have to bring up your own drinks). When you step into the Alkistis's two-story marble lobby you may have trouble believing you're in a Class C hotel, but one look at the rates and you'll be persuaded that this is another of the city's remarkable bargains. Summer rates are about 2,750 drs ($21) in a single with bathroom, and breakfast, 3,800 drs ($29) in a double with same. These low rates are reduced by 10% in the off-season. *But get your reservations in early—the Alkistis is one of the most popular Class C hotels in Athens. Note:* Platia Theatrou is kitty corner from the Omega Hotel, below.

The **Hotel Nestor,** 58 Aghiou Konstantinou (tel. 5235-576), has a rather olive-drab exterior but the 50 rooms themselves are bigger than usually found in this category, bright, with handsome furniture, pastel-colored walls and balcony, and all have bath or shower. There's an outdoor café, and a dining room enlivened with fresh flowers on every table. The friendly, 50-room, seven-story Nestor has been popular for years with Scandinavians: now it's the turn of the Americans. Singles are 4,500 drs ($35) and doubles are 5,900 drs ($45) in peak season.

Another gleaming, marble-façaded hotel with its front steps in the market is the **Omega Hotel,** 15 Aristoghitonos (tel. 312-421). This one has a roomy, wood-paneled lobby, a pleasant lounge and coffee bar. All of its 54 rooms have private bathroom, but the furnishings are fairly basic. Still a good bet at 3,545 drs ($27) double.

Platia Exarchia is a charming triangular plaza lined with trees and cafés, with its apex at the **Hotel Exarchion.** This Class C hotel, built in 1973, has 64 rooms (all with private bath or shower, most with balcony), and there's a splendid view across the city from the rooftop bar, six floors up. Double rooms are 3,396 drs ($26); breakfast is an additional 300 drs ($2.30) per person. If your first stop in Athens is the National Archeological Museum, and you want to be in an area that's Athenian rather than touristy, then this is a good address to head for—55 Themistokleous (tel. 3601-256).

The **Hotel Museum,** 16 Bouboulinas St. at Tossita Street (tel. 3605-611), is a friendly, pleasant, spotless C-class hostelry located right behind the National Archeological Museum. Of its 59 rooms, 52 are doubles with balcony, all at the front, and the remaining seven are singles, all at the rear; all 59 come with private shower, telephone, and taped music. The mezzanine floors are given over to a cafeteria and bar/lounge. Singles cost 2,200 drs ($17) and doubles run 2,900 drs ($22)—which makes the Museum popular with visiting professors and students.

ROCK-BOTTOM ACCOMMODATIONS FOR ADVENTURERS AND STUDENTS

In a city like Athens, where 1,560 drs ($12) will set you up in a single room in a very nice hotel in the off-season, you hardly need to bother with the local rock-bottom prices. However, thousands of young (and some not so young) people arrive in Greece each year with minimal dollars in their pockets and backpacks on their shoulders, and Athenians seem to go out of their way to cater to them, although in 1983 the government started to clamp down on many of the pensions and hotels offering dormitory-type accommodations.

The **YWCA**, or **X.E.N.** as it's known in Greece, hardly deserves the title rock-bottom, because it's in a big, modern building that at first glance seems more like a first-class hotel, in a convenient location—at 11 Amerikis St. (tel. 3624-291), just a couple of blocks from Syntagma and the American Express office. X.E.N. has a hairdressing salon and library, as well as kitchen and laundry facilities on every floor. Each room has beds, tables, chairs, marble floors; there's no air conditioning, but the sunless rooms at the rear are cool even at midday in midsummer. June through October, rates for stays of one to three nights are from 780 drs ($6) for a single without bath, double that for a double room with bath.

The **Athens Youth Hostel** at 57 Kypselis St. (tel. 8225-860) charges about 450 drs ($3) to 600 drs ($5), with facilities for breakfast and light meals. It's open all year, but you need an International Youth Hostel Card (you can buy one on the spot for 1,200 drs, or $9.25 and it's valid all over the world). *Note:* The hostel now organizes group tours at appropriate rates. Ask for details.

Since the government decided to eliminate most dormitory-style accommodations for backpackers and students, Cleo's Guest House has gone and now there's only **Cleo's Hotel** (or Cleopatra, in the official listing), consisting of a dozen small but clean rooms (some rooms have Acropolis views), at 3 Patrou St. (tel. 3229-053). It's located more or less in the Plaka, across the street from the Hotel Hermes, and a few blocks from the cafés of Constitution Square. All rooms come with shower and telephone; doubles are 4,133 drs ($32); triples 4,740 drs ($36).

CHAPTER VI

DINING OUT IN ATHENS

□ □ □

You may have heard some people say Greek food is dull. Dull? Try this for starters: *caravides*—fried crayfish with Russian dressing; *koheli*—lobster, mussels, crab, shrimp, or red snapper baked in a shell with cognac; *moussaka*—chopped meat with eggplant, cheese, and béchamel sauce; *teropita*—those delicious little cheese puffs filled with feta; *yigantes*—white lima beans in tomato sauce; *dolmadakia*—vine leaves stuffed with meat, onions, and spices, and served with lemon sauce.

That's not a random selection from many menus. It's not even a random selection from one menu. It's only the start of one recent meal, what the Greeks call *mezedes*, or hors d'oeuvres—which was concluded with mixed grill of lamb chop, veal, and kidney, tomato and spring onions, followed by a deep-fried fritter served in a hot sugar sauce, followed by apple spiced in honey.

So let's straighten out some of the facts about dining in Athens. Greek food is *not* dull. Maybe if you're staying there for a week or longer, your palate may lose its enthusiasm for more Greek food because so much of it is cooked in oil and flavored with lemon, or because so often it's lukewarm when served (on the theory that hot food is not good for you). But for the average visit of two or three days, you won't have time to sample all the dishes you're going to want to sample. If you do stay longer and you do want a change of pace, you can always go to one of the restaurants serving American or continental cuisines in their infinite variety.

Most Greek restaurants also serve a few dishes that are popular in Greece but that are not Greek dishes. Most of the inexpensive restaurants feature spaghetti, cannelloni, wienerschnitzels, omelets, and steaks. Remember, Greeks have been entertaining tourists from other European countries for a long time now, and try to cater to them. There always has been a choice of French and Turkish eating places, but now Athens has acquired Chinese and Japanese restaurants, even an English pub or two.

The other rumor you hear about Greek food is that it contains some unsavory ingredients. This is sometimes true in the country, and in the lambing season partially true in Athens. If anyone ever asks you if you'd like to try *ameletita,* just smile and say no thank you. Even in Greek it means unmentionables. Plural. Or if someone suggests *kokoretsi,* decline. It's second cousin to a Scottish haggis and we all know what a yummy that is. And don't be surprised if you take your Greek date to a seafood restaurant over by Piraeus and she gobbles up the entire fish—head, eyes, and all. It's not that she's starving. It's simply the Greek custom. You don't have to follow suit.

If you're tentative about what you eat (and when you're traveling, changing time zones, and generally rushing around, you have every right to be), stick to basic dishes like roast lamb and veal. They're cooked on the spit, with only a whisper of spices.

Unfortunately, as you'll see a few pages from now, inflation has been catching up with kitchens in Athens, and some of the basic Greek dishes are getting close to the point where they're not worth the price. Nevertheless, if you're on a tight budget your dollars will buy you more sustenance in Athens than in most European capitals. If you're really counting your leptas rather than drachmas, stick to restaurants *(estiatorion)* rather than tavernas, to *ouzeri* rather than cafés.

TYPES OF EATING PLACES AND DINING TIPS

TYPES OF EATING PLACES: The one thing that Greece has that most countries don't have is **tavernas.** There probably was a time when a taverna was something quite distinct from a restaurant—and even more distinct from a nightclub. But that's no longer the case. A taverna can be a pub, a restaurant, a café, a nightclub, or a combination of all of them. Since many of them provide music, and are really for an evening on the town, you'll read about them later on the chapter on nightlife.

The other unusual feature about Athenian eating places is the **roof garden.** Apparently the roofs of Greek houses used to be flat in order to collect rainwater, which was then drained off and fed into a tank under the soil; when proper plumbing and water systems came along, people didn't need their roofs as dams, but they then discovered that they were refreshingly cool places to spend an evening. So they started turning them into gardens, or at least terraces. The idea spread to restaurants. Now many of the new hotels in Athens include a roof garden, and you should certainly plan to spend at least one evening up there. There are also basic, authentic roof gardens on tavernas in the Plaka.

Athens at midday in midsummer is often too hot for sitting down to a meal, and this has probably given rise to the city's varied types of **snackbars**—the Western-style snackbar, the tea and pastry shops, the fig-and-nut store, the pastry vendor, and the souvlaki shop. Keep these snackbars in mind if you're on a budget, or if you're having problems adjusting to the curious meal hours in Athens (a subject I'll come to in a minute).

The Pastry Vendor

He's the local equivalent of the pretzel man. He sells two, sometimes three, items. First, there are rolls and hero-style breads, plus a bread known as *koulouri*—a large, thin bagel with sesame seed on top. It costs only a few drachmas—the perfect inexpensive snack. The pastries include plain *bourekia,* a sort of doughnut with sugar sprinkled on top. You can buy bourekia either in a "long-john" shape, or in a rounded shape with a small smidgen of jelly in the middle. *Bougatsa* is a pastry pie with cream inside, and sprinkled with powdered sugar. When filled with apples rather than cheese, it's known as *milopitta*. Some pastry vendors also have ham sandwiches, or *piroski* (bread with sausage inside).

Fig-and-Nut Shops

They sell figs, dates, prunes, walnuts, pistachios, almonds, honey, raisins, syrup, and so on. You buy by the drachma, and these goodies hit the spot if you're on a budget, or if it's a long time until your nine o'clock date.

Picnics

What with all that sunshine and all those scented lemon trees, you may want to find a corner of some centuries-old agora and have a picnic. To stock up, visit a grocery store or the Pris-Unic-Marinopoulos supermarket. Start with some cheese. The main types are *graviera* (Greek-Swiss), *feta* (Greek goat cheese), *kefalotiri* (a yellow, salted cheese), *kasseri* (a hard, yellow cheese), and *roquefort* (which in these parts is any kind of bleu cheese). The olives are stored in large wooden barrels and aged for months (order them by the drachma). Yogurt is ladled from large vats and spread onto wax paper. Ten drachmas' worth is probably your limit. You'll never taste fresher yogurt than in Greece (try it served with honey for breakfast). You may also want to check with the restaurant the **Stagecoach** at 14a Voukourestiou, which lists picnic boxes on its menu—mostly salads and sandwiches—for 910 drs ($7) or thereabouts.

Pastry Shops

The Greeks have sweet tooths. Shamelessly so. *Baklava* is a gooey goody made of layers of paper-thin pastry called *filo*, honey, nuts, pastry, honey, nuts, etc. *Kataifa* is equally gooey but filled with sweetened nuts and shreaded wheat, and in its most glorious state, served with a mound of chantilly cream. *Galaktoboureko* is much simpler—a hollow pastry filled to overflowing with custard cream. Greek chocolate, like Greek olives, is bitter, and you can sample it in the form of layer cakes, tub cakes, or flaky mounds. Many pastry shops (or *zacharoplasteions*) in Athens also sell coffee, so you can sit down and enjoy yourself right there and then—simply pointing to what you fancy.

Cafés

As in most Mediterranean countries, people pop into a café or *cafenion*, at the slightest opportunity. In winter, they'll have a quick espresso as a pick-me-up; in summer, something cooler. The café is an institution. Almost an epidemic—Constitution, or Syntagma, Square can seat 3,000 imbibers at one time. The café waiter is no less immaculately attired or competent than his counterpart in a real restaurant. Even the simplest order is attended to with style. Ask for a lemon juice and he'll bring you a tall glass with freshly pressed lemon juice, a carafe of water, and sugar on a silver tray—all for something like 230 drs ($2). And having paid your dues, you're free to sit in this informal "club" all afternoon watching the world go by, flirting, dozing, writing postcards. In Athens, as in other parts of Europe, it's perfectly proper to sit at an empty chair even when there are other people at the table.

DINING TIPS: The following few nuggets of information will make eating your way around Athens easier.

Refreshments

Coffee: Ordering a cup of coffee for the first time in Athens is almost as bewildering as trying to order a sandwich in New York if you're a stranger (white, whole-wheat, rye, pumpernickel, toast, etc.). The list of coffees on café menus in Athens goes roughly as follows—espresso, cappuccino, French, Viennese, Nescafé, Greek (which had been known as Turkish coffee until the troubles flared up in Cyprus in 1974). If you just say coffee, you get either Greek (if the waiter thinks you look Greek) or Nescafé (if he thinks you look American). What you probably want is, in fact, French. Nescafé is instant coffee brought to you with a cup and some hot water and you mix your own. Cappuccino comes from those hissing Italian coffee machines, and is a combination of coffee and cocoa with a white froth on top, sometimes served with a pinch of nutmeg or cinnamon. Coffee for the Greeks comes in three degrees of sweetness: *metrio*—medium strong, medium sweet; *variglyko*—strong and sweet; *sketo*—no sugar. Most Greeks seem to drink it *metrios,* and that's the way you'll probably prefer it. Besides, it's the easiest to say.

Wines and other liquid refreshments: You can't *not* drink wine in the land of Bacchus. Most people think of *retsina* when they think of Greek wines, but there's more to it than that. Retsina is resinated wine. Originally the resin was added to preserve the wine, then everyone liked it so much that way the resin stayed there. However, it's an acquired taste. Most visitors prefer the regular Greek wines, from the bottle rather than the barrel. There are hundreds of them, some good, some okay, some *yuggh*. Order the following and you won't go far wrong:

Reds: Demestica or robust Castel Danielis, both from the Peloponnese; Caviros or Cellar from Attica (the closest thing to a local Athenian wine); Naoussa from Macedonia; or Chevalier de Rhodes from Rhodes. Of these, Demestica is the least expensive, Caviros the most expensive. Porto Carras is a sturdy wine from new vineyards associated with a new resort in the north.

Whites: Again, Demestica, Santa Helena, or the muscadet-like but light Santa Laura, all from the Peloponnese; Robola from Cephalonia; Pallini, or the pricey Cava Cambas and Elissar from Attica; and Domaine Carras blanc de blanc from Porto Carras.

Rosés: Roditis, Cimarosa, King, Cellar.

Be adventurous and ask for half a kilo (yes, wine is measured by the kilo) of the open wine if they have it. This will be the local wine—the white will probably be resinated, the red probably not. Although retsina is an acquired taste it's surprising how fast many foreigners do acquire the taste, and at prices around 130 drs ($1) a kilo, who can blame them? Obviously you take pot-luck, but the wine from Attica, the region behind Athens, is usually good.

The main Greek apéritif is *ouzo,* a clear anise drink that turns misty gray when you add water. *Mastic* is a thick white gum from a tree that grows only on the island of Ios—it's dropped into a glass of water still clinging to the spoon and it's stickier and sweeter than anything in the world.

There seem to be no Greek beers these days, so the most popular brews are the Dutch Amstel and Heineken, and Henninger, all of which are brewed in Greece. Beer is sold in two sizes—550 grams and 330 grams; remember to ask for a small beer (330 grams), about the size you're accustomed to back home.

Water

It's one of the most refreshing drinks in Athens, and comes automatically to the table—even when you order coffee—but without ice. If you prefer bottled water, carbonated water is more reliable than the still variety, but if you order the latter at the table you'll probably get a large 1½-liter bottle. In the country, never drink water that has come straight from a well. A popular Greek refresher is the lemonade—fresh lemon juice, the real kind, squeezed into a glass, and usually served with a separate glass of water so that you can mix to your own taste. You can spend an entire afternoon in a café nursing one lemon juice. Two other popular Greek refreshers, on sale almost everywhere: Coke and Pepsi.

Dining Hours

Lunch is closer to 2 p.m. than to noon, and nobody thinks of starting dinner before 9 in the evening (even later in summer). If you have a date, arrange to meet for drinks at 9 p.m., then go on from there. If you're accustomed to eating earlier, you'll have problems. Most restaurants don't start serving dinner until 9 p.m., but a few (mostly in the budget category), which are probably accustomed to serving tourists from northern Europe, will serve you a meal from 6 or 7 p.m. on. Now you know why there are so many snackbars in Athens! (Memo to business travelers: In Athens you're more likely to be invited to a business *dinner* than a business lunch.)

Prices

This is probably the most tempting part of the subject, despite inflation—you can go to the finest restaurant in Athens, pick out the most expensive dish, and still end up spending less than you would on an average meal back home. If you want to shoot the works, Athens is the place to shoot. If you have to survive on pennies a day, you needn't get skinny in Athens. There are plenty of restaurants in this guide where you can eat, and eat *well,* for under 1,300 drs ($10).

Restaurant prices, like hotel prices, are controlled by the government, specifically by an organization referred to on the menus as the Marketing Police. Each type of restaurant is fitted into a category and must supply meals within those limits. Individual items will vary on the à la carte menus of different restaurants, but all restaurants within a given category, except deluxe, must supply fixed meals at a fixed price.

Column A and Column B

Most menus in Athens have two columns of prices. The first column is the price of the dish. The second is the price of the dish plus service and taxes. You'll be charged the price in the second column, and I've no idea what will happen if you try to pay the price in the first column. Theoretically, it's probably a good idea to show customers how much they're tipping—except, as in the case of hotel service charges, people may still feel obligated to tip more. See below.

Tipping

Despite the service charge, most people round out the figure on the bill and leave the change as a bonus tip. You don't have to, but some Greek restaurants, even the humblest, are swarming with busboys and assistant waiters who rely heavily on tips. If your busboy, or *micro,* is particularly attentive about getting rid of empty plates and so forth, tip him separately by placing a few 20-drachma coins *on the table,* not the saucer.

RESTAURANT DINING

Now for the restaurants themselves. What you will find in the following pages is a listing of Athens dining spots arranged by type (Greek, steakhouses, international) in the case of the moderately priced and expensive restaurants, followed by a roster of recommendations (restaurants, snackbars, and cafés) where you can dine for 1,300 drs ($10) or less. Since you've come to Greece for local color, I'll begin with restaurants and tavernas that have a distinctive Greek flavor and ambience.

THE TAVERNAS: Nothing could be more Greek than the taverna. The simplest tavernas (and for many people, these are the most enjoyable) are plain rooms in nondescript buildings, or in patios and gardens under arbors and olive trees; furnishings usually consist of plain-jane wooden tables and chairs, the tables covered with white paper on which your waiter sets glasses of water. The kitchen is usually open to view, and the selection of food is either still in the pots or spread out in glass-enclosed showcases—diners simply walk over to the pots or display, size up the various dishes, then indicate to the waiter what they want. Simple—especially for foreigners who don't speak Greek. Most menus follow the same basic pattern—that is, moussaka, dolmadakia, arni souvla, barbounia skara, and some regional variations of these basic dishes.

In some tavernas, on the other hand, you have no choice, and it matters not whether you speak Greek or Swahili because waiters simply arrive at your table with platters of food, beginning perhaps with the selection of *mezedes,* or appetizers, mentioned at the start of this chapter.

In Athens, the most famous of these fixed-menu tavernas is **Taverna Myrtia** at 35 Markou Moussourou-Mets (tel. 7012-276), somewhere behind the Panathenium (or old Olympic) Stadium, about a 260-dr ($2) taxi ride from Syntagma; it's fairly typical of its kind, with rush-matting walls, beamed ceiling, a collection of island pottery and copper lamps, a few paintings. Myrtia also regales you with a strolling trio. It's the most expensive of the tavernas listed here, about 3,200 drs ($25) per person, fixed price, including wine, for a meal of innumerable courses (probably more food than you can manage). It lends itself to convivial evenings: the tables are covered with jolly red cloths, and waiters squeeze and maneuver through the crammed tables with platefuls of shrimp, mussels, meatballs, followed by moussaka, and tas kebab, followed by lamb stew, roast pork, and fruits. Myrtia also has garden seating during the summer. You must always call ahead for a reservation.

Steki Tou Yianni at 1 Trias St. (about five minutes from the National Archeological Museum by taxi) sounds like a steakhouse but in fact the name translates as "Yianni's Lair." Like Myrtia, it's an excellent introduction to Greek food for those who feel they ought to try some traditional fare but may be nervous about doing so. Decor is basic Greek rustic: walls paneled to the waist with wood, the remainder with that basket-weave that's almost *de rigueur* in tavernas, and as you enter, you walk past a row of aging barrels filled with the house wines. Typical dishes are squid in batter with a cocktail sauce, seafood pie served from an oyster shell, moussaka, tiropitakia with spiced sausage and beans, dolmadakia, and finally, stifado (or Greek stew). Followed by (if you can still cope) Greek desserts. Yianni's fine house wine comes from Attica, and is served in attractive earthenware jugs. Reckon on spending about 5,000 drs or thereabouts ($38 to $40) for two with the house wine. Steki Tou Yianni's is closed on Sunday and for a month or two in summer.

Many Athenians will tell you that one of the best traditional tavernas is **Xynou,** at 4 Angelou Geronta St., a back street in the Plaka (tel. 3221-065). It's basically a cluster of leafy courtyards with soft lights, murals of life in ancient Athens, and a trio of balladeers singing gentle songs. Xynou is where well-to-do Athenians

GREEK MENU TERMS

Hors d'oeuvres

Taramosalata	Fish roe with mayonnaise
Tiropita	Cheese pie
Spanakopita	Spinach pie
Melitzanosalata	Eggplant salad
Tomates yemistes me risi	Tomatoes stuffed with rice
Midia fassolia salata	Dandelion salad
Piperies yemistes	Stuffed green peppers
Tzatziki	Cucumber with yogurt

Fish

Astakos (Ladolemono)	Lobster (with oil and lemon sauce)
Bakaliaro (Skordalia)	Cod (with garlic)
Barbounia (Skara)	Red mullet (grilled)
Caravides	Crayfish
Garides	Shrimp
Glossa (Tiganiti)	Sole (fried)
Kalamarakia (Tiganita)	Squid (fried)
Kalamarakia (Yemista)	Squid (stuffed)
Oktapodi	Octopus
Soupies yemistes	Stuffed cuttlefish
Tsipoura	Dorado

Meats

Arni souvla	Spit-roasted lamb
Arni yiouvetsi	Lamb in tomato sauce
Arni avgolemono	Lamb with lemon sauce
Brizola moscharisi	Beef or veal steak
Brizola hirini	Pork steak or chop
Dolmadakia	Stuffed vine leaves
Keftedes	Fried meatballs
Kotopoulo souvla	Spit-roasted chicken
Kotopoulo yemisto	Stuffed chicken
Loukanika	Spiced sausages
Moussaka	Meat and eggplant (or potato)
Paidakia	Lamb chops
Pilafi, risi	Rice pilaf
Souvlaki	Lamb (sometimes veal) on the skewer
Youvarlakia	Boiled meat balls with rice
Yuvetsi	Lamb with noodles

dine (you'll see more jackets here than in most tavernas); prices are moderately expensive: a good meal with house wine should cost less than 2,500 drs ($19) a head. Call for reservations. Open 8 p.m. to 2 a.m.; closed Sunday.

One block behind the National Archeological Museum and popular with students and well-to-do Athenians as well as with visitors, **Taverna Costoyannis** serves consistently good meals in a big, rambling, busy taverna at 37 Zaimi St. (tel. 8220-624). Unlike other restaurants that remove only the roof in summer, Costoyannis discards its walls too, so you can dine virtually in a garden surrounded by whitewashed walls and luxuriant creepers. Costoyannis has a stunning selection of appetizers, with a special recommendation for shrimp with bacon, tzatziki, eggplant Imam, and swordfish souvlaki. Visit Costoyannis with a few friends, order half a dozen dishes, and dip in. Call for a kilo of the house wine, called "brusco," or "kokkinelli," and you'll still be amazed when your bill comes—about 1,400 ($11) a head! If you want to splash out, or if you can squeeze in yet another dish, the grills, both meat and fish, are excellent. Costoyannis fills up from 9 p.m. on, so go early or reserve unless you don't mind waiting for a table. A taxi from Syntagma will cost another 260 to 390 drs ($2 to $3) each way. Costoyannis is closed for lunch and all day Sunday.

Three typical neighborhood tavernas are located in the residential district known as Kolonaki: **Rodia** at 44 Aristipou St. (tel. 7229-883), in a whitewashed courtyard in summer, a pink-walled chamber in winter; **Rouga** at 7 Kapseli St. (tel. 7227-934); and **Philippos** at 19 Xenocratou (tel. 7216-390), where in summer the tables overflow on to a tiny terrace notched into the precipitous street and the half-dozen tables fill up with local artists, writers, and actors attracted by the moderately priced fare, around 2,600 drs ($20) for two with a modest wine.

Note: See next chapter for names of additional tavernas in the Plaka.

OTHER TYPICALLY GREEK RESTAURANTS: The following selection is similar in style and cuisine, but these are considered restaurants rather than tavernas.

Gerofinikas, at 10 Pindarou St., between Syntagma and Kolonaki (tel. 3636-710 or 3622-719), is considered by many to be the finest of the Greek/Levantine restaurants, and it certainly is not the sort of place where you can expect to be seated without a half-hour wait if you forget to make a reservation. You enter it through a long, unprepossessing passageway that leads you into a surprisingly leafy indoor "courtyard," which is air-conditioned in summer; displays of Oriental desserts and great bowls of fresh fruit greet you at the door, and off to the left there's a big open kitchen with the day's dishes set out for your inspection—lamb fricassee, eggplant Beyendi, doner kehap (grilled veal) and mouskari, or veal with vegetables cooked in a paper bag. The succulent desserts include the syrupy sweet ekmek kataif, topped with chantilly in summer, with thick cream in winter. With prices of main dishes in the 1,000-dr ($8) to 1,500-dr ($12) range, Gerofinikas is one of the best buys in town, but if you want to dine there you'd better call ahead for a reservation. Open 12:30 to 11:30 p.m.

Vladimiros, at 12 Aristodemou St. (tel. 7217-407), is a delightful restaurant on the way up to the Lycabettus funicular. It's an ideal spot for American visitors—a neighborhood restaurant catering to a local clientele who may want a change from their native moussaka, so without acting like a tourist you can enjoy beef, pork, lamb, and veal dishes cooked over charcoal and garnished in continental style. Vladimiros is equally popular in summer for its garden beneath the pine trees of Lycabettus, in winter for its piano bar and cozy rooms filled with paintings. Budget 1,450 drs ($11) to 1,700 drs ($13) for main courses. Open daily from 8 p.m.

A few streets closer to Syntagma at 36 Loukianou St., **Jimmy's Cooking** is located at the point where a steep street becomes steep steps. There's a cozy, comfortable interior, but the main attraction is the small warm-weather terrace shaded by a canopy and screened by greenery. Jimmy's cooking consists of a variety of Greek and continental dishes in the 700-dr ($5) to 950-dr ($8) range.

One of the brightest little restaurants in Athens is **Fatsio's,** 5 Efroniou (tel. 717-421), a few blocks from the Hilton and fewer still from the Caravel, where walls and ceilings are hand-painted in the style of Thessaly, with cornucopias and flowers in sunny blues, yellows, and reds. Even the linen napkins are sealed in clear plastic. The display of dishes includes baked veal with eggplant, baked swordfish, veal with tomato sauce—none of them over 950 drs ($8). Call for reservations. Open for lunch only, noon to 5 p.m.

The air-conditioned **Corfu** at 6 Kriezotou (tel. 3603-411), just around the corner from Panepestimiou, is classed as a "luxury" restaurant although the decor suggests something more modest. Likewise the food. As its name might lead you to expect, it features several Corfiote specialties, like beef "Pastitsada," which is boiled beef and spaghetti, at 850 drs ($7), and sirloin of beef "Sofrito," which is sliced beef in a wine sauce with noticeable amounts of garlic, at 950 drs ($8); the rest of the Corfu's menu ranges from moussaka at 520 drs ($4) to lobster (priced according to season). A place to drop into in a thunderstorm if you can't make it to one of the better spots near here; but you can call ahead for a reservation. Open daily from noon to midnight.

The number-one spot for dramatic dining (and highest in the city) is the **Dionysos Restaurant** on top of Mount Lycabettus (tel. 7226-374), with an eclectic menu of salads, Greek food, and continental dishes like escalope Holstein and chicken Negresco. A full dinner here will cost about 3,120 drs ($24) to 4,680 drs ($36) a head, but lighter meals could be as little as 1,560 drs ($12); and when you add in the view, lunch is also quite a bargain at 780 drs ($6) to 910 drs ($7).

Farther down Mount Lycabettus, **Le Grand Balcon** fills the roof of the St. George Lycabettus Hotel at 2 Klemeou St. (tel. 7290-710). In winter you're tucked into the flashy new Grill Room; in summer you have views of the entire city. In both cases, you'll be entertained by a combo (there's a dance floor too), and à la carte dinners will cost somewhere between 1,900 drs ($15) and 2,800 drs ($22).

> **An Early Dinner with a View.** You can get an even closer view of the Acropolis from the Roof Garden of the **Astor Hotel,** 16 Karageorgi tis Servias (tel. 3255-555), one of the city's few year-round eyries (in winter it's enclosed in glass that doesn't block the view). This is another place for lingering, although it *closes* when most Athens restaurants are just warming up. Once you get up there, order a bottle of Santa Elena or Cimarosa, and slowly scan the menu; you'll be reluctant to rush through your meal and get back down to earth, literally and otherwise. Enjoy roast lamb, shish kebab, or the complete 1,700-drs ($13) dinner with moussaka or soup as a first course, roast lamb or chicken with rice, dessert, and/or feta cheese. If it's still too early to drag yourself away, order some Greek coffee. Then follow it up with a Metaxa. Two people can still leave with change from 4,550 drs ($35)—having enjoyed a better view (better value) than diners in the pricier places. Open to 10:30 p.m. only.

FRENCH AND CONTINENTAL RESTAURANTS: The **Balthazar,** 27 Tsocha St. at Vournazou Street (tel. 6441-215), near the American Embassy, a 325 drs ($2.50) to 390 drs ($3) cab ride from Syntagma, is an imposing corner town house with a curving driveway, steps at the front, and a secluded garden for summer dining in the rear. The first things that greet you as you come in through the main door are crystal chandeliers, beautiful walnut paneling, lofty ceilings, and marble fireplaces. The three-story mansion was built at the turn of the century for a well-to-do Athenian family (not shipping—textiles), but in recent years it was rescued from decay by a young consultant economist, Nikos Paleologos, who had his passport removed by the regime of 1967, so he had plenty of time on his hands to put the place in order. He has imported a special craftsman from London to restore the elaborate ceilings, decorated the walls with his private collection of contemporary Greek art, and decked the windows with his private collection of antique glass bottles (some of them are real curios). The setting may be elegant, but the Balthazar is, in fact, fairly casual about its elegance: the waiters are in shirt sleeves, and Paleologos commutes from the kitchen to the tables in blue denims. The name, by the way, comes from a reference in *Cyrano de Bergerac*—"faire un Balthazar," meaning have a feast or big meal—and that seems to be the clear intent of Nikos Paleologos and his wife. Their meals are hearty. Some suggestions from their varied menu: minute steaks with brandy and mushrooms, the daily Eastern curries served with homemade chutney; for openers, try the spiced cheese log which is a blend of island cheeses and herbs. Menus vary from season to season, but you can expect main dishes to be in the 1,300 to 1,950 drs ($10 to $15) price range. A large open-air bar was added to the restaurant's summer garden—so you can always drop by just for a cocktail. Dinner only, from 7 p.m. to 2 a.m.

The **Athens Hilton** at 46 Vassilissis Sophias Ave. can now boast two of the most popular eating spots in the city. The classy **Ta Nissia** is a brighter, pastel-and-planter version of the old Taverna Ta Nissia, while retaining its distinctive wooden ceiling and hand-carved stone walls. The menu, too, retains many of the old favorites (suckling pig on the spit, for one) but augments them with a few international dishes (prime ribs), seafood (turbot—the only place where it's served in Athens), and innovations (deep-fried phillo dough stuffed with mince meat—even the ancient Greeks never thought of that one). Entree prices are from 1,350 drs ($10) to 1,800 drs ($14). The self-service "salad" bar is an inviting roundup of Greek *mezedes,* available as an appetizer for 950 drs ($7) or as an entree for 1,750 drs ($14)—and nobody seems to check the quantities! Evenings only, 7 p.m. to 12:30 a.m.; for reservations, call 7220-201.

The Hilton's **Kellari,** "The Cellar," just across the foyer from Ta Nissia, is completely new—a sort of upscale version of the local *ouzeri,* where guests can sample ouzo and wines while nibbling on *mezedes.* Kellari's *carte des vins* runs to 150 wines from every region of Greece, priced from an incredibly low 500 drs ($4), with many of them available also by the glass; and each evening there's a selection of appetizers set out on a buffet, at an inclusive price of 950 drs ($7). Evenings only, 6 p.m. to 1 a.m.; no reservations accepted.

The next restaurant is over on the far side of the Acropolis, near the Herod Atticus Theater and Philopappos Hill, with one of the best views of the Acropolis in the entire city. The **Dionysus** (tel. 9233-182) is difficult to fit into one category, since it's several restaurants in one: it serves Greek food and continental food (escalope Holstein, chicken Negresco, crêpes Suzette) in its glass-walled restaurant and terraced garden; and snacks in its vine-covered courtyard café, which is almost right opposite the main entrance to the Acropolis. Dinner in the restaurant will cost about 2,800 drs ($15) to 2,800 drs ($21) a head; in the courtyard, there are tourist menus for under 1,600 drs ($12), and simple dishes like omelets, spaghetti, and sandwiches cost well under 1,500 drs ($12). With these prices, and this setting, Dionysus is a very popular place, so call for reservations.

One of the most highly regarded French restaurants in town is the award-winning **Prunier,** a pretty little three-room bistro at 63 Ipsilantou (tel. 7227-379), two blocks from the Hilton. Interesting menu, attentive service. At the **Brasserie des Arts** (tel. 3255-301), the dazzling glass-and-copper dining room on the second floor of the Hotel NJV Meridien, a French chef oversees the nouvelle cuisine brochette d'espadon and carré d'agneau; the pastry chef has his farm-fresh butter flown in from Normandy; and it's the only eating place in the city with tableside telephone service. Expensive, and marred by an amplified combo that's more obtrusive than it should be in a space like this (although they're actually playing in the lounge). Open daily from 1 to 4 p.m. and 8 p.m. to 1:30 a.m.

Opened in 1985, **Bajazzo** (tel. 7291-420) is the big-city branch of a popular summertime dining spot on the island of Hydra. It's located in an elegant old town house in fashionable Kolonaki, at 35 Ploutarchou, at the point where the precipitous street gives way to precipitous steps. Upstairs, the bar/bistro is decked out with turn-of-the-century antiques, while downstairs the petite 30-seat restaurant is dressed up in contemporary colors and fabrics (too chic in the case of the carpeting—a pale melon color that was never designed for wear and tear and crumbs). One wall is decorated with the animated puppet clowns that give the restaurant its name. The German chef/owner offers a varied, serendipitous bill of fare: appetizers like "Mushroom Treasure" (morilles wrapped in a crêpe basket), spring roll with duck, or strawberry salad are brought to the table for inspection in wicker baskets. Main courses might include "Typsy tournedo" (with cognac) or pork medallions with mushrooms. Entree prices are around 1,550 drs ($12) to 2,600 drs ($20); appetizers and the sumptuous desserts, 1,350 drs ($10) to 1,550 drs ($12)—slightly less at lunchtime. Air-conditioned. Call for reservations; open in winter only.

Most of the continental restaurants I've been talking about here serve only indoors, but up in Kolonaki, at the corner of Xenokratous and Aristodimou, **Je Reviens** (tel. 7223-605) has a stylish indoor salon (with piano music and chanteuse in the evenings) *and* a pleasant terrace with checked tablecloths and lanterns strung from the mulberry trees. For a dinner featuring coq au vin or cotelettes de veau, expect to pay around 2,200 ($17) to 3,100 drs ($24), but for a light lunch of omelet and salad you can get by on 780 drs ($6). Call for reservations. **L'Abreuvoir,** next door at 51 Xenokratous (tel. 7229-061), is the oldest French restaurant in town and for many Athenians still the best, but many visitors find it too stuffy and expensive.

Number 14 Voukourestiou, a lovely turn-of-the-century building recently restored, is now the **Stage Coach** (tel. 3635-145), which has moved there from Kolonaki. In summer a few tables overflow onto the pedestrian mall; indoors, the street level is given over to a long wooden bar with mahogany stools, while upstairs the setting is somewhat fancier, with circular booths upholstered in print fabrics (and taped music that doesn't enhance the setting in any way). Downstairs, lunchtime specials include plain omelets for 450 drs ($3), "stuffed spuds" for 440 drs ($3) to 510 drs ($4), and two eggs with sausage for 510 drs ($4); the upstairs menu is more elaborate, from Rocquefort hamburger steak and beef shish kebab to Chateaubriand at prices from 1,420 drs ($11) to 3,200 drs ($25). Both rooms are air-conditioned, and you should call for reservations. Open from breakfast to midnight, with the congenial bar staying open until 2 a.m. Closed Sunday.

One of the most interesting restaurants to open in Athens in recent years is the new **G. B. Corner** (tel. 323-0251) in the prestigious Hotel Grande Bretagne, with one entrance in the glittering, elegant lobby, the other on Panepistimiou Avenue. The G. B. Corner has an Edwardian, masculine air, all dark wood and cut glass, brightened by clusters of globe lamps. The most surprising feature of this newcomer is its moderately priced menu and its innovative dishes—including hamburger chasseur. A welcome addition to the Syntagma scene, it's a pleasant place to visit any time of the day or half the night (it's open until 2 a.m.) for a drink, a coffee, or a full meal, which could be as little as 1,200 drs ($9) or as much as

2,080 drs ($16). **Le Bistrot Athenian** (tel. 325-5301), on the next corner of the same Syntagma block, adjoins the lavish Brasserie one floor up in the new Meridien but serves less expensive fare— say, omelettes aux choix, hamburgers, or *croque monsieur* for 900 drs (less than $7). Open 7 a.m. to 1 a.m.

What used to be McMilton's in the Plaka is now just plain **Milton's** (tel. 3249-129), all spiffed up in decor (white and wicker and islandy) and menu—the budget-priced snacks were replaced by moderately priced Greek and continental dishes. Some people probably wish it had stayed cheap and simple, but it does have a pleasant candlelit terrace, facing the bustling intersection of Flessa and Adrianou (at no. 91, officially). Air-conditioned indoors, it's open from noon to 2 a.m.

ITALIAN, ORIENTAL, ET AL.: Each year Athens is becoming

more and more cosmopolitan, and although you're probably not coming to the land of olives and feta cheese to eat pizza and tempura, you may like to know that they are available—together with the cuisines of Lebanon, Turkey, Spain, Korea, China, Mexico, Cyprus, and even Polynesian at the Ledra Marriott's Kona Kai and Asian barbecues at the Inter-Continental's Kubla Khan. Here's a sampling of international ethnic restaurants.

The smartest Italian restaurant in town is **Da Walter** (tel. 7248-726), located in a modern apartment building at 7 Evzonon St. at the corner of Anapiron Polemon in Kolonaki, between the American and British Embassies. The decor, in tones of mocha and coffee, is chic and modern (although the thickly upholstered modular sofa/chairs would probably be more appropriate in the lobby next door), and the fresh flowers and lemon-colored napery tell you that the dapper staff takes a pride in the place. Prices are moderate to hefty—peti di pollo al marsala or filetto Voron of (veal in a cognac and mustard sauce) will cost 1,040 drs ($18) to 1,430 drs ($11), but if you avoid pricey appetizers like prosciutto crudo and salame de Milano, you can dine well for under 2,340 drs ($18). Dinner only, from 8 p.m. to 1 a.m. daily. Call for reservations; taxi fare from Syntagma is about 260 drs ($2). If even these prices are too stiff, the **Al Convento Pizzeria** is just around the corner at 4-6 Anapiron Polemon (tel. 7239-163), open from 8 p.m. to 1 a.m. (closed Sunday).

At the **Kona Kai** in the Ledra Marriott, 117 Syngrou (tel. 9347-711), the lower-level location is deftly disguised with waterfalls, pools, hanging batiks, and a striking backdrop photograph of a South Sea isle matched in extravagance only by the exotic cocktails (try the "Kona Grog," served in a skull mug. Deadly.). In addition to Polynesian fare there are also several Japanese tepanyaki tables. Expect to pay $25 to $30 a head, depending on your resistance to the fancy drinks. Dinner only, 8:30 p.m. to 1 a.m.; closed Sunday. The Kona Kai is one of the most popular restaurants in Athens, so reservations are essential.

Tucked away in a narrow street (near Farmaki Square) in the Plaka is a Japanese restaurant, **Michiko,** 27 Kidathineou St. (tel. 3220-980), in a Japanese courtyard, complete with fish pond, fountains, butterfly bridge, and kimono-clad waitresses. The 20-odd tables are distributed along flagstone paths on two raised terraces beneath frilly red awnings, and the whole place is sheltered by a venerable tree and decorated with colored lanterns. Sukyaki and tempura may not be what you've come to the Plaka to savor—they're not exactly bargains here at 1,690 to 2,730 drs ($13 to $21)—but they're there if you feel like a change of pace from moussaka and eggplant some evening. Open to midnight; closed Sunday.

If you have an uncontrollable longing for the flavors of Canton and bamboo furniture, the place to be is **China** at 72 Efroniou (tel. 7233-200), near the Caravel. Expensive. Call for reservations.

STEAKHOUSES: The Steak Room, at 6 Eginitou between the Hilton and the American Embassy (tel. 7217-445), is one of those restaurants you might want to try if you weary of moussakas and veal. Some people will tell you it serves the best steaks in Athens, prepared in the American manner and served with baked potato and sour cream or butter. The Steak Room's owner, Michael Papapanou, a Greek who spent ten years in Canada, gets his beef loins from the north of Greece, ages them, then cuts them right at the charcoal fire. For any cut (from porterhouse to filet steak), the price ranges from 1,200 drs ($9) to 1,820 drs ($14). His stint in Canada also taught Mr. Papapanou the mysteries of extra-dry Beefeater martinis and Irish coffee.

The air-conditioned Steak Room is open from 7 p.m. to 1 a.m. for dinner; closed Sunday. The Steak Room claims to have been the first steakhouse in Athens, and if so, it started quite a trend. They're now all over the place.

Templars' Grill, the steakhouse in the Royal Olympic Hotel (tel. 9226-411 for reservations), is the most spectacular. It flies its Aberdeen Angus steaks in from the U.S. and they're reputed to be the tenderest in town, prepared and grilled by a chef who spent several years in the States. Open daily from 8 p.m. to midnight. Prices for main courses are 850 drs ($7) to 2,000 drs ($15).

Flame Steak House is only a few blocks from its rival the Steak House, at 9 Hadjiyanni Mexi (tel. 7238-540), on the corner of Michalakopoulou, near the Hilton. Restaurateur Elias Dialektakos picked up the tricks of his trade in Chicago, then packed up some American-style light fixtures, amber glassware, and ashtrays, and returned to his homeland. His 17-year-old eatery has knotty-pine paneling and bar, and comes equipped with air conditioning and taped stereo, and hand-hammered copper plaques depicting Michelangelo paintings, all set off by burgundy rugs and peach tablecloths. Most dishes on the menu are charcoal-broiled—like filet mignon at 1,250 drs ($10)—but there are also items like golden french-fried shrimp for under 750 drs ($6). One of the restaurant's nicest features is a roomy terrace for sidewalk dining, with a brown-and-tan awning and trellised greenery to shut out the traffic. Open daily 11 a.m. to 1 a.m. Call for reservations.

MEALS FOR UNDER $10
RESTAURANTS, CAFÉS, AND SNACKBARS

Despite the steady rise of prices in Athens in the past few years, there are still many entries in this category thanks to the devaluation of the drachma. Some of those restaurants and tavernas mentioned above have a few items on their menus that could, with judicious selection, bring you a meal for under 1,300 drs ($10); conversely, some restaurants in this section list a few expensive dishes which *could* put your meal over the 1,300 drs ($10) figure. On the whole, however, you should have no problem keeping within your budget at any of the restaurants, cafés, and snackbars listed below. There's no need to detail the menus in each of these places: they all follow a basic pattern—moussakas, dolmadakia, keftedes, and various lamb, veal, and pork dishes in assorted Greek styles (such as those listed earlier in this chapter). Many of them also have a sprinkling of international dishes like omelets, spaghetti, schnitzels, and escalopes (but not too much seafood, which is now relatively expensive throughout Greece). In most cases, the waiter will offer you a menu in English. You can expect a cover charge of 30 drs (25¢) to 50 drs (40¢), and a small charge for bread and butter.

RESTAURANTS AROUND SYNTAGMA: The two-story, air-conditioned, wood-paneled **Delphi,** just off Syntagma at 13 Nikis (tel. 3234-869), has a wide-ranging menu with budget-priced grilled chicken with rice at 450 drs ($3) and shrimp with rice for around 1,300 drs ($10), as well as a selection of dishes within that price range—rice with minced meat, veal with okra, moussaka, and a choice of unusual salads featuring squash, dandelion, beetroot, and cabbage. Don't come looking for a leisurely, relaxed meal—those waiters *move*. The Delphi is open daily from 11 a.m. to 11:30 p.m.

Just around the corner at 10 Exnofondos St., the tables of the new **Diros** spill out on to the sidewalk beneath the stoa. A refrigerated glass case displays some of the attractions within—roast veal at 600 drs ($5), moussaka at 400 drs ($3), omelets from 140 drs ($1) to 220 drs ($2), grilled grouper or grilled shrimp at 850 drs ($7) to 1,350 drs ($10). Side dishes cost around a dollar; a half bottle of retsina is 500 drs ($4). In other words, you can easily put together a meal with wine at Diros for under 1,560 drs ($12). Air-conditioned.

In a city where misspelled menus are two a drachma, **Sintrivani** at 5 Filellinon takes some kind of prize, for where else in Athens have you been offered "duddelions"? Nobody, to our knowledge, has actually partaken of this intriguing vegetable dish, but if you're prepared to settle for an excellent egg-lemon soup followed by lamb or swordfish kebabs, at about 450 drs ($3), then you won't be disappointed by Sintrivani tou Syntagmatos—"the fountain of Syntagma." Go through the main room in summer and you can dine in a very pleasant garden; service is friendly, and it's only a two-minute walk from the square.

Another restaurant in this down-to-earth Greek style, with moussakas, dolmadakia, omelets, and spaghetti in the 350-dr ($2.75) to 500-dr ($4) range, is the **Kentrikon,** which overflows into the arcade just off Kolokotroni Square, next to the National Historical Museum.

The Drugstore, located at 4 Korai St. (tel. 3226-464), in a shopping arcade off Klathmonou Square and Stadiou, doesn't have quite the personality of its Parisian namesake. But if you're in no hurry, you can linger over items from an eclectic menu, from cheese pie at 300 drs ($2) to hamburgers at 720 drs ($6), to a tasty variety that includes octopus, pastroumas, and "haughty fish" in the Oyzeri section for 135 drs ($1) to 650 drs ($5). Open seven days a week from 8 a.m. to 2 a.m.

SNACKBARS AROUND SYNTAGMA:
First, two with similar names: the **American Coffee Shop,** on the corner of Nikis and Karageorgi tis Servias Streets, offers nostalgic dishes for just less than a couple of dollars—fish and chips, char-broiled hamburgers, or two eggs any style. Open from 7 a.m. to midnight. The **American Snackbar** is located directly across from the post office at 3 Mitropoleos, and greets you with signs announcing the day's special—which is liable to be hamburger with french fries for around 450 drs ($3); inside, there are cozy booths where you can

try the nondaily specials—breaded fish fry with french fries and salad, fried chicken, pancakes with syrup, or complete lunches and dinners for around 870 drs ($7).

Another pleasant stop for refreshment in this general area is **Hermion,** in the arcade at 715 Pandrossou, on your way to the Flea Market. In warm weather it spills into the colorful canopy-topped courtyard; otherwise it's a clean and shiny 20-table restaurant attended by smart-jacketed waiters. Even the most expensive items, like roast lamb and potatoes, costs less than 800 drs ($6). Open for breakfast, lunch, and dinner.

In the Plaka, the people-meeting place is **Café-Restaurant Posidon** (or Possithonos), in tiny Kapnikareas Square opposite the Roman Agora. The menu is extensive, but if you prefer, and if there are tables to spare, you can spend the evening nursing a beer as you watch busking hippies, old ladies selling fluffy shawls, and Greek Adonises sizing up the latest influx of Swedish maidens.

Near Kolonaki Square, **Jimmy's Café,** at Valaoritou, serves a variety of light meals from donuts and pastries on up. Higher up the hill, the snackbar/coffeeshop of the **St. George Lycabettus Hotel** goes al fresco in a comparatively quiet, tree-shaded terrace of whitewashed stone with white wrought-iron chairs and comfy green padding; the "everything" menu has hamburgers, pizza, spaghetti, salads, steaks, and an omelet Hill (with sausage, potatoes, and a Basquaise sauce) that's a meal in itself for just over 520 drs ($4).

DINING AROUND OMONIA SQUARE:

Over in the Omonia Square area prices tend to be a few drachmas cheaper than around Syntagma. One of the busiest eating spots (at least at lunchtime) in this neighborhood is **Ellinikon** at 3 Satovriandou, just off the square, with seating for 100 diners. Prices are modest—275 drs ($2) to 500 drs ($4) for items like moussaka, pastitsio, spaghetti, or meat pie. Directly across the street, prices are a few drachmas higher at a newer establishment called **Taygetos,** the place on the corner with the yellow walls and smart wooden trim. Here main dishes are in the 500- to 700-dr ($4 to $5) range.

While you're in the square, you might also take a look at two hotel restaurants—those of the **Omonia** and **Asty;** both serve a three-course lunch or dinner for 1,000 drs ($8).

The best of the snackbars in this neighborhood is probably the **Floca Self-Service,** two blocks from the square at 16 Emanuel Benaki St. Since it's a member of the Floca chain, it's reliable, spotless, and good value: stuffed vine leaves, moussaka, roast chicken

—in other words, a tasty Greek meal for 300 drs ($2) to 400 drs ($3). The Floca was recently outfitted with modern, new booths; air-conditioned.

Also on Benaki, this time at no. 3, between Panepistimiou and Stadiou Streets, you'll find one of the most attractive and spacious restaurants in this area—the wood-paneled **Nea Olympia.** Its extensive menu includes dolmadakia and omelets for less than 300 drs ($2), veal dishes for around 600 drs ($5).

Still near Omonia Square but a block or two toward Syntagma, at 46 El. Venizelou, the **Ideal** serves omelets at around 130 drs ($1) and various meat dishes from 550 drs ($4) to 1,290 drs ($10), plus a "grillerie" for kokozetsi, in an attractive pseudo-rustic setting, and a brick-and-wood entrance flanked by displays of seafood and fruit.

Where Panepistimiou meets Omonia Square there's a narrow, quiet street called Themistokleu with bargain eats: the **Gelateria/Cafeteria Esperando** has a wood-trimmed, two-level interior with wood-trimmed decor and, in summer, a few red chairs, tables, and umbrellas under the arcade. It's self-service, with hearty cheese pies for 80 drs (60¢) and assorted hot dishes for 260 drs ($2) to 390 drs ($3).

THE CONVIVIAL CAFÉS OF ATHENS: The third type of eating place in this price group is the café. In some cases the cafés are also snackbars; in some cases they also have restaurants. They're listed here because their *main* role is as a café—a place where you can idle away hours over a coffee, lemon juice, Coke, or ice cream, or enjoy a light lunch of pan pie, cheese puffy, or sandwiches.

There are three main centers for cafés in Athens—Constitution Square (Syntagma), Kolonaki Square, and Fokionos Negri Street.

Syntagma is the largest, with 3,000 chairs (armchairs at that) deployed around its sidewalks and around the fountain in the center of the square, shaded by cypress, laburnam, and three palm trees. These cafés serve sandwiches—veal, ham, cheese, at 310 drs ($3) to 530 drs ($4)—pastries at 280 drs ($2) to 380 drs ($3), orange or lemon juice and tea or coffee for around 195 drs ($1.50). If you're longing for pastries, go to a *red* chair in the square and you'll be served by the excellent **Dionysus** kitchen (notable for especially good pastries from its associated restaurants, Zonar's and Dionysus, two favorites in town).

For Americans, the most popular café is **Papaspyrou,** the one surrounding the American Express office, on the west side of the square, now both waiter service *and* self-service. Papaspyrou is at its busiest around 5 in the afternoon, when the mail arrives at American Express and the tables fill up with beaming or crestfallen faces, depending on the mailman.

Phivos, 2 Othonos, is the café with the blue awnings and green chairs at the corner of Syntagma and Filellinon. It bills itself as a patisserie/cafeteria/snackbar, so you can satisfy any degree of hunger here. But take a peek inside at the pies, pastries, baklavas, and chocolates, and you'll probably decide to settle for something light. And sweet. Hot dishes—like hamburgers, dolmadakia, cannelloni, and moussaka—are around 600 drs ($5).

A café where you can get an exceptionally good cup of coffee is the **Café Do Brasil** in the arcade that cuts the corner between Constitution Square and Stadiou. The Brazilian is part of a chain, with a stand-up counter downstairs and tables upstairs where executives look down on the tourists scurrying among the stores in the arcade. Coffee costs from 125 drs (95¢) to 165 drs ($1.25); pastries, 115 drs (85¢) to 198 drs ($2).

Another attractive coffeeshop in the Syntagma area is the **Brazilian Coffee Stores,** at 1 Voukourestiou, the sort of stand-up place where you pop in for a quick espresso or cappuccino and enjoy a pastry and the aromas of a dozen types of coffee. A few doors down, on the corner of Voukourestiou and Stadiou, the new **Everyday** is a cavernous, split-level mecca for coffee imbibers, this time with chairs and tables and a menu of snacks and light meals. For sweet tooths there are two new tea room/confiseries in town: the dainty **Désiré** at 6 Dimokritou in Kolonaki, and **De Profundis,** at 1 Angel Hatzimihalis St. (near the Center for Folk Art), with French decor, English and exotic teas, and taped classical music (but closed for most of August).

A few blocks from the Hilton, near the Caravel Hotel, **Le Palmier** is a bright new café on the corner of Andinoros and Iofondos Streets, its white-on-white interior opening to a small terrace with wood-topped tables and wicker chairs. If you just want to while away an hour reading your *Herald Tribune,* you can order salads for around 380 drs ($3), crêpes with minced meat, cheese, and tomato at 480 drs ($4), or chicken with cheese and bananas for 490 drs ($4).

A few blocks down from the American Embassy, the tall eucalyptus and pine trees of Venizelou Park offer respite from the noise and sun; tucked into the northwestern corner of the park, the **Monirro** snackbar/taverna has a terrace facing lawns, hedgerows, and flower beds and a menu that ranges from omelets and teropita to fried cheese and meatballs, all in the 250-drs to 900-drs range ($2 to $7). Ice creams are 400 drs ($3) to 510 drs ($4), and there's a refreshing *frappé,* or iced coffee, for about 130 drs ($1). The menu is in Greek only, but chances are the fellow at the next table is an attaché from the embassy and will be happy to translate for a peripatetic taxpayer.

In recent years, the square in front of the cathedral, Plataeia Mitripoleos, has been cleared of traffic, relaid with cobblestones, and generally spruced up; now there's also a new café/patisserie/confiserie on the corner of Pandrossou—**Café Metropolis,** with a sprightly interior and a spacious terrace where you can observe the comings and goings at the cathedral while sipping a fancy ice cream concoction (380 drs, $3, and up) or a *café frappé* for about 130 drs ($1).

Syntagma is where the tourists go, but **Kolonaki Square** is where the Athenians sip their coffee, and talk business or gossip. Kolonaki Square is only a few blocks from the National Gardens and Syntagma, just off Vassilissis Sofias. It's something of an oasis (although at times it looks more like a parking lot), with a grove of trees and a fountain in the center and a café on almost every corner. Pick almost any café on Kolonaki Square. By day your choice is determined by the position of the sun; at night, by wherever you can find a seat.

Fokionos Negri, our third café haunt, is over in Patission, the residential neighborhood just beyond the National Archeological Museum and slightly off the beaten tourist track. But if you're spending more than a couple of days in Athens, and you want to get beneath the surface of Athenian life, hop into a taxi, or take the no. 3 trolley bus and ask the conductor to let you off at the stop nearest Fokionos Negri. Now blessedly traffic-free except at intersections, this street is sometimes called (but never by Athenians) the Via Veneto of Athens, and you'll soon see why: it's a broad, plaza-like street with hedgerows, fountains, café tables and umbrellas in the center, and a café, it seems, on each corner. The remainder of the street is taken up by boutiques, flower shops, food shops, and other services pampering to the needs of Athenian society. Here again, you can choose almost any café (or wherever you can find a table and chairs), but if you want to sit outdoors, head for the **Select** or **Floca,** or if indoors for the comfy **Oriental.** For dining, there are a couple of modest but good-value tavernas (**I Thraka** and **Violetta**), but generally speaking it's easier to find cannelloni and coteletta than a good moussaka—at **Il Forno** (no. 37) or **Italika** (no. 50), where pizzas range from 450 drs ($3) to 880 drs ($7), pasta dishes from 300 drs ($2) to 850 drs ($7), and grills from 800 ($6) to 1,300 drs ($10).

The perfect Athenian evening spent in Fokionos Negri would be a leisurely apéritif at Select or Oriental, a stroll around the street scanning the menus, a leisurely dinner beneath the acacia and mulberry trees, helped along with a bottle of Boutari, followed by coffee and pastry at Floca. Then a 450-drs ($3) taxi ride will get you back to Syntagma in about five minutes.

SELF-INDULGENCE ON PANEPISTIMIOU AVENUE.

One of the most famous *zacharoplasteions* in Athens is, in fact, on none of these squares, but on Panepistimiou Avenue, one block from Constitution Square. **Zonar's** is the huge café on the corner with a row of red tables and chairs beneath a bright-red awning. The interior of Zonar's is an Expo for sweet tooths—with display cases piled high with candies, chocolates, pastries, baklavas, galaktoboureko, and bougatsas, as well as the classical pastries you'd find in Vienna or Munich. Even the decor carries through the theme—chocolate-brown walls, cream-colored ceilings, icy chandeliers, and marble-topped tables (although the management is whispering about redoing it). At the rear, a few steps lead up to the restaurant, and a few more lead down to the cozy American bar. You can have snacks here—sandwiches are 330 drs ($3) to 650 drs ($5)—but most people come to savor the pastries at 300 drs ($2) to 410 drs ($3) and sip the espresso, cappuccino, Viennese coffee, Nescafé, French coffee, and Greek coffees. Zonar's is a haven for self-indulgence. Don't miss it.

Much to the dismay and regret of Athenians (and who knows how many thousands of visitors), the 100-year-old *zacharoplasteion* next door to Zonar's, the delightful **Floca,** closed its doors for the last time in 1988—to be transformed into, eventually, a bank. But the joys of Floca live on despite progress and big bucks in various branches around the city—the nearest Floca being on the pedestrians-only square known as Korai, a few blocks along Panepistimiou, opposite the university.

THE OUZERI OF ATHENS: Here's a leisurely, carefree, and relatively inexpensive way to sample some local color—visit an *ouzeri*. The *ouzeri* is a sort of neighborhood bar/pub/café where Athenians stop in at any time of the day for a quick pick-me-up of *ouzo,* wine, or coffee accompanied by bite-size delicacies like *sagnaki* and *dolmadakia.* Decor is usually basic and functional, the clientele mostly male, the conversation mostly soccer or politics. Now the *ouzeri* is making a comeback, partly because of the new working hours, partly because of a general tendency to eat lighter food—and now the clientele is more mixed and the decor more inviting.

One of the city's old-style *ouzeri* is just three blocks from Syntagma, in the arcade at 10 Panepistimiou, where the high-ceilinged Apotsos lines its well-worn walls with posters and mirrors advertising the pleasures of biscuits, whisky, and mustard. Other traditional spots are **Athinaikon** at 8 Santaroza St., near Omonia Square, a gathering place for lawyers and judges from the nearby law courts; and halfway up Lycabettus Hill, a godsend for thirsty, camera-toting pilgrims bound for the white church up top.

Among the newcomers, two are particularly attractive for visitors, both located in the Kolonaki district and ideal for shoppers and museumgoers. **Grafio** fills the first floor of a former town house on the corner of Platia Dexameni, just down the hill from the St. George Lycabettus Hotel. It's fancier, more stylish, and a shade pricier than the traditional *ouzeri,* with white-on-white contemporary decor designed by its architect owner—hence the framed engravings of classical buildings and the name, Grafio, or "Design." The menu is in Greek only but the open kitchen just inside the door displays all the goodies available that day so all you have to do is point. A simple but tasty meal for two, with a half-bottle of wine, should cost around 1,900 drs ($15). For about the same price, maybe slightly less, you can while away a leisurely hour or two at **Yali Kafines,** 18 Plutarchou. Again, the decor is contemporary/traditional—dark wood and polished brass—and in summer a few tables are set up at an incline on the sidewalk, where you can sip your *ouzo* and nibble on your *sagnaki* and *dolmadakia* under the acacia trees.

RESTAURANTS OUTSIDE OF ATHENS: In summer, most
Athenians don't come into the center of town for dinner: they drive out to their favorite hideaways on the outskirts of town—in the countryside or by the sea. You might want to follow suit, in which case here are some tips on where to go.

Kifissia
Kifissia is a village some ten miles from the city center, once primarily a resort, now both a resort and residential suburb, which in recent years has become a home away from home for many Americans who have come to live and work in Greece. It's not the sort of place you'd come to if you're in Athens for only a few days, but you may want to spend an hour or two here to cool off in summer, or stop off for a meal on your way to Delphi or other points in the hinterlands. You can get to Kifissia for 30 drs (about 25¢) on the subway from Omonia Square, or by taxi for about 910 drs ($7) to 1,040 drs ($8); once there, take a 20-minute, 300-dr ($2) ride

around the town center in a horse-drawn carriage before or after your meal, or pay a brief visit to the **Goulandris Natural History Museum** and its displays on flowers and zoology.

Some of the most popular restaurants in Kifissia are the **Edelweiss, Blue Pine Farm, La Belle Hélène, Alt Berlin,** and the small but stylish **Lotophagus.** At the restaurant of the **Grand Chalet Hotel,** you can sit in the garden as you sip or dine and look across at the marble quarries on Mount Pentelicon. (You may have gathered from reading the chapter on hotels that the Greeks use marble the way Americans use Formica, much of it from Pentelicon; and in case you were thinking that by now the mountain must be a molehill, take a look across the valley—Pentelicon still stands.) These are all pleasant spots for a meal, but they are "international" rather than Greek in flavor; for more typically Greek settings go to Varsos or Taverna Moustakis.

Varsos, just off the main square, is a cavernous pastry shop that's been pleasuring sweet tooths for over 100 years, where dinners linger over kataifa, baklava, and that unique ice cream with a texture like Turkish delight known as kaimaki, 24 hours a day, 365 days a year.

Taverna Moustakis (tel. 8014-584) serves its Greek delicacies indoors in winter (in a cluster of wood-and-wicker rooms around an open kitchen where you can order your meal by pointing), in a tree-shaded courtyard in summer, serenaded by strolling bouzouki players. The Moustache is a popular spot with Kifissians, so call ahead for a reservation (and directions, if you're driving). Open also for lunch on Saturday and Sunday.

Mikrolimano

The other popular dining spot on Athens's outskirts is in the opposite direction, by the sea, 650 drs ($5) or so away by taxi. Until a few years ago it was known as Turkolimano ("Harbor of the Turks"), but in post-Cyprus Greece the signposts now direct you to Mikrolimano, "Little Harbor." Little *and* circular. It's a marina filled with sailboats from the seven seas, and crowned on the far hill by the ultra-chic Royal Hellenic Yacht Club. The entire waterfront is ringed with seafood restaurants, each with its terrace set up beneath brightly colored awnings across the street by the edge of the quay. Some of these restaurants have no-nonsense, unadorned interiors; others (the newer ones) are interior-decorated; on the whole, they're expensive. A few of them have their own fishing boats, or their own sources of supply, and theoretically they should sell less expensive fish, but it doesn't always work out that way as you'll discover on a stroll along the waterfront checking out prices. *Note:* All fish prices are quoted automatically "per kilo," but are invariably sold *whole;* therefore the price you pay is the price per kilo times the weight of the fish.

When you visit Mikrolimano, here's the procedure: check out the restaurants and menus to see what the day's catch has been, and how much you'll have to pay. Next, find yourself a table across the street by the quayside, order an ouzo or a bottle of Demestica. Then go back to the restaurant, ask the waiter to open the icebox with the fish, and make your selection—*barbounia* (red mullet), *garides* (shrimp), *glossa* (sole), and so on. Have your waiter weigh the fish right there and then and tell you how much your choice will cost. Finally, tell him how you would like to have it cooked—*skara* (grilled) or *tiganiti* (fried). Before returning to your waterfront table, select as an appetizer one of the Mikrolimano specialties—baked shrimp with tomatoes and feta cheese, or pikilea, a sort of seafood hors d'oeuvre (one portion is usually enough to appease two appetites until the main course is ready). Then you can settle back and spend the rest of the afternoon or evening sipping your wine, listening to the water lapping the hulls of the schooners and yawls. Afterward, get one of the weathered boatmen to row you around the harbor for a half an hour at about 1,000 drs ($8) for the boat, which will hold up to six passengers. You could almost be in Hydra or Mykonos or one of the other romantic Greek islands—yet you're only a 650-dr ($5) to 780-dr ($6) cab ride from your hotel.

Every Athenian has his favorite restaurant in Mikrolimano, although there is really only a marginal difference in prices, usually in the region of 1,900 drs ($15) to 2,200 drs ($17) a kilo—which should work out to 3,800 drs ($30) to 5,600 drs ($43) a head per meal, without wine (prices used to be much lower, but fish are getting scarce and no one wants to go fishing anymore, even in Greece). In summer, you may have little choice between one restaurant or another—you simply grab whatever table is available; if not, you should check out **Semiramis, Zefiros, Ta Prasina Trehantiria, Kokkini Varka,** the newish, three-story **Aglamer,** or, perhaps most famous of them all, **Canaris.**

Zea Marina

If you go one bay beyond Mikrolimano you come to a larger but equally circular harbor known as Zea Marina, which is the part of Piraeus given over to pleasure boats rather than cruise ships; and if you're joining one of the Greek shipping tycoons for a cruise, chances are this is where you'll come to board his floating palace. Zea Marina is a pleasant spot to keep in mind on a stifling Athens day when you want to get a breath of fresh air. Take the subway or bus to Piraeus and join the folks on a stroll around the promenade, stopping off now and again to admire a particularly handsome yacht, or taking a break in one of the cafés in the main square (there's usually music and dancing on weekends in summer). If you want to mingle with the owners of the yachts, have a drink or meal in the newly renovated **Landfall**, 3 Makriyianni at the far end, on the side farthest from Mikrolimano (tel. 4525-074). If you're hungry, drop into one of the local tavernas for a meal (try **Vasilena**, at 72 Etolikon [tel. 4612-457] and you won't go far off course). Better still, check out one of the marina cafés and sit by the edge of the marina dreaming of a Mediterranean cruise on the three-masted schooner *Créole*.

CHAPTER VII

NIGHTLIFE IN ATHENS

□ □ □

Breaking Plates in the Greek Tradition

Athenians don't paint the town red—they say "Let's go and break a few plates together!" It's an old Greek custom. When the audience is enjoying itself, it's expected to show its appreciation exuberantly. Greeks used to do this by smashing plates or glasses, or throwing flowers on the stage. The plate- and glass-smashing is now banned by the police, and the audiences started throwing flowers or plastic baubles instead; but you'll still find occasions when the music, the stars onstage, the stars above, and Dionysus combine to rouse the audience to smashing pitch. Just in case it happens some night when you're around, don't insist on a ringside table. Sit well back. (And don't break any plates because the taverna will charge a hefty premium for them.)

Athens itself is, of course, the greatest show of them all. The way to enjoy it is simply to go to the nearest café, find a table, and watch the performers—the lottery sellers, the sponge sellers, the souvlaki vendors, the taxi drivers, the stately old ladies all dressed up for a gala at the Grande Bretagne.

If you insist on paying for your entertainment, there are plenty of options open to you. Athens has a few ideas on nightlife you'll find nowhere else in Europe. Take your pick. You can watch ancient Greek drama in a theater dating from the time the plays were written. You can relive the history of the Acropolis in the awesome Son-et-Lumière, or Sound-and-Light, spectacle. You can sit on a roof garden beneath the floodlit Acropolis and watch a folklore show—or you can get up and dance a Zorba-like *syrtaki*. You can listen to a world-famous orchestra playing Beethoven in a 2,000-year-old amphitheater. And so the possibilities go on and on.

Whatever you decide to do, you'll soon discover one of the most appealing features of nightlife in Athens. Not only is it varied, not only is it unique, but it's priced so low you can enjoy almost everything it has to offer—even if you're on a tight budget. The only restraint on living it up right through the night is the thought that tomorrow you still have so many ancient wonders to see.

The entertainment pages of *Athens News* and *The Athenian* are the best guides to local events in Athens, what's playing in theaters, concerts, operas, cinemas, nightclubs, tavernas, and restaurants.

STA BOUZOUKIA (TO THE BOUZOUKI CLUBS)

Long before the movies *Never on Sunday* and *Zorba the Greek* there was bouzouki. This six-stringed lute-like instrument was popular with *rebetes,* men who scratched out a living on the fringes of society in places like Piraeus, persecuted by the police for their crimes and drugs. Unsavory characters indeed, but their music had an appeal that reached out and touched Greeks everywhere. No one knows exactly when *rebetika*—the songs of the *rebetes*—began to be sung, but it was probably in the 1820s, around the time of Greek independence; they were played by the poor and the social outcasts, in bitter but stoical protest against the injustices of their lives—much like the early blues songs. With the songs came the dances: the *zebekiko,* an intensely individualistic dance which the *rebetis* performs for himself and not for the people around him; the *hasapiko,* another traditional *rebetic* dance for two or three men, no more, and again a private introverted dance. What you may recall from *Zorba the Greek* was *syrtaki,* which is a modified and faster version of the *hasapiko.*

Over the years bouzouki became fashionable with all strata of society, reaching its peak in the early 1950s. Then it declined, due mainly to commercialization; to make the instrument more versatile another pair of strings was added, then the instrument itself was electrified. Instead of just the traditional guitar for accompaniment, the sophisticated Athenians who went out for a night *sta bouzoukia* (to the bouzouki clubs) came to expect guitars and drums and piano, and possibly double bass and electric organ, besides a couple of bouzoukia. This is basically what you'll hear today when you go *sta bouzoukia;* the unamplified bouzouki has all but disappeared, and the districts where the *rebetes* themselves used to hang out have all been pulled down. However, you can still hear good modern bouzouki music in several taverns in the Plaka, in downtown clubs in the winter months, and in the seaside clubs in summer.

At some point during your visit, you should try to listen to this authentic Greek music. Even their pop tunes have retained that haunting, bittersweet quality. Their love songs are not so much about falling in love as being clobbered by love (some samples, roughly translated, from the current repertoire: "I hate my eyes since I've looked at you/you've made my eyes a little toy." . . . "Talk to me, talk to me/I've never kissed you/and I can only kiss you in my dreams." . . . "Believe that you met me some night in a dream/but for me it wasn't a dream"). Even when the songs are not about love, they're not exactly joyful jingles—"The worry beads broke/and fell on the ground/and all the men started to cry/the lamp has blown out/and the last ship has sunk. . . ." If you have active tear ducts, better take along plenty of tissues when you set off for a night on the town in Athens.

IN THE PLAKA: Until recently, to take a few steps inside the Plaka was to realize that pandemonium is indeed a Greek word. Before World War II there was only one taverna in the Plaka (it's still there) and the other buildings were private homes. Now every home seems to be a taverna and every other sidewalk and rooftop an extension of a taverna. Tavernas set up their tables in patios, on rooftops, even on the stepped streets climbing up to the base of the rock. Most of the tavernas have music, which would be fine if they didn't also have amplifiers to blast out their sounds, reverberating through the alleyways and across the rooftops. Into the bargain, the Plaka had acquired a form of entertainment known as the open-air light show, a rooftop discothèque pounding kilowatt upon kilowatt of *noise* into the air.

Fortunately for all of us (and especially homeowners and hotel guests within earshot), the new minister concerned with the environment has banished rooftop discos and light shows, cut down on other noise, and encouraged authorities and people to gut and restore all those wonderful old buildings. A few years from now the Plaka will once more be a unique experience. Meantime, if you're not in the mood for curling up with Aristotle it can be a lot of fun. Tremendous fun. If you don't want to get yourself involved in the raucousness, you can still find an occasional taverna without music in a quiet (well, relatively quiet) terrace or courtyard, with the music arriving distantly across the rooftops.

Finding Your Way Around in the Plaka

Finding a particular club is not easy since most of the streets are identified in Greek only. However, you'll get there if you follow these basic directions. First, go to Cathedral Square. From the steps of the cathedral (facing out to the square), turn left and follow Palieloghou Venizelou Street until you come to a modern white marble building on the corner; bear right, past the Greek art shops, Stathis and Zorba's, until you come to Adrianou Street, at right angles. Now go left on Adrianou, past a few gift shops until you come to Milton's bar-restaurant on the left, a streetful of boutiques dead ahead. The street on your right is **Flessa Street,** and you'll know you're in Flessa because on the right there's a building that looks something like a misfit from Kyoto, which is the Taverna Palia Athena. Continue up this street to the fork in the road and bear right. This puts you on **Lissiou Street,** which is where most of the action is—here and on **Mnisikleos Street,** which runs at right angles to it.

Coming *from* the Acropolis, follow the path past the Areopagus, past the **Café-Bar Acropolis** (which has a magnificent view from its pathside terrace); there's an intersection on the left, but keep going along the path at the base of the hill, past an old church, then follow a curve to the left and down to a white wall; now go right. From that point follow the bustle, and from there you'll have to negotiate steps cluttered with tourists just listening to the music, tables filling up every inch of flat surface, waiters trying to get to the tables, people trying to get to the tables, people trying to get to the Acropolis, and occasionally someone trying to pinch a bottom.

Picking a Place in the Plaka

Once you're in the Plaka, how do you go about selecting a taverna?

On a busy weekend, the only valid piece of advice is: grab the first table you come to. There's really not so much difference in food or decor or service between one restaurant and another; if you can, get to the Plaka about half an hour before you're likely to feel ravenous, wander around and look the places over until you see something you fancy—in a patio, on the sidewalk, on steps, or on a rooftop. Yes, rooftop. In summer, the warm and cozy tavernas become barren ghost rooms and everything moves onto roofs rimmed with potted plants and usually covered by a removable awning. The important thing here is the *view*—if you're going to sit outdoors on the roof you might as well at least be in a position to watch the Acropolis as you dine. As you walk through the streets of the Plaka you'll be importuned by countless waiters promising that their rooftop has the best view. Don't take their word for it—go up and have a look for yourself before committing your evening. Some tavernas (like the Allo-Allo a couple of pages from now) are positioned in such a way that diners can look out on the Acropolis *and* Lycabettus *and* the lights of Athens.

Check out the prices too as you go along. Tavernas with music cost more than tavernas without music; tavernas with shows cost more than tavernas with only music. To give you some idea of what you can expect to pay, here is a sample of prices from **Taverna Kalokerinou** at 10 Kekropos St. (tel. 3232-054): main dishes (lamb chops, shrimp) from 1,100 drs ($8) to 1,920 drs ($15); appetizers cost anywhere from 130 drs ($1) to 360 drs ($3); desserts, 280 drs ($2); a bottle of local wine will be 320 drs ($3) to 580 drs ($4); and there's a cover charge of 100 drs (75¢). Work all that out and you'll find that an evening here, or in a similar taverna, will cost about 3,800 drs ($29) to 5,600 drs ($43) a head, with wine. This figure may be higher in other tavernas, depending on such variables as music tax, entertainment tax, show tax, and who is performing. *Prices in tavernas without shows are a few dollars less.* Most tavernas are open seven nights a week in the summer.

Taverna Kalokerinou (above) is one of the most reliable of the tavernas with shows (folk dancing and belly dancing from 10 to 11:45 p.m., and nonstop music from 9:30 p.m. for singing, dancing, or just plain finger-snapping and foot-tapping). The management here bans tour groups, so that couples and foursomes can get well-placed tables rather than being shoved into a corner. Like most other tavernas in these parts, the show is indoors in winter, on the roof in summer.

The corner of Lissiou Street and Mnisikleos Street is where you'll find one of the liveliest concentrations of tavernas, one on each corner.

I'll start with the **Mostrou,** because it's the only one around that has its name in large English characters on a sign above the door. It's your landmark, as well as a potential destination, if you don't mind spending an evening surrounded by other tourists. It's a big place with a roof garden for warm weather (the remainder of the year, you're in a semirustic room with a ceiling that looks like a TV studio with its complex of lights and spots for the floor show). The Mostrou show, indoors or outdoors, features a modern band and vocalists for dancing, six dancers (in folk costume), and the inevitable singer with hand-held microphone who always manages to sound like Barbra Streisand doing an imitation of Judy Garland. The show is at its best when the dancers and band cut out the jazz and get down to some serious Greek dancing. Then you can't even catch the waiters' attention. The Mostrou menu is probably one of the biggest in the Plaka. It's more expensive than most —grilled swordfish at 1,350 drs ($10), chicken dishes at 940 drs ($7)—but then it has a bigger floor show than most. The music begins at 9:30 p.m., the show runs from 11 p.m. to 12:30 a.m., followed by more music. Closed on Sunday.

Directly across the street is another multifloored taverna with a roof garden—**Dionysus** (not to be confused with the restaurant of the same name mentioned in the previous chapter). It's more relaxed than Mostrou, prices are a few drachmas less, and here you have a chance to inspect what you're going to eat when you walk past the display case and kitchen at the entrance. Under its new management, it's been spiffed up, the waiters are courteous, the atmosphere much more welcoming than at Mostrou, but the breaking of plates is banned. For reservations, call 322-7589.

Across the street are two tavernas in the simple, peasant style, popular with Greek families (no tour groups), and consequently much cheaper. The one on the right as you face the steps that take you up the hill is the **Taverna Kritikou,** and you'll probably hear it before you see it. Its tables spread over the steps and through the doors to the dance floor, and if the only free table is at the rear, allow yourself three or four minutes to squeeze through. This was the first taverna in the Plaka, by the way. There's a minimum of decor here—a few murals in Plaka-primitive style and a less-than-classical arch of corrugated plastic above the band. It's a four-piece combo—with electric organ, guitar, drums, and bouzouki—but it gets the place going, encouraging a steady stream of men getting up to dance, egged on by the audience to perform wilder, more contorted leaps than their predecessors. Its attractive menu is decorated with paintings of the beast, fowl, or fruit you're about to order—and the attractive prices include moussaka for 460 drs ($4), chicken or squid for 960 drs ($7) to 1,080 drs ($8); Cretan wine from 620 drs ($5).

Again across the street—**Plakokiti Taverna O Fandis,** which translates as Jack's. This is another boisterous place that caters mainly to Athenians but welcomes out-of-towners. If anything, it's even more basic, more congested, and noisier than Kritikou, but it's spread out through three small rooms separated by arches and decorated on every inch of wall and pillar with the traditional Plaka-primitive murals. The band is raised to shoulder height, and the stamp-size dance floor is half in one room, half in another. It's an infectious place, and most visitors probably wish they could do Greek dances. Some visitors actually try. To enjoy the fun you have to eat, but that's no strain on the budget. The Fandis has an inexpensive and varied menu: shrimp or octopus for less than 1,600 drs ($12), veal and potatoes or veal and onions for less than 1,200 drs ($9). Retsina costs about 620 drs ($5) a kilo, and domestic white or red wine is 700 drs ($5) to 1,440 drs ($11) a bottle. Open seven evenings a week.

Up the hill, a couple of doors beyond O Fandis at the corner of Thrasyvilou, the taverna on the right has the unlikely name of **Allo-Allo** (tel. 3250-332) and while I might not recommend its food or service in the winter, in summer it's blessed with one of the best rooftops—with 360-degree views. There's also a trio of barely amplified musicians to add to the magic of the Acropolis and Lycabettus. Moussaka, listed under appetizers, costs 480 drs ($4), country salad 300 drs ($2). Beef kebab at 800 drs ($6) is probably your best bet among the main courses—the steak is disappointing, the fish too expensive (and, in any case, the light is too dim for fiddling around with finicky bones). Wines are priced at 600 drs ($5) and up, and they're not available by the glass.

Some Other Plaka Tavernas

Taverna Klimatiria is located in a quiet corner on the outskirts of the Plaka, just under the Acropolis, at the corner of Thrassyvoulou and Klepsydras Streets. Climb the steps into the taverna and you are in what appears to be a very noisy, roughly decorated cellar with brick arches in the walls, the whole area crammed with tables, apart from the end where the musicians stand in a niche beneath one of the brick arches. Klimatiria has all the usual *mezedes* and a large selection of wines from all over Greece, from retsina to Robola; main courses are principally grills —shish kebab, veal chops, and beef steak. In summer the roof comes off and the music (a couple of guitars, piano, and bouzouki) fills the air until about 2 a.m. A nice, friendly place, this one, where dinner for two should cost 3,800 drs ($29) or less.

When you decide you've had enough of music while you eat, try a meal at **Café Restaurant Aerides** at 3 Markou Avriliou. This is on the edge of Plaka and in summer you eat on the pavement opposite the Tower of the Winds; from here you also have a glimpse of the Erechtheon up on the Acropolis, and hills away in the distance. They also have a raffia- and greenery-covered patio and a couple of rooms upstairs in an old Plaka house. You can get a three-course meal for 1,060 drs ($8) to 1,380 drs ($10). Or, if you're really only here for the view, there's moussaka, dolmades, and stuffed tomatoes at 430 drs ($3) each. Good selection of wines and several varieties come in half bottles. Service is courteous. Unlike most tavernas, Aerides is also open for breakfast and lunch.

Head down Diogenou away from the Tower of the Winds and in 30 seconds you'll find yourself in a quiet, shady little square with tables and chairs under the trees, and **Taverna O Platanos** and a little *cafenion* facing each other. Another taverna without music for your battered eardrums, this is one of the oldest in Plaka and specializes in grills. Try a brizola moscharisi for 530 drs ($4) to 640 drs ($5) and a Greek salad at 400 drs ($3); a perfectly acceptable kilo of open wine from the barrel is a mere 200 drs ($2). Lots of Greeks go there—perhaps they too like to get away from meat and music sometimes. When you've finished, slip over the square to the *cafenion,* have a cup of Greek coffee, and ask for a backgammon set as you digest your brizola moscharisi. The official address for O Platanos is 4 Diogenou. Open for lunch from noon to 3:45 p.m., for dinner from 8 p.m. to midnight (sharp!); closed Sunday.

Tavernas, like everything else these days, have their ups and downs, and it might be wise to check with your hotel receptionist to see which are the brightest, liveliest places when you are in town. A current favorite—the tree-shaded terrace of **Taverna Nefeli** at the top of Panos Street (at no. 24), opposite the Kanellopoulos Museum, is an attractive, quieter spot for "outdoors" weather, but the interior is dull and dreary. However, the prices are reasonable—roast chicken for less than 510 drs ($4), veal with rice for less than 920 drs ($7).

When you walk around the Plaka looking for these places, you'll pass dozens of others, and if you see one that looks interesting, just drop in; the list above doesn't claim to be *the* top ten or whatever, but simply a sampling to let you know what to expect.

NIGHTCLUBS BY THE SEA (AND IN ATHENS)

At midnight, when coaches turn into pumpkins, Athenians turn into swingers. Drop into any Athens nightclub just after dinner and you can almost certainly have a choice of ringside tables, overwhelming service, and a dance floor all to yourselves. At worst you may have to dodge a few tangoing tourists (until midnight, all the bands sound like Guy Lombardo). Come midnight, the whole atmosphere changes. The local swingers start filing in, the bouzoukis are plugged into their amplifiers, and the air fills with bittersweet Greek melodies. Everything keeps blasting away until three or four in the morning, or until the last plate has been thrown.

Before listing a few of the more popular clubs in Athens, here are some ground rules about nightclubbing in the city. You don't have to dress to the nines, but you'll find that most men wear jackets and ties. Most nightclubs don't have a separate minimum or cover charge. They usually incorporate it in the price of the first drink—somewhere in the region of 2,000 drs ($15) to 2,400 drs ($18), regardless of what you drink. Subsequent drinks are usually a bit costly as well. If you have dinner to while away the evening until midnight, your drinks will cost less, but, of course, you'll still end up paying at least 4,400 drs ($34) if you have Greek dishes, up to 7,600 drs ($58) if you order steaks. It's expensive, but consider what you're getting in return—three, four, five, or six hours of entertainment, frequently with one of Greece's top singing stars, plus dancing.

Athens nightclubs set such a hot pace that the air conditioning can't keep up with them; so when the weather warms up the nightclubs pack up for the shore, and set up their music stands and stages all the way from Piraeus to Vouliagmeni. The night owls of Athens then scan the newspapers to find out where their favorite stars are singing and follow them. The actual club is relatively unimportant—it's the performers that count. If you plan to follow suit, here are some of the names to watch for—Marinella, Dalaras, Bithikotsis, Zambetas, Voskopoulos, Dionyssiou, Tsitsanis, and Kokotas. They're the ones who get the plates flying.

One of the newest and swankest of the shoreside nightclubs is **Delina** (tel. 8940-205), in a dazzling year-round anchorage out near the airport. You enter it through a tunnel of aggressive multihued spotlights, which lead into a softly lit big circular bar; a concealed door then guides you into a vast area like a circus big top, so vast it could almost house the entire menagerie of Barnum & Bailey. The seaside end of this area is taken up by a large stage normally filled with a 22-piece *(twenty-two)* orchestra. The international floor shows are at 11 p.m. and 1 a.m. Minimum charge is around 3,000 drs ($23), which is the cost of your first scotch and soda, but that will, if you wish, keep you going until the club closes at 2 a.m. Dinner will set you back about 9,750 drs ($75), with wine. A stunner of a nightspot. Call for reservations.

Heading south along the coastal highway, there's the **Neraida** in Kalamaki (tel. 9812-004), possibly the loveliest setting, by the sea, beside a new marina. Minimum charge is around 3,000 drs ($23). **Fantasia** (tel. 9810-503), by the beach, opposite the old airport, is the least sophisticated of the group, but currently one of the most popular. And the **Athinea** at Glyfada Beach (tel. 8946-898), which is part of the hotel-bungalow complex, an attractive, modern, red-and-white taverna opening to the bay, the beach, and the sky, and worth the cab ride; this is a sophisticated taverna with music rather than a cabaret, and most of the music is international pop. Dinner is around 13,000 drs ($100), with wine, per head.

Note: None of these clubs is more than 1,300 drs ($10) by taxi from downtown Athens, and you can always get a taxi to bring you home in the wee hours.

Back to Athens, the new **Copacabana,** behind the Royal Olympia at 4 Kallirrois Ave. (tel. 9232-648), bills itself as a nightclub/music hall, featuring a six-piece orchestra, a juggler, exotic dancers, belly dancing (sort of), striptease (sort of), assorted singers, and a Greek folk troupe—all adding up to a show that lasts three hours somewhere between 10:30 p.m. and 2 a.m. A meal at the Copa (no relation to its New York namesake, by the way) will cost you from 7,800 drs ($60) a head, domestic wines about the same price per bottle (without dinner), and a full bottle of champagne or scotch (probably the best bet in the long run) costs 2,800 drs ($22) to 3,800 drs ($29). Call for reservations.

DISCOTHÈQUES

With all that lively Greek dancing going on around you there's not much need for discos. However, if your feet start to itch for the big beat, here are a few suggestions.

Since discos tend to boom in and out of fashion in Athens as elsewhere, your best bet is to pick up a copy of *Athens News* or *The Athenian* and study the latest listings; alternatively, ask someone at your hotel to recommend something that fits your tastes. Generally speaking, discos have no entrance fee, but drinks will cost around 1,170 drs ($9). That said, some of the current "in" spots are **Nine Plus Nine,** at 5 Aghras St. near the Olympic Stadium (tel. 7222-258); **14,** right in Kolonaki Square; and **Papagayo,** at 37 Patriarchou Ioakim St. in Kolonaki (tel. 7230-135).

Another well-established favorite with Athenians is **Akritiri,** on a promontory at Aghios Kosmos in Glyfada, with dancing on a breeze-cooled patio beside a pool in summer (in winter, everything moves indoors). A hotel disco much frequented by well-to-do locals and visitors is the **Horizon Dancing Bar** of the Caravel Hotel, again on the roof with a dazzling view.

OTHER NIGHTSPOTS IN ATHENS

THE BOÎTE: If you think the decor in a taverna is fairly basic, wait until you see a *boîte.* The typical Athenian boîte is small, crowded, smokey, and the seating may be "kindergarten" stools rather than chairs—but it can be a lot of fun. The boîte is strictly for music—*rebetika,* folk songs, pop hits, and occasionally resistance songs (although you may have trouble in determining what they're in resistance to). Performers are usually unknowns, but occasionally you may have an opportunity to hear one of Greece's more famous singers or composers. There are usually two shows nightly (the first one is never before 9 p.m.), and the admission charge of 550 drs ($4) to 660 drs ($5) usually includes the first drink. Since the evenings can be long (you may have to sit through supporting acts until the star arrives), your best bet usually is to order a bottle of wine and make it last the evening.

LATE-NIGHT BARS: "Late" is relative, of course, in a city where most people don't even get around to eating dinner until 9 or 10. There's no shortage of late-night spots in Athens, and you may have found your favorite on your first night in town. If not, here are some suggestions for nightcaps: **Montparnasse** at 30 Haritos in Kolonaki, popular with the neighborhood's writers and artists, and decorated with 1920s posters, glass-topped tables, and overstuffed cushions in the shape of fruit; **Larry's Bar,** near the top of Likavitou Street (at no. 20), is another favorite with the Kolonaki night owls. A couple of fine restaurants where the barflies may linger beyond the regular dining hours are **Stage Coach** at 14 Voukourestiou, just off Syntagma, and **Balthazar** at 27 Tsocha, near the American Embassy. Among the hotel lounges and bars, the **G.B. Corner** in the Grand Bretagne and the rooftop **Galaxy** in the Hilton are especially popular with both locals and out-of-towners.

OTHER NIGHTTIME ACTIVITIES

MOVIES: You probably hadn't planned on taking in a movie on your trip to Athens, but if you're going to be in town for several days you may feel like one some evening as a change of pace from Aristophanes and Euripides. In any case, movie-going in Greece is an experience in itself. Around the end of May the indoor cinemas close up for the summer and take to the open air—wherever there's a space that's not currently a construction site or car park. The movies are usually reruns, but no matter, since you have a chance to catch up on something you've missed. If you go to the first performance, around 8:45 or 9 p.m., the sound is audible but the picture is faint; if you wait for the second show, after the sun has properly set, the picture may be clear but the sound may be almost inaudible so as not to antagonize the people living in nearby apartments (who have been known to show their resentment by turning their own radios and TVs up loud and switching on every available light). The films themselves are shown in their original language with Greek subtitles. Grab a Coke or beer and a bag of potato chips as you go in (everyone does). It may not be for the serious movie buff, but on a warm evening a visit to a movie can be fun, and inexpensive—rarely more than 300 drs ($2).

In case you want to call ahead for starting times, here are the telephone numbers of some of the leading *indoor* movie houses in Athens, open in winter only:

Asty, 4 Korai St. (tel. 3221-925).

Attikon, 19A Stadiou St. (tel. 3228-821).

Embassy, 5 Patriarchou Ioakim (tel. 7220-903).

Pallas, 1 Voukourestiou St. (tel. 3224-434).

Radio-City, 240 Patission and Lissiatrion (tel. 8674-832).

DORA STRATOU DANCE THEATER: The south side of the Acropolis can be a congested spot in summer. The crowd that's not heading for the Pnyx and the Son-et-Lumière show is probably on its way up the Hill of Philopappos following the sign for the Dora Stratou Dance Theater. The Dora Stratou Company is a group of folk dancers that was founded about 35 years ago and has earned a lot of bravos since then, both in Greece and on tours around the world, including the U.S.A. The show consists of a warm-up overture by the Zygia, a small orchestra made up of clarinet, violin, lute, santouri, and drums. The players are dressed in typical Greek native costumes, which differ from region to region, but include black waistcoats, miniskirts, blouses, white stockings, and snub-nosed shoes—like evzones in mufti. The dances and songs are dances and songs that Greeks have been dancing and singing for 2,500 years, and there's no finer place to watch them than under the feathery trees, on an Athenian hillside, a stone's throw from the Acropolis. You can almost see Pan and the nymphs dancing here. A typical program might include the Florina-Kratero from Macedonia, the Dodoni from Epirus, and the Ierissos from Chalkidiki.

You can get to the Dora Stratou Dance Theater by bus 9 from Constitution (Syntagma) Square. The dances are performed every evening at 10:15 p.m., from May through October. On Wednesday and Sunday there are "matinees" at 8:15 p.m. Admission prices range from 550 drs ($4) to 750 drs ($6), and your ticket reserves a specific seat in the amphitheater (real seats, not bleachers).

CONCERTS AND OPERA: There are performances of opera and ballet by the **National Opera** in the Olympia Theater, 59 Akadimias (tel. 3612-461); November through May; concerts by the **Athens State Orchestra** (its regular house, the Kotopouli Theater at 48 Venizelou, burned down and its concerts are given in other locations); and there are often recitals and chamber concerts at the **Gloria Theater,** 7 Ippokratous (tel. 3626-702). Check with the Athens Festival (tel. 3230-049) for ticket prices, but expect them to be in the 300-dr ($2) to 700-dr ($5) range.

Nearby Piraeus has recently developed into a miniature cultural center, and you can sometimes take in concerts, operas, and recitals in that rejuvenated seaport.

The best place to find out about all these events is in the pages of *The Athenian,* or *Athens News,* or from the concierge at your hotel. He'll also tell you how to go about getting tickets, and in the better hotels he'll probably get them for you.

SON-ET-LUMIÈRE: If you arrive in Athens anytime between the beginning of April and the end of October, make a point of spending at least one evening watching the Sound-and-Light spectacle at the Acropolis. Son-et-Lumière involves batteries of lights —1,500 in all—that are flooded onto the Acropolis hill and the Parthenon in various combinations, to tie in with a commentary relating the history of the city. It's a stupendous show (with a pretentious commentary). It takes place every evening at 9 and 9:45 p.m. in English, except on Good Friday.

To see the Sound-and-Light show, you go to the small hill called Pnyx, which is on the south side of the Acropolis—the *far* side, if you're near Omonia or Constitution Squares. If you don't want to walk, take bus 230 that goes along Dionysus Areopagitou, past the Acropolis, and get off one stop past the Herod Atticus Theater, where you'll find a sign that says Son-et-Lumière. (Or take a taxi—it should cost no more than 300 drs, less than $3, from either square.) From there, just follow the crowds. The 45-minute show costs 400 drs ($3) (half price if you show a student card). If you don't want to spend even a couple of dollars, go to the Areopagus Hill; from that vantage point you can see the show, but you won't hear the commentary or the music.

The Son-et-Lumière show is part of a much more broad-ranging show—the Athens Festival.

THE ATHENS FESTIVAL: The Athens Festival takes place from mid-July to mid-September at the 1,800-year-old **Herod Atticus Theater,** on the slopes of the Acropolis. There you can sit on marble bleachers (now with free plastic cushions), beneath the stars, and watch some of the world's finest orchestras, musicians, singers, dancers, and actors in a setting unsurpassed anywhere in the world. The theater (sometimes known as the Odeon) was built by Herod Atticus as a memorial to his wife, Appia Annia Regilla, so the architecture is Roman, not Greek. It holds 5,000, every seat has a perfect line of vision, and the acoustics are extraordinary, even for a Chopin nocturne.

Programs are never available until a month or two ahead of opening night, but to give you an idea of the caliber of performers, recent visitors have included the Royal Philharmonic Orchestra with Vladimir Ashkenazy, the Netherlands Dance Theater, Natalia Makarova, Rudolph Nureyev, the Vienna State Opera and Philharmonic, the Utah Symphony Orchestra with Maurice Abravanel, Béjart's 20th Century Ballet, the Royal Swedish Ballet, the Washington National Symphony, and, in 1988, the Bolshoi Ballet and New York Philharmonic under Zubin Mehta. When you add to that the splendor of the setting, the balmy night air, and the stroll back to your hotel or the Plaka, you have the ingredients for the evening of a lifetime. Here's your chance, for example, to see local companies such as the National Theater, the Amphi-Theater, and the Art Theater perform plays by Euripides, Sophocles, Aristophanes, in an almost authentic setting. They will be in Greek (you can buy a synopsis) but there's plenty to enjoy even if you don't understand the words. (However, if you don't want to wait for the last act, at least wait for an intermission before you get up and leave.)

Ticket prices, like the programs, are never established until the last minute, but they are very inexpensive compared to other European festivals—probably in the 500-dr ($4) to 3,500-dr ($27) range. You can get details and tickets from the Athens Festival Office in the Spyrou Miliou Arcade at 4 Stadiou St., which is one block from Constitution Square (tel. 3221-459 or 3223-111, ext. 240). You can also get tickets from the box office at the Herod Atticus Theater (tel. 3232-771 or 3223-111, ext. 137). English summaries of the Greek plays, at either location, are 100 drs (75¢).

(*Note:* Additional performances sometimes take place at a second outdoor theater on Lycabettus Hill.)

A NIGHT AT THE TABLES: If nightclubbing is too tame, take a taxi to **Mount Parnes** and try your hand at blackjack or roulette. The casino on top of Mount Parnes is one of the largest in Europe (17,000 square feet of glitter and plush) with girl croupiers (some from England, most from Greece). About 1,500 gamblers a day make the trek up the hill to have their fling at blackjack, roulette, punto banco, baccarat, chemin de fer, boule, and craps. And it is a trek. Mount Parnes is an hour's drive from Athens; when you get there you can either drive all the way up the mountain, or you can take the *téléferique* from the base at 200 drs ($2) each way, a five-minute ride (but it runs only every half hour or so).

The casino is open every day, except Wednesday, from 8 p.m. until 2 a.m. All you need to get in is a jacket and tie, and a passport;

be prepared to fill out at least one form. The casino is out of bounds to civil servants and bankers. For information call 3229-412.

NIGHTTIME TOURS: The simplest way to sample the nightlife of Athens is to take one of the special "Athens by Night" sightseeing tours. This kind of tour is more fun in Athens than in most cities because it usually includes a drive past the floodlit Acropolis, then along the edge of the sea to Castella in Piraeus, with refreshments in a typical taverna and dinner at a Greek nightclub, complete with floor show and folk dancing. **American Express, CHAT, Key Tours,** and **Viking** operate these "Athens by Night" tours and "Theater Night" tours that take you to performances of the Sound-and-Light Spectacle *and* the Greek dances at the Dora Stratou Theater. The "Theater Night" tour costs 2,700 drs ($21), including tickets but without dinner, and the "Athens by Night" tour costs 4,000 drs ($31) with dinner.

CHAPTER VIII

SIGHTSEEING
IN ATHENS

◻ ◻ ◻

If you have only one day in Athens, your best bet is to take a guided sightseeing tour. But even if you're staying a few days and plan to do a lot of sightseeing, it's still a good idea to take the tour to get an idea of the lay of the land, and find out what really interests you. Then you can go back yourself and take in the spots you want to cover in depth.

Let's assume, however, that you plan to see the city on your own, and you've decided to begin with breakfast in **Syntagma,** or Constitution Square. The square itself is a sightseeing attraction (you've already read about its cafés). On the bottom side you have one of the highlights of the square as far as Americans are concerned—the office of **American Express,** usually surrounded by swarms of visitors, young and old, rich and poor, student and professor, booking trips to the islands, waiting for mail and/or money from home. The mail is delivered at 5 p.m., by the way, and this is the time to be there to meet old friends, catch up on gossip, make new friends, and sympathize with those who didn't get that check. The café on the corner, Papaspyrou, gets the brunt of the sorrow and elation. You have to move nimbly to get a table here.

However, the main sight of Syntagma is the former Royal Palace, now the **Parliament Building.** This is a large, squarish yellow building with a marble forecourt facing the square. Apparently, this site was chosen personally by young King Otto (the Bavarian who was put on the throne after the war with Turkey), and his site-selection technique was to hang pieces of meat in various parts of town and select the location where the maggots were slowest to develop. The main attraction here, apart from the constant arrival or departure of dark limousines, is the **changing of the guard.** This ceremony, complete with evzones and their pompoms, takes place every hour, 20 minutes before the hour, and on

Sunday at 11 a.m., accompanied by its regimental band. If you get there late, you can always photograph the new evzone on duty at the **Tomb of the Unknown Soldier,** in front of the building.

You can spend whole days sitting in the cafés of Syntagma, enjoying the daily routine of the city—the crowds cramming into the offices in the morning; the lottery ticket sellers promising riches; the sponge sellers, more interested in sitting in the shade than selling a record number of sponges; the jet-setters dashing in and out of the NJV Meridien and Grande Bretagne; the tourists checking into the airline offices; the limousines heading for Parliament; the Americans clustering around American Express; the shoppers disappearing into the arcades of Ermou and Karageorgi tis Servias Streets; the crowds cramming out of their offices and cramming into the buses; young hippies; young blondes; young Greeks trying to pick up the blondes; the elderly gentlemen who've been congregating here through several reigns and regimes, as timeless as the Acropolis.

But sooner or later you'll want to leave the comfy café chairs and the shade of the awnings and go see the other sights of Athens, mainly the Acropolis. *Note:* In the following paragraphs, where mentioned, the winter period is from November 1 to March 31, and summer is from April 1 to October 31—but there's a lot of leeway.

ARCHEOLOGICAL SITES

THE ACROPOLIS: "Future ages wonder . . ." and they admire, and huff and puff up the hill for a closer look. The Acropolis (meaning "upper city") is built on a rock 515 feet above sea level. The rock has been there, presumably, since the Creation; the walled fortress on top of it has been there for many millennia; but the Acropolis you see today, with its temples and its Parthenon, is a creation of the 5th century B.C. Let's simplify the upper city. The "Acropolis" is the entire plateau; it contains four ancient buildings and one very discreet modern building, which is the Acropolis Museum.

The first of these ancient structures is the **Propylaea,** an imposing entrance consisting of a central gateway with two wings (one of which was originally a picture gallery, the Pinacotheca). Just to the right of the Propylaea is a small temple known as **Athena Nike,** or Nike Apteros ("Unwinged Victory"). It was built in the 5th century B.C. to commemorate the victories of the Greeks over the Persians, and its beautiful friezes portray scenes from that war.

The **Erechtheum** (pronounce it er-ek-the-*um*), was begun in 421 B.C. and completed in 407 B.C., on the site of a temple to Erechtheus, a legendary king of Athens. In some ways this is the most hallowed spot up on the hill, because it is the spot where, so the legend says, Athena herself, the guardian of Athens, created the first olive tree. Legend also has it that the invading Persians destroyed this tree, but when they were driven off the tree miraculously grew again. It's a curious temple by Athenian standards: it's built on two levels, it's asymmetrical, and its two porches have no relationship to each other. The smaller porch of the two is the famous one supported by the six **caryatids,** or stone maidens. During the Turkish occupation, the military governor housed his 40 wives here.

But the crowning glory of the Acropolis is the great temple dedicated to the virgin goddess herself, the **Parthenon.** At one time the temple sheltered a gigantic statue of Athena, finished in ivory and gold, and its anterooms were stacked high with the treasures of the city. The Parthenon was built during the time of Pericles, between 447 and 432 B.C., and designed by what may have been the most successful architectural team of all time—Phidias, Ictinus, and Callicrates. They started out with a very uneven foundation, so that one end of the building rests on 35 feet of marble to bring it level with the rest of the structure; the temple lies east to west, with 17 columns on the north and south walls and 8 columns on the other two sides.

But the numbers mean little compared to the grace and grandeur of the temple's lines. The Parthenon has no straight lines. Horizontal lines curve in the middle and the 50 columns bulge in the center then taper off toward the top. Traces of iron in the marble (from the hill of Pentelicon, on the edge of the city) give it a golden glow. In its youth the Parthenon had statues and friezes and other decorations, but over the years they've been removed by various conquerors or explorers (the British Museum's famed Elgin Marbles come from the Parthenon). But long before Lord Elgin scrambled up the hill, the Parthenon had undergone various humiliations—for 1,000 years it was a Christian church, then it became a Muslim mosque complete with minaret, and then a Turkish arsenal. It was hit by a Venetian shell during a siege in 1687, and that one hapless shell destroyed the interior and the roof of the temple. All the bits and pieces that were left lying around were put back into place during a restoration project that began in the 19th century and didn't end until 1930.

Take a breather now. What you see from up here (with the exception of the museum)—the Stoa, the Plaka, the Areopagus, and Pnyx—was the extent of the city of Athens in its Golden Age.

This was where the action was. Pericles, the orator, aristocrat, general, and statesman, was the grand panjandrum. The plays of Euripides, Aeschylus, Aristophanes, and Sophocles were being premiered at the **Theater of Dionysus**. Philosophers and men of learning were gathering there and exchanging their wild ideas: Anaxagoras with his absurd theory that the universe was an organized system; Democritus mumbling about all matter being made up of atoms; Herodotus, the so-called father of history, researching his book on the Persian Wars. It must have been an extraordinary, exciting place.

Now for the rest of the Acropolis. The **Acropolis Museum** is a low structure tucked into the southeastern end of the plateau, hidden from the outside world. It was built in the last century to store the various statues and fragments of stone reliefs found on the surrounding hills—pediments, friezes, the *Moschophoros* (man with calf), *Athena Meditating,* and a collection of statues of women, known as "Korai," famous for their smiles (which certainly make a change from *Mona Lisa* and her mystic smile). The museum helps you visualize how the buildings must have looked centuries ago.

The Acropolis is usually open Monday through Saturday from 7:30 a.m. to 7:30 p.m., to 5 p.m. during winter (on Sunday and holidays from 8 a.m. to 6 p.m.). The Acropolis Museum's hours are the same as those of the Acropolis, except on Tuesday (noon to 6 p.m.). Admission to the Acropolis site and the museum is 600 drs ($5). Please check these facts and figures when you get to Athens, before hiking up that hill, because they may change, due to preservation work to counteract the effects of air pollution —and too many admirers. The preservation of the Erechtheum is nearly complete; the caryatids have been moved to the museum for preservation; replicas stand in their stead. The actual temple will reportedly soon be open to visitors. On the whole, the preservation work will continue for several years, but there's a good chance that the priceless treasures will survive for a few more centuries.

THE AGORA: We can still stay within the orbit of the Acropolis and feel its presence over our shoulders. The second most important corner of antiquity is the region around the Agora, at the base of the Acropolis on the northwest side. In Ancient Athens the Parthenon was the center of religious life, but the Agora was where the business was done and the fun was found. Pericles's Aspasia probably headed right for this spot. One of the former arcades, the **Stoa of Attalos** has been rebuilt (by the efforts of the American School of Classical Studies) and now houses a museum filled with the bits and pieces found around the Agora, including models of the Acropolis and the Agora, which will help you understand both sites better—so go there first. Originally, the stoa was the market, and housed some of the first government offices of a democracy. The dominant feature here, however, is the majestic **Temple of Hephaistos,** usually referred to as the "Theseion," or "Theseum." It's as old as the Parthenon, and unquestionably it's the best preserved of all Greek temples. The Ancient Agora Museum in the Stoa of Attalos, to use its full title, is open from 9 a.m. to 3 p.m. Monday through Saturday; 9 a.m. to 2 p.m. on Sunday and holidays. The museum, but not the site, is closed Tuesday. Admission is 400 drs ($3) each for the site and the museum.

Other sites in this neighborhood include the old **Dipylon Gate,** which used to be the first landmark on the road from Athens to Thebes; the **Keramicos,** the cemetery of Ancient Athens where you can still see some old sculptured memorials and stelae in the graveyard itself, and funerary tablets and ceramics dating from the 11th century B.C. in the adjoining museum. The Keramicos Archeological Museum (to give it its formal title) is open from 9 a.m. to 3 p.m., on Sunday and holidays from 9:30 a.m. to 2:30 p.m.; closed Tuesday. Entrance fee is 200 drs ($2).

Still in this general region, but not in the Agora itself, you can visit the so-called **Tower of the Winds,** a clock built in the Roman period in the shape of an octagonal tower, with figures of the winds, a weather vane, and a unique hydraulic mechanism.

Farther to the east, between the Acropolis and the National Garden, is the **Temple of Olympian Zeus** (what a resounding name!), at the junction of two avenues—Amalias and Olgas—facing the southern entrance to the National Gardens. Begun in the 6th century B.C., the temple was built on a terrace 225 yards long, but today it's very much a ruin, and most impressive when it's floodlit in the evening. The best place to admire it from is not the site itself but from the lounge of the Royal Olympic Hotel, or the roof of the new Athens Gate Hotel. The temple site is open from 9 a.m. to 3 p.m., from 9:30 a.m. to 2:30 p.m. on Sunday and holidays. Nearby **Hadrian's Arch,** built by the Emperor Hadrian in the 2nd century B.C., marked the boundary between the ancient quarter of the city and the new Athens, or Adrianople as it was then called.

THE MUSEUMS

NATIONAL ARCHEOLOGICAL MUSEUM: At 1 Tositsa St. (but the public entrance faces Patission Avenue).

Don't rush in. Enjoy the setting first. From Patission you walk through a spacious garden with cafés beneath palm trees, up to a long, classical façade above a sweep of marble steps—usually crowded with footloose young travelers in search of a heritage, or a companion, and crowds of tourists pouring from sightseeing buses. It's not unusual for 8,000 people to visit this museum in one day.

Once in the exhibition rooms proper you're left with no doubt that here is the world's grandest collection of antiquities. Years after you've visited the National Archeological Museum, its treasures will be imprinted on your mind. You need several hours, if not several days, to see everything here. Go on your own rather than on a tour, when you'll be whisked through so quickly you won't remember a thing; on the other hand, if you have time for several visits, it might be an idea to take a tour first time round, make a mental note of exhibits you want to see in a more leisurely manner, then return again on your own.

All the treasures from Mycenae are here in Athens, and the distant site really comes alive before your eyes when you see the fantastic collection of objects discovered at the dig by the famous German archeologist Schliemann. Note the magnificent beaten-gold mask of a man with beard and moustache taken from the fifth Shaft Grave: Schliemann claimed, having removed the mask, to "have gazed upon the face of Agamemnon." The Mycenaean Hall contains a staggering variety of finds: intricate gold and silver dagger blades, gold-leaf portrait masks, breastplates, swords, libation cups, and many representations of animals and birds—all dating from around 1550 B.C.

Contrast these objects of exquisite craftsmanship with the comparatively crude statues of the 7th and 6th centuries B.C.— the stiff, upright *Kouros* or youth is represented naked with one foot forward and the *Kore* or maiden is draped. Examples of this sculptural style have been found all over mainland Greece and the islands. Another remarkable category of exhibits (not grouped together) consists of bronzes, some of which have lain beneath the sea for the past 2,000 years.

You should also visit the exhibition of the finds from Santorini (or Thira, as it has now been officially named), the frescoes alive with colorful representations of swallows, monkeys, dolphins, and elegant figures of youth and maidens. Thira/Santorini was an island civilization that flourished at the same time as the Minoan, back in the second millennium B.C. The islanders built luxurious homes and decorated them with gorgeous murals and pottery. But one day, as legend has it,

"Enkeladus in the bowels of the Earth was roused with undescribable fury," and the ensuing earthquake wiped out Thira (you'll read more about this in the chapter on the Greek Islands).

These paragraphs describe maybe one-millionth of this museum's treasures; unless you have time to pay several visits, confine your tour to a couple of halls, and within each focus on a couple of showcases—such as the displays of gold rings, bracelets, and seals. Otherwise you'll go daffy.

Museum hours are Tuesday through Sunday from 8 a.m. to 5 p.m.; closed Monday. Admission is 500 drs ($4).

There are three other museums adjoining the National Archeological Museum, mostly of specialized interest—the **Epigraphical Collection** (inscribed monuments from all parts of Greece), the **Numismatic Collection,** and the **Display of Plaster Copies of Antiquities** (both for display and for sale). The hours are similar to those of the National Archeological Museum and the same 500 drs ($4) ticket will get you into all of them.

BENAKI MUSEUM: At 1 Odos Koumbari (corner of Vassilissis Sofias Avenue).

It is, of course, almost *de rigueur* to visit the National Archeological Museum in Athens, and if you're a classical scholar you'll be excited by its thoroughness. If you're not, it may stagger you with its size. The Benaki, on the other hand, is a manageable museum. It's more human, which is probably how its founder, the late Anthony Emm. Benaki, would have liked it. This mansion was in fact his home, and most of the exhibits are part of his own collection, which his family turned over to the state after he died. Judging by the exhibits, Benaki must have been a man of wide-ranging interests, because here you'll find relics of the Greek War of Independence, ecclesiastical treasures, textiles, ceramics, glass, costumes, and furniture of Greek, Turkish, and Islamic craftsmanship.

The museum's on three floors, and the room arrangement is rather odd, so buy the 400-dr ($3) guidebook in English. Some highlights: the portable writing desk of Lord Byron; antique pistols and rifles impeccably decorated with silver and engravings; an intricately carved wooden door from Baghdad (9th century); a virtually complete 17th-century reception room from Cairo with mosaic floor, fountain, basin, and tiled pilasters; a pair of early works by El Greco; some fascinating Coptic fabrics and embroidery; a whole roomful of Egyptian, Roman, Mycenaean, and French silver and gold jewelry; one-third of the magnificent collection of Chinese art that once belonged to Georgiou Eumouphopoulos (the other two-thirds is in London)—Han, T'ang, Sung, Yuan, Ming, and Chin dynasties. There are also collections of household embroideries and festive costumes from the islands, golden embroidered coats from Epirus, liturgical seals, distaffs, and musical instruments.

The Benaki is well worth the short walk up from Syntagma, or down from Kolonaki Square. Open 8:30 a.m. to 2 p.m.; closed Tuesday. Admission is 200 drs ($2); free on Sunday.

NATIONAL GALLERY: The **Ethniki Pinakothiki** and **Museum Alexandre Soutsos,** or National Gallery, is the gleaming new building at 46 Vassilissis Sofias Ave. opposite the Athens Hilton. The National Gallery was established in 1900; its new home was inaugurated, however, in 1976, and it's a beauty. The collection includes a Goya (*Fiesta*), Correggio (*Guardian Angel*), Poussin (*The Holy Family* and *St. Anne*), van Dyck (*Portrait of a Nobleman*), and half a dozen El Grecos. Unfortunately, they're not always on view. A large gallery is given over to temporary exhibits, and there's a sculpture garden at the rear. Open from 8:45 a.m. to 3 p.m.; on Wednesday, 9 a.m. to 2 p.m.; on Sunday and holidays from 9:30 a.m. to 2:30 p.m.; closed Monday. Admission is free.

BYZANTINE MUSEUM: At 22 Vassilissis Sofias Ave., the museum is at the far end of a pleasant courtyard lined with fountains and sculpture fragments, rather like a Florentine palazzo. It has two floors of mosaics, sculpture, fragments, altars, garments, archbishop's staffs, and Bibles. The descriptive signs are in English and Greek. Open from 8:45 a.m. to 2:30 p.m.; closed Monday; on Sunday and holidays, 9:30 a.m. to 2:30 p.m. Admission is 300 drs ($2).

MUSEUM OF GREEK FOLK ART: At 17 Kidathineou St., Plaka. Folk art here includes vestments, embroidery, pastoral woodcarving, icon stands, reliquaries, carnival costumes, and a roomful of murals from Mitilini. Open daily from 8:45 a.m. to 3 p.m.; Sunday and holidays, 9:30 a.m. to 2:30 p.m. year round; closed Monday. Admission free. The museum's collection of folk ceramics is displayed in a former mosque at 1 Areos St., Monastiriki Square.

HISTORICAL AND ETHNOLOGICAL MUSEUM: Kolokotroni Square. Modern history's equivalent of the National Archeological Museum—the story of Greece from the Balkan Wars through more or less the present day. Open 9 a.m. to 2 p.m.;

closed Monday and the month of August. Admission is 400 drs ($3); free on Thursday.

THE WAR MUSEUM OF GREECE: At 2 Rizari St. (corner of Leoforos Vassilissis Sofias). "War" in this fabled corner of the world means Achilles vs. Hector, Neoptolemos vs. Paris, Greek vs. Persian, Alexander the Greek vs. the rest, and continues all the way through recorded history to World War II and the Korea Campaign. The collection includes Neolithic cudgels, obsidian hammers, Corinthian helmets, diagrams of ancient battlefields, paintings, uniforms, ship models, a glittering armory of swords and sabres, and in the courtyard, an exhibition of howitzers, torpedos, and antique fighter planes. Refreshment corner in the basement. Open daily, except Monday, from 9 a.m. to 2 p.m.; admission free.

CENTER FOR FOLK ART AND TRADITION: At 6 Angeliki Hatzimichaeli St., Plaka. Opened in 1981, the center is in the refurbished town house of a wealthy Athenian family—and feels lived-in, as though the family had just left to vacation on Skiathos. Door frames, mantels, and window seats are of dark wood, elaborately carved in classic and folk designs of ships, birds, and mythical creatures. Exhibits include tiled fireplaces, Skyros plates, hand-woven fabrics, stained-glass windows, and family portraits. Free admission. Open Tuesday and Thursday from 9 a.m. to 9 p.m.; on Wednesday, Friday, and Saturday from 9 a.m. to 1 p.m. and 5 to 9 p.m.; on Sunday from 9 a.m. to 1 p.m.; closed Monday.

KANELLOPOULOS MUSEUM: In the Plaka, at the top of Panos Street (near the Taverna Nefeli). In a private neoclassical house, this private collection of classic Greek artifacts includes vases and figurines, Byzantine ikons, religious embroideries, and Persian *objects* in gold and crystal. Admission is 200 drs ($2). Open weekdays and Saturday from 8:45 a.m. to 3 p.m.; on Sunday and holidays from 9:30 a.m. to 2:30 p.m.

MUSEUM OF CYCLADIC ART: 4 Neophytou Douka St., off Vassilis Sophias, just beyond the National Gardens. This is the world's first museum devoted solely to art from the Cycladic islands that circle the holy island of Delos. And a beauty it is, in its own striking, modern building of glass and marble, endowed by the foundation of a former shipowner, Nicholas P. Goulandris. The permanent exhibition, beautifully displayed against midnight-blue suede, features statuettes, figurines, jewelry, and vessels in clay or translucent marble, covering a period of 5,000 years—from as far back, in fact, as 3000 B.C.—yet extraordinarily "reminiscent" of much modern art and sculpture. There's a café in the basement, and the lobby gift shop has stylish replicas of the exhibits (the jewelry is particularly attractive). Open daily except Tuesday and Sunday: from 10 a.m. to 4 p.m. weekdays, to 1 p.m. on Saturday. Admission is 200 drs ($2), free on Saturday.

CITY OF ATHENS MUSEUM: On Klafthmonos Square, halfway along Stadiou Street. Another newcomer, this museum is in a refurbished "palace" once occupied by King Otto I. You'll see paintings, prints, royal memorabilia—and a striking scale model of Athens as it appeared in 1842. Open Monday, Wednesday, and Friday from 9 a.m. to 1:30 p.m. Admission is 100 drs (75¢).

SOME NOTES ON MUSEUMS: The following notes should be of interest to the serious museum-goer.

Hours
Subject to change. If you can, check with the Tourist Organization or your hotel receptionist. Unless indicated otherwise, all museums are closed on Tuesday.

Admission
Admission to all state museums is *free* on Sunday unless otherwise noted (but again, double-check). Naturally, this means that museums are busiest on those days, and if you want peace and quiet you'd better be prepared to pay some drachmas.

Public Holidays
Museums and archeological sites are *closed* on New Year's Day, March 25 (the National Holiday), Good Friday (after noon), Easter Sunday, and Christmas Day. For other holidays, check with the Tourist Organization.

Free Passes
People who can prove they belong to the following categories are allowed into museums free of charge: directors of studies and students of foreign archeological schools; foreign archeologists, architects, and artists on a study visit; foreign interpreters and guides; foreign professors of classical studies; foreign students of classical studies (high school or university level); and children up to age 12. To get your free pass you have to go to the office of the **Directorate of Antiquities and Restoration,** Department of Museums, 14 Aristidou St. (tel. 3243-015). The office is open Mon-

day and Friday from 11 a.m. to 1 p.m. only. Take along your passport, plus proof of who and what you are. On second thought, it might be easier just to pay.

Cameras

There are some curious rules here: (a) if you pay the equivalent of the general admission charge you can take pictures, *provided* you don't use a tripod or flash cubes; (b) you can use a tripod in museums if you pay an extra fee; (c) you can use a tripod in archeological sites if you pay a fee (*Note:* The Acropolis is classified as an archeological site); (d) if you're using a tripod you may not photograph "a person or persons together with an antique object."

MINOR SIGHTS OF ATHENS

Two of the more popular destinations for tour buses are the **Olympic Stadium** and the **Presidential Palace,** both within a couple of blocks of each other, beyond the National Gardens. The stadium (which now is also referred to as the Panathenium Stadium, to distinguish it from the *new* Olympic Stadium) was built on the site of the ancient Panathenaic Stadium, but this version was completely rebuilt in white marble for the first modern Olympic Games in 1896. The Royal Palace was the home of King Constantine before he went into exile; it's a handsome, French-style château, but you can't see much of it behind all the trees. Most people go there to see the evzones' changing-the-guard ceremony. Don't expect to see anything like the ceremony at Buckingham Palace. In fact, don't bother visiting the Royal Palace and the Stadium unless you have oodles of time.

Surrounding the Parliament Building, back at Syntagma, is the **National Garden** (often referred to as the Royal Garden). It's a formal garden, with a remarkable mixture of trees, lots of shady nooks, swan lakes, duck ponds, terrace cafés where orchestras play Viennese waltzes, and a beautiful palace-like building called the **Zappeion,** which is used occasionally for temporary exhibitions and European Common Market meetings.

One place you should visit, though, even if only briefly, is the **Cathedral of Athens,** or **Mitropoleos,** halfway between Syntagma and the Plaka, a red pile in Byzantine style, its interior draped with icons which in turn are draped with silver votive offerings like necklaces on an ample-bosomed dowager. The votive offerings are usually small effigies of people who have been blessed or cured by the particular saint. The cathedral genuinely *looks* like a place of worship, even to the black-garbed priests shuffling around in the rear.

The baby cathedral right next to it, the **Church of Aghios (or**

Saint) Eleftherios, a tiny church dating from the 13th century, is as austere as the cathedral is ornate. This is a gem of Byzantine architecture, but it was built from marble and stone filched from pagan temples of the classical period. There are many of these venerable Byzantine churches around Athens. Your favorite may well be the minuscule 11th-century **Church of Aghias Dynamis** (Divine Power), squatting in the middle of the sidewalk, beneath the arcade of the modern Ministry of Education, on Mitropoleos Street, or **Aghias Kapnikareos,** in the middle of the street halfway down Ermon.

THE VIEW FROM THE TOP

Athens has a couple of vantage points, besides the Acropolis, from which you can get superb views of the city. **Lycabettus Hill** is really a limestone rock reaching almost 1,000 feet into the once-crystalline Athenian sky. In the evening the top half is floodlit, and from the Acropolis it looks something like a giant soufflé. By day it's a green-and-white hill topped by a tiny, glaringly white church, **Aghios Georgios.** It's a nagging challenge, and sooner or later you're going to want to climb it. Don't try to walk up (pilgrims used to, but it's an Everest for the faithless), and don't try to take a cab, because it only goes halfway and you still have quite a hike to get to the top. Take the two-minute funicular up the southeast flank. To get there follow the "télépherique" signs to the corner of Kleomenous and Ploutarchou Streets, between Kolonaki Square and the Athens Hilton. The fare is 170 drs (about $1) round trip. The panorama from the top is priceless—all the way to Mount Parnes in the north, west to Piraeus and the Saronic Gulf, with the Acropolis sitting like a ruminative lion halfway to the sea. There's also a café/restaurant up there, which you've read about in Chapter VI on dining out.

Philopappos Hill is the big hill west of the entrance to the Acropolis. It gets its name from the monument to a versatile fellow who was a Syrian prince, Roman consul, and Athenian magistrate which was erected sometime between A.D. 114 and 116. On some maps you'll see a sign on the northwest flank saying "Prison of Socrates." It's a cave, and maybe it was and maybe it wasn't the philosopher's prison.

Lower down this great outcropping of rock you come to the hill known as the **Pnyx** (pronounced p-nicks). You may visit it some evening because it's now used as the auditorium for the Son-et-Lumière show, but you may not have time to reflect on what a hallowed spot this is. Free speech was born here. During the days of Pericles the Assembly met here; the Assembly, or Ecclesia, was nothing less than a quorum made up of as many of the city's

150,000 free citizens as felt like attending. The Ecclesia gathered here about 40 times a year and listened to the great orators who addressed them from the speakers' podium (which you can still see). The amphitheater seated 18,000, and, just to make sure it was well filled even when the Ecclesia was discussing something tedious, the police went around with ropes dipped in wet paint and herded the citizens up the hill to the Pynx. Some of the most fateful decisions in Athenian history were made right here on this beautiful hillside; some of history's most rousing speeches were delivered right here on this speakers' podium.

Still another historic hill, to the northeast of the Pnyx, closer to the Acropolis, is the **Areopagus.** The name means the "hill of Mars," and according to legend this is where Ares (that is, Mars, the god of war) was tried for murdering one of Poseidon's sons. He was acquitted. So was Orestes, when he was tried here for murdering his mother. And it was probably on this hill, in the spring of A.D. 54, that St. Paul delivered his sermon to the Athenians. Nowadays, when you walk past here on a soft Athenian evening, the great hill is suffused with the silhouettes of young lovers and travelers.

How do you get to these hills? You can, of course, take a taxi, but to absorb the full significance of paths that have known the footfall of so many Olympian personalities, you really have to walk. Slowly.

THREE WALKING TOURS OF ATHENS

Athens isn't really such a big city, and most of the places you're likely to be visiting, at least by day, are grouped in clusters. Many of the clusters are within walking distance of each other. The best way to get around is undoubtedly to walk. For one thing you'll be able to experience the exotic sights, sounds, and smells of the city as you go along. You'll *feel* the city.

From Syntagma, the cathedral, the Plaka, the Temple of Olympian Zeus, the Benaki Museum, and the Byzantine Museum are all five to ten minutes on foot. Even the Acropolis is not insurmountable on foot.

However, strenuous walking is really only possible in the early morning, late afternoon, or evening. And you can't always plan things that neatly, especially if your visit is short. Fortunately, public transport is inexpensive (see Chapter IV for details on buses, taxis, etc.).

Anywhere you stroll in Athens you'll find the unusual, the exotic, the surprising, the ancient, or the elegant. The three tours below will give you some idea of the possibilities. The first tour is a general sightseeing tour, the second could be called a shopping tour, the third is a museums tour, but of course all three overlap. They all begin in Syntagma.

TOUR A—THE SIGHTS: From Syntagma, stroll down Mitropoleos Street (it's the one on the southwest corner) down past the shops to the **cathedral** and the Church of Aghios Eleftherios; when you leave the cathedral or the church, turn left, walk one block, then turn right onto **Pandroussou Street** and enjoy the Oriental bazaar atmosphere of its leather, antique, souvenir, and jewelry shops.

When you get to the square at the bottom of the street you're in Monastiriki; go left and you're at the **Library of Hadrian,** then round the curving street to the left until you come to the **Tower of the Winds** and the **Roman Agora.** Now walk down Pikilis Street and you're at the archeological site with the **Stoa of Attalos,** the **Agora,** and the **Temple of Theseus.** From there you can walk up the hill to the **Acropolis,** or double back to the nearest taverna in the Plaka.

TOUR B—SHOP-AND-STOP TOUR: From Syntagma, leave by Mitropoleos Street; before you reach the cathedral, turn right and walk one block to Ermou Street, the main shopping street in this area. Continue up Ermou to Nikis, then turn left to Karageorgi tis Servias Street, go through the shopping arcade and into Stadiou Street, cross at the lights and walk up Amerikis Street to Venizelou Avenue, where you can stop for a coffee or lemon juice at Zonar's.

When you've built your strength up, continue up Amerikis Street to Akadimias Street, turn right and walk one block to Voukourestiou Street, then back to Venizelou Avenue. If you're bushed you can call it a day here and scramble over to Zonar's, or, better still, you can go left one block to Kriezotou, walk up the hill via Pindarou Street, to Tsakalof Street, then go right past the boutique shops there and so down the hill to the nearest café on Kolonaki Square.

Check this itinerary against the list of shops (see Chapter IX, "Shopping in Athens"), and mark on this page which streets you really want to visit. That way you can probably shorten this tour. How long it takes depends on how much window-shopping you do. It could last a whole day, in which case you'd have lunch in Zonar's or one of the cafés on Kolonaki.

TOUR C—MUSEUM TOUR: From Syntagma, take Stadiou Street (between the tourist office and the NJV Meridien Hotel) to the **Historical and Ethnological Museum.** From there, cross

Stadiou, walk up Amerikis Street to Akadimias Street, where you turn right, then bear left at Kanari Street and walk the one block to Kolonaki Square. Leave Kolonaki Square in the bottom right-hand corner (Koumbari Street), and at the corner with Vassilissis Sofias Avenue you're at the **Benaki Museum.** When you leave the Kenaki, continue up Vassilissis Sofias to no. 22, the **Byzantine Museum** or farther along to the **Museum of Cycladic Art.** (If you're still feeling energetic after that, walk up the hill to the funicular and take a two-minute ride to the top of Lycabettus Hill, or walk back to Syntagma via the Parliament Building and the National Gardens.)

SIGHTSEEING TOURS OF ATHENS

One of the simplest, most relaxing ways to get around the sights of Athens is to call one of the tour operators, make a reservation for the next morning, and have the bus come and pick you up at your hotel.

A company like **American Express, Key,** or **CHAT,** will pick you up in an air-conditioned coach, a comfortable 52-seater with a guide who'll speak English plus one other language. Both companies offer a choice of four or more sightseeing tours in Athens. Here are two examples:

The **Morning Half-Day Tour** (9 a.m. to 1 p.m.) includes the National Archeological Museum (except on Tuesday when they substitute the Benaki), National Library, University, Academy, Royal Palace, Stadium, Temple of Olympian Zeus, Hadrian's Arch, the cathedral, and Aghios Eleftherios. Price: 2,200 drs ($17).

The **Athens By Night Tour** in Athens is more fun than usual because in winter it includes a drive past the floodlit Acropolis, then along the edge of the sea to Castella (Piraeus), with a visit to a taverna for dinner and a floor show. In summer, the tour starts off at Son-et-Lumière, and ends with dinner and a taverna show in the Plaka. These tours last from 8:30 p.m. until 1:30 a.m., and cost from 4,000 drs ($31) with dinner.

An alternative evening choice is the Sound-and-Light spectacle (English-language commentary) plus Greek folk dances. This tour, available nightly from May through September, lasts from 8:30 p.m. till midnight; the cost is 2,700 drs ($21).

CHAPTER IX

SHOPPING IN ATHENS

□ □ □

People don't go to Athens for a shopping spree as they might to London or Amsterdam or the Caribbean. But there are stores enough and temptations enough in Athens to lure you from ogling the antiquities, so be sure to bring along some spare cash for gifts and souvenirs—especially since there are so many attractive items that you can buy only in Greece.

What are the favorite buys in Athens? That's hard to pin down, but generally speaking Americans are impressed by the jewelry (especially gold items, and the reproduction of the patterns and designs of antiquity), flokati rugs, hand-knit sweaters (made by village women in winter, priced in some cases less than the wool back home), leather goods, hand-woven and hand-embroidered blouses and dresses, local pottery from the islands, tagaria (beach bags of cotton or wool), furs, and icons. There are many more, as you'll see when you wander around the streets of the city—or when you skim through the roundup below.

WHEN, WHERE, AND HOW TO SHOP: To help relieve traffic congestion and thereby pollution, the Greek "siesta" break is officially over. By law, shops must now stay open Monday, 1 p.m. to 7 p.m.; Tuesday through Friday, 9:30 a.m. to 7 p.m.; Saturday, 9 a.m. to 3 p.m. Not a universally popular decree and "come July and August, who knows?" so it's best to check at your hotel desk.

As for the kiosks and the Flea Market, they're nearly always open; and shops in the Plaka usually stay open late to catch the revelers.

The main shopping centers in Athens are concentrated in the streets around Syntagma Square, around Kolonaki Square, and the side streets between Stadiou and Panepistimiou. To generalize, you might say that the gift and souvenir stores were more numerous around Syntagma; that the Athenians' everyday shopping was done around Stadiou and Patission Avenues (this is where some of the major department stores are to be found) or on bustling Ermou Street, between Syntagma and Monastiriki; and that cosmopolitan Athenians shopped in the streets between Syntagma and Lycabettus. But these are only generalizations, and you'll find quality shops in the most unlikely neighborhoods.

Of course, the most interesting shopping streets can change from year to year; right now, for example, **Tsakalof Street** running off Kolonaki Square is turning out to be one of the most interesting shoppers' streets in Athens. It will unveil a steady procession of boutiques (for men and women), jewelry, furniture and fabric stores, pastry shops and restaurants. Other browsers' streets in Kolonaki are **Skofias, Souidias,** and **Patriarchou Ioakim**—but many Kolonaki streets, even the steep ones, are worth the stroll for isolated boutiques (like, for example, the self-explanatory and charming **Patchworks** at 10 Ploutarchou).

Traffic has been banished from one of the city's most fashionable shopping streets, **Voukourestiou** (two blocks from Syntagma, between Panepistimiou and Lycabettus), which, with a few adjoining streets, has been transformed into a mall with potted plants and globe lamps.

BARGAINING: Should you bargain in Athens? Before you run out and start haggling, be warned that not all the city's shopkeepers take kindly to it. You can tell by the look of the place whether you can or cannot. Save your bargaining for the streets, especially the Flea Market—but when you do it, do it with gusto.

Some Rules: Take your bargaining seriously—don't have the family gawking in the background. Totally disregard the vendor's first offer; reject out of hand his second. If you have a Greek friend, let him do the bargaining for you. And never rush. If you like something with a special passion, begin bargaining for the item next to it, then "settle" for the one you want. When in doubt, don't buy. It's cheaper next door.

KIOSKS: If you can't find it anywhere else in Athens, you'll probably find it at one of the numerous sidewalk kiosks (or *peripteros),* a unique Greek institution. They're open 18 hours a day (in some cases, around the clock, though you may find kiosks outside the center of town closed on Sunday afternoons), and sell an incredible assortment of goods: chocolates, magazines, newspapers, dolls, postage stamps, cigarettes, cakes, pharmaceuticals, chewing gum, films, pens, lightbulbs, detergents, cosmetics, books, and on and on and on. And you can use their telephones for local calls for just a few drachmas.

ATHENS MARKETS: Centering on Pandrossou Street, and spreading out to surrounding streets, the **Flea Market** is just what you'd expect it to be: a monumental assortment of cast-offs, some of it junk, the treasures or otherwise from the attics of Attica. You might like some of the brass and copper ornaments, jewelry, 1930 Victrolas, icons, lamps, woven bags, or old used clothing. Make a special point of visiting the crafts shops in the restored arcade at 15 Pandrossou (watch for the Hermion Café sign). A visit to the Flea Market can be quite exciting, especially if you try your hand at bargaining. Save this trip for a Sunday.

If the Flea Market should put you into a general market mood, then head as well for the **Meat Market,** at 81 Eolou. A tiny entrance beckons the unsqueamish into a passageway of butchers' stalls, with red meat hanging everywhere. Twenty steps in, the passageway is transformed into a giant cross of stalls. The **Fish Market** is here too.

On the other side of the Meat Market is **Sofokleous Street,** home to dozens of little cheese, olive, and grocery stores. Go there for a lunch of feta cheese, black/brown olives (they're loaded with vitamins A and C), a loaf of bread, and your choice of wine.

In addition to these two flea markets there are several street markets (called *laiki*), following a tradition that dates back to the Middle Ages. Stalls are piled high with fruit and vegetables as well as clothing and country wares brought into town by itinerant merchants. These markets are held in different neighborhoods on different days (invariably from early morning until 2 p.m.); ask at the hotel reception desk for the day or location of the market nearest to your hotel.

HANDCRAFTS AND SOUVENIRS

You'll find the handcraft/jewelry/souvenir/"Greek Art" type of shop everywhere in Greece, and it often doesn't make much difference which one you step into. The prices and merchandise, all "typically Greek," are similar at most of them. In this section, however, the listing concentrates on shops selling handcrafts that are of better quality than the usual souvenir-type trinket.

Before you start racing from store to store, however, you might first take a look at what's available by stopping off at the exhibition of Greek handcrafts in **Hommex** at **9 Mitropoleos St.,** two blocks down from Syntagma. Here you'll find examples of ceramics from the islands, silverwork, hand-painted wooden utensils, leather desk accessories, embroidery, dolls, necklaces made from ahatis stone, and various types of traditional rugs. The staff will help you with questions or sales, although they're really there to help *commercial* clients since this is officially the Hellenic Organization of Small and Medium Size Industries and Handcrafts, or Hommeh, for short.

The **National Welfare Organization** channels the work of poor families and schoolchildren from all over Greece; it supplies the designs (invariably adapted or copied from museum pieces) and the families do the rest. Their handiwork makes excellent gifts, easy to pack, easy to carry, and some, easy on the wallet: a package of two embroidered linen guest towels for under 1,540 drs ($12), sets of four napkins and placemats for 13,800 drs ($106) and up, hand-embroidered tablemats for upward of 6,000 drs ($46) each. These prices are about one-third less than you'd pay for the comparable articles in New York, and all profits go to charity. The N.W.O. has shops at 24a Voukourestiou St., 135 Vasilissis Sofias Ave., and 6 Ipatias St. Open daily, except Sunday, from 8 a.m. to 8:30 p.m., with no lunch break.

Leshki, at 19 Pindarou St., is the kind of hole-in-the-wall shop you miss if you blink, but in fact it's worth a detour if you're interested in bookbinding or unusual leather wall plaques depicting characters from traditional Greek shadow theater at prices from 6,000 drs ($46). Everything here is done by hand (two hands only —the proprietor's), ranging from hand-painted note cards for less than 260 drs ($2), to leather photo albums embossed with Greek ships, 25,000 drs ($192) to 40,000 drs ($308).

One of the most delightful handcraft shops in Athens is **To Anoyi** at 1 Sotiros, one floor up in a quaint little Plaka house with a bookbindery in the basement. When you climb the stairs to iconographer Katherine Apostolou's workshop you may find her painting to the music of Mahler. Her dazzling display of crafts includes attractive enamel ashtrays with delicate designs of boats and animals, bronze candle holders, hand-blown glass, Greek pottery, cotton scarves with traditional regional designs, decorative wooden eggs in traditional designs. There's something here for every taste and every budget, including the most modest.

Deros, 4 Stadiou St., is one of two fine shops located in a large corner building, three floors of which are bulging with china, glassware, housewares, and crystal chandeliers. You'll find the prices reasonable enough, even though the store is the exclusive importer of some of Europe's leading crystal, porcelain, and tableware.

Other handcraft and "Greek Art" shops include **Stathis** at 2 Palaealogou Venizelou St. (just off Cathedral Square); **Cleo's** in the Hilton arcade (bags, dresses, necklaces, bracelets, leather pitchers, rings); **Mati** at 20 Voukourestiou St., where you can buy "mati" stones for keeping the evil eye away, as well as old monastery lamps, candlesticks, glass and silver, and all sorts of *unexpected* things; **Greek Corner** (Sam Pessah and Son), 10 Karageorgi tis Servias St., bursting with every sort of "authentica" available, including blouses of hand-woven "cheesecloth" trimmed with traditional embroidery from 1,950 drs ($15) to 2,470 drs ($19), as well as silver and gold jewelry.

ADC, short for Athens Design Center, is a small outlet for the works of a group of designers in ceramics, silver, bronze, and pottery. It's at 4 Valaoritou St., and its displays include saucers, cups, plates, bowls, flowerpots, and one-of-a-kind ceramic sculptures. Unusual pottery pieces include turtle doves and boxes, an interesting collection of silver-and-bronze jewelry, and unusual bronze candleholders for as little as 1,800 drs ($14).

Tanagrea, 15 Mitropoleos, at the corner of Voulis and Mitropoleos Streets (near the little church in the middle of the sidewalk), sells "Les Faïences de la Grèce, all handmade items," in classic and contemporary designs from all the islands and areas of Greece.

Cantoros, at 28 Voukourestiou, specializes in ceramic lamps and bangles, and assorted household items—ideal gifts at reasonable prices.

Pandora, 12 Voukourestiou St., is one of the more attractive shops selling artifacts, jewelry, and gifts; it's clean and well laid out, and its owner, Mr. Sakellaridis, quite clearly takes pride in the place.

SUMMER THINGS: When it's time to shop for beach bags, sun hats, or espadrilles (especially espadrilles—in solids, stripes, polka dots, and dozens of colors), head for **A.J. Maggioros** in the arcade that connects 3 Akidimias with 14 Kriezotou. In spring, the Maggioros windows overflow with bunnies and candles, at Carnival with noisemakers and masks, but at any time of the year the store is filled with toys for the kids left at home.

Museum Shops: Greek arts and jewelry are also available in several museums, including the **National Archeological Museum** (reproductions of vases, figures, and statues), the **Benaki Museum** (table linens, prints, matchbooks, etc.), and the new **Museum of Cycladic Art** (jewelry, figurines, scarves). All three of them, of course, also sell books, which are useful as souvenirs and gifts.

Additional suggestions for handcrafts and gifts: for handwoven, hand-knitted sweaters, **Helen de Luca** at 4 A. Hatzimhali

St. (two doors down from the Hotel Nefeli); for hand-woven fabrics for upholstery, cushions, or bedspreads, priced from 1,150 drs ($9) to 5,200 drs ($40), **Village Shop** at 30 Tripodou St. in the Plaka; and for one-of-a-kind textiles made into wall hangings, mats, and cushion covers, **Ilakat** at 46 Amalias, near the Royal Olympic Hotel (but open at odd hours).

JEWELRY

This is one of the most popular shopping items in Greece, and the range of merchandise ranges from souvenir trinkets based on ancient designs to chic avant-garde creations in gold and precious stones.

Voukourestiou Street might be the place to begin your expedition, since the city's finest jewelers are located at the corner with Panepistimiou, and the new mall is lined with reliable shops.

Some of the most original and imaginative gold jewelry in the world is designed by **Ilias Lalaounis** and handcrafted by his artisans in a workshop in the shadow of the Acropolis. Lalaounis introduces two new collections a year (sometimes more when he receives a special commission from a sheikh). A typical collection might include a dazzling array of gold necklaces, bracelets, and rings evolved from the shapes of aboriginal and prehistoric tools and statuettes, priced in the thousands of dollars. However, visit any of the Lalaounis stores and you'll find items costing as little as 7,000 drs ($54). The main store is at 6 Panepistimiou, with branch boutiques in the lobbies of the Hotel Grande Bretagne, the Athens Hilton, and on Corfu, Mykonos, and Rhodes.

Neck and neck, so to speak, with Lalaounis in quality and price is the other great name in Greek jewelry—**La Chrysothèque Zolotas** at 10 Panepistimiou, with branches in several deluxe hotels and museums throughout the islands and mainland. **Charles Pentherondakis** is at 19 Bucharest St., and on Voukourestiou Street itself you have **Agnostoupolous** at no. 13, **E. Athiniotakis, Petradi** at no. 20, and **Petra Nova** at no. 19. The latter two feature *petradi,* or semiprecious stones (amethyst, tiger's eye, lapis, turquoise, and sodalite are the most popular here), set in imaginatively designed pins, necklaces, rings, earrings, pendants, and what have you, at prices ranging from 12,000 drs ($92), to well over 400,000 drs ($3,077). Athiniotakis has a particularly interesting selection of unusual "art-to-wear" jewelry, with most popular items selling for about 78,000 drs ($600).

At 10 Nikis St., **VIP** stocks Byzantine seals and brooches copied from originals in the National Archeological Museum, mostly from the Mycenaean and Alexander the Great periods, mostly priced above 16,000 drs ($123).

There are more museum copies at the showroom of archeologist Maria Antoniades (one floor up at 6 Apollonus St.), as well as original modern designs in gold, silver, and precious stones. Prices ranges from a few hundred dollars to 650,000 drs ($5,000). **Gold Coin Jewelry,** 17 Stadiou St., actually sells *you* money—a unique collection of unusual coins, all of it copies of ancient Greek currencies.

If you admire the Lalaounis concepts but cannot afford the price of gold, visit a store called **The 4 Lamda** in the Athens Tower skyscraper. It's actually another branch of Lalounis, with the same imagination and flare in design, but most of the items are crafted in silver, with scores of gifts in the 5,200 drs ($40) to 7,800 drs ($60) range, as well as more substantial items.

WOMEN'S FASHIONS

This is a subject you have to look at from two angles: local designs and fabrics on the one hand, high fashion and international chic on the other. Sometimes they overlap, with intriguing results. Generally speaking, shopping is more varied and rewarding in Athens now that Greece is a full-fledged member of the European Common Market, and nowhere is this truer than in matters of fashion. Hitherto, many of the designer shoes on sale in fine stores in Paris or Rome or New York were actually made (but not sold) in Greece; now they are, at prices way below what you'd pay elsewhere. Fashions (for both women and men) are rapidly shrugging off their traditional gray-serge conservatism for flashier colors and linens. To be in tune with these new styles, watch out for the labels of the new fashion stars—Billy Bo, Polatof, and Loukia—alongside the Lanvins, Courrèges, and Trussardis. But many of the local designers who have been turning out classics for years are still major draws, among them Yannis Travassaros and Nikos & Takis.

These designers are now in the forefront of design not only in Greece but throughout Europe, catering to a jet-set clientele. In addition, with the spur of the Common Market, the *quality* of Greek-made clothing has improved, and is now on a par with Paris and London.

Yannis Travassaros has his main boutique in the Athens Hilton. He designs virtually everything he sells, and in most cases he also weaves his own fabrics, or trims coats or dresses with old embroidery and authentic *bibiles* (needlework borders) from his own collection of old Greek costumes. Most of his creations are for dressy winter wear—pant suits, *zigouni* (sleeveless coats like jackets worn by Greek shepherds), evening coats, evening dresses.

The other two hot-shot designers work as a team—**Nikos & Takis,** two ex-painters who got fed up with people who expected to bargain a $2,000 canvas down to $200, so they started designing clothes. Their boutique is at 10 Panepistimious Ave., near Syntagma Square (with branches at the Astir Palace in Vouliagmeni, and in the old city in Rhodes). Again, the inspiration for the designs comes from classical Greek and Byzantine costumes and decoration. Since they're both designers and manufacturers, Nikos and Takis offer reasonable prices, and they keep sizes 10, 12, and 14 in stock but can usually run up other sizes, or make alterations, within 24 hours. Their favorite fabrics are cotton, wool, silk, mohair, and raw silk.

Tseklenis on upper Boukaristio St. is named after its owner-designer whose trendy clothes are also available in the States.

For more ladies' fashions, less pricey than in the boutiques of Kolonaki, check out the windows of the following stores, all on Ermou Street: **Sinanis** at no. 9 (with a branch at 23 Voukourestiou), **Tsantilis** at no. 23 (with a branch at 4 Stadiou), and **Papagiannis** at no. 47.

Just around the corner from Syntagma, at 4 Panepistimou, the **Contessina** boutique has an interesting array of fashions and gifts at reasonable prices.

Lizard (14 Kriezotou St.) and **Gianari Gallani Boutique** (on the corner of Kolonaki Square and Skoufa Street) both have elegant selections of leather goods—including shoes, belts, and jackets.

MEN'S FASHIONS

If you want to look over suits, jackets, and shirts by Europe's top-flight designers (particularly Italian), the appropriate stores seem to be concentrated near the intersections of Akadimias Street with Pindarou Street, Voukourestiou Street, and Amerikis Street (for example, **Simbolo**, at no. 18). A few of the trendiest new men's boutiques have now set up shop in Kolonaki, mainly along Tsakalof Street.

Ascot, at 29 Nikis St. (just off Syntagma Square) and 6 Kapsali St. (just off Kolonaki Square), features a wide selection of suits, sportcoats, slacks, shirts, sweaters, ties, and toiletries. **Perla**, with a classy branch in the arcade at 5 Stadiou St., and other stores throughout the city, also has a fine selection of men's shoes and assorted menswear.

SANDALS

Head up Pandrossou Street from Monastiraki Square to no. 89 and inside you'll find the "poet-sandalmaker" of Athens, **Stavros Melissinos.** Look in the dusty window and you'll see several yellowing newspaper articles about this remarkable man, in among the sandals, straps, and tools of the trade; inside the small shop, you'll find up to 30 different styles of sandals ranging in price from 900 drs ($7) to 2,300 drs ($18), in sizes 19 to 45. If your feet are bigger or smaller, Melissinos will make you a special pair. He counts among his clients various celebrities including Jackie Onassis, and framed certificates above his workbench testify that Harvard College Library and Bodleian Library in Oxford, England, have copies of his books in their collections. (You could buy one for your collection, too; just ask Stavros.) An unaffected, gentle, and friendly man, Melissinos will chat about his poetry with you while helping you choose your sandals. His brother-in-law's workshop, **Tony's Sandals,** at 52 Adrianou (near the Roman Agora), is the place to go when you want a comfortable pair of shoes or boots—casual style.

FURS

A high priority on your fur-stalking list should be **Voula Mitszakou** at 7 Mitropoleos, where the charming Mrs. Mitszakou herself runs the business her father founded over 75 years ago; any of her helpful assistants will be happy to explain the entire process of making fur coats, and serious customers (with emphasis on the serious) will be treated to a tour of the workshops downstairs. (Mitszakou employs 25 people, each an expert in one specific stage of the process.) Mink jackets here will cost you from 84,500 drs ($650) to 299,000 drs ($2,300) (six different qualities of mink are involved), a full-length multicolored mink coat from 227,500 drs ($1,750), Persian lambs from 78,000 drs ($600), and Greek red fox jackets are 136,500 drs ($1,050) or thereabouts. You can take your pick from 25 to 30 varieties of fur (from Greek wolf to French rabbit to sable) and get Mitszakou to design a coat especially for you (in which case you add a minimum of 10% to the off-the-peg prices). Mitszakou has full cold-storage facilities, and exports fur coats to clients all over the world.

OLD ESTABLISHED COMPANY. The fur stores listed here are fine for most people, but if you have a chauffeured limousine waiting for you at the airport to whisk you to a suite at the Grand Bretagne, then you'll probably be able to persuade someone to take you to a rather special place—**J.A. Sistovaris & Sons, Inc.,** at 14 Voulis St. (up one flight), 4 Ermou St., or 9 Venizelou. This old, established company, now in its fourth generation, uses only the finest quality furs for the finest quality clientele. Expensive, naturally.

George M. Trahos & Sons, 7 Filellinon St. (tel. 3228-256). Everyone refers to it as the Fur House, so the Fur House it is. It has been in business for over 100 years and it has its own expert fitters. Pick your favorite fur—Persian lamb, natural Greek stone marten, autumn haze natural mink, tourmaline natural mink, or palomino mink. Indian lamb is particularly popular because it combines lightness with warmth. Pick your favorite style—full-length, three-quarter-length, cape-stole, bolero jacket, or straight stole. You'll have a choice of hundreds of coats, stoles, jackets, hats, and scarves—and prices that will make you feel you've got a bargain (but, of course, it pays to know something about furs and prices before you buy). Mailing service is available.

ANTIQUES, MUSIC, ART

Antiqua, 4 Amalias (tel. 3232-220). This is a proper, elegant antique shop owned by a family that knows and loves its wares. The store is filled to the brim with clocks, jewelry, paintings, ancient Greek votive dishes, ivory statues, icons, Chinese vases and carvings, and French and Venetian furnishings. The shop is a bit off Syntagma, and the prices range from 2,340 drs ($18) to 302,900 drs ($2,330). The family has a second antiques gallery at 2 Messoghion St., Athens Tower.

Tassos Th. Zoumboulakis, 7 Kriezotou St. (tel. 3634-454) and 20 Kolonaki Square (tel. 3608-278). Founded at the beginning of the century, the gallery (it's air-conditioned, by the way) collaborates with several of the finest art dealers in Europe and the United States, so it's not restricted to works by Greek artists. Nevertheless, those are the works that will probably interest you most, and here you'll find a selection by Greek artists who are known only within their homeland, and others who have earned reputations abroad. Among them are Tsazouchis, Chryssa, Matta, Alan Davie, and Fassianos. Also occasional works by Calder, Max Ernst, Rauschenberg, Magritte, and other contemporary artists. Zoumboulakis also specializes in Greek folk art and the jewelry of Greek national costumes (brooches, pendants, rings, and things) from 3,250 drs ($25) to 25,350 drs ($195), as well as embroideries from the native dresses (mostly 17th, 18th, and 19th century) of Attica, Crete, Naxos, Rhodes, and Patmos (they make exquisite wall hangings, but you'd better talk directly to the owner about prices).

C. Haritakis Antiques, 7 Valaoritou St. (tel. 3621-254), has a fine collection of paintings, furniture, prints, porcelain, and icons.

Les Amis de Livres, in a short passageway at 9 Valaoritou, is everything its name promises to lovers of books—rare books, prints, engravings of Greek scenes. Open 9:30 a.m. to 3 p.m. Monday through Saturday in winter; closed Saturday in summer.

Gallerie Antiqua, Queen Sophias and 2 Messoghion (tel. 7705-881), is an elegant shop housing the works of noteworthy Greek and foreign painters, exquisite art objects, and furniture of high quality and good taste. Near the American Embassy.

Three other galleries where you will see temporary exhibits of works by local and international artists: **Athens Gallery,** 4 Glyconos in Kolonaki (tel. 713-938); **Desmos,** 28 Akadimias (tel. 3609-449); **Jean Bernier Gallery,** 51 Marasli (tel. 723-5657; Monday through Saturday; 10:30 a.m. to 1:30 p.m. and 6 p.m. to 11 p.m.; international contemporary art); **Hydrohoos Art Gallery,** 16 Anapiron Polemon St. in Kolonaki (tel. 7223-684).

RUGS

There's a bewildering choice of designs and colors in Greek rugs—Horassa, Hamadan, the Lobanof with its playful lions, Greek designs from the Acropolis, blue-and-yellow Byzantine designs, the Sykrion (based on motifs taken from a village cemetery near Corinth), the Greek classical designs with their stark blues and whites and subtle flecks of ochre, some Oriental designs that look like woolen Jackson Pollocks (and beautiful enough to hang on a wall).

One store with an especially interesting selection of rugs and carpets are **Arts and Crafts,** on the corner of Voukourestiou and Valaoritou Streets, a branch of the National Welfare Organization specializing in Greek designs—Cassandra, Mistra, Didoni, and Ionia. The main enclave of carpet stores is on Patission Avenue, beyond the National Archeological Museum.

Flokati rugs are among the most popular purchases for visitors to Greece, and most visitors flock to one of the two showrooms just off Syntagma—**Karamichos Flokati** on the corner of Voulis and Apollonos and **A. Kokkinos** at 3 Mitropoleos St. These flokatis come from the city of Trikala in central Greece; they're made from a combination of wools (from Greece for wear, from New Zealand for softness), softened under fresh spring waterfalls in Trikala before being woven by hand or machine to make thick, close piles. Both showrooms display a variety of flokatis in natural tones or kaleidoscopic patterns. Prices range from 4,160 drs ($32) for a two-by five-foot rug in natural colors. Karamichos and Kokkinos will pack, insure, and mail your purchases.

MISCELLANEOUS

Shoes: If you didn't pack adequate shoes for clambering over all those ruins and archeological sites, try **Mouriades** at 4 Stadiou

St. and branches throughout the city, which most people consider the best shoe shop in the city, with prices from 7,500 drs ($58) to 16,000 drs ($123), including some Bally models.

Books: When you want to bone up on your Greek history and need English-language books and paperbacks, go to the **American Bookstore** at 23 Amerikis St., **Pantelides** at 11 Amerikis, **Eleftheroudakis** at 4 Nikis St. (around the corner from Syntagma and the best bookshop in town), or the bookstand in the **Athens Hilton.** Newspapers you can buy almost anywhere, especially at the ubiquitous **kiosks.**

Gifts: For gifts for sons, daughters, grandchildren, nephews, and nieces, head for one of these toy shops: **Panhellinios Agora,** 9 Stadiou St.; **El Greco,** 30-32 Kreontos St.; or **Tsokas,** 52 Aiolou St. For children's colorful, smart clothing, check out **Free Kit,** at 19 Anagnostopoulou in Kolonaki.

Crystal and China: Illum, at 19 Stadiou, has two floors of it by makers like Noritake, Kosta Bode, Royal Copenhagen, and Arabia.

Leather Goods: At 21E Voukourestiou St., **Peau d' Ange** has a fine collection of small leather goods—wallets, picture frames, shoes, purses, bags, desk sets, diaries, and calendars—in unusual designs. A good spot for gifts. There's more leather—wallets and luggage—at **Magasin Scourletis,** 8 Speusippou, in Kolonaki.

Fabrics: *Argaliou* means loom and *Brailas* is the name of a family that looms, so **Argaliou Brailas,** at 7 Filellinon St., is the place to head for top-quality hand-woven silks. *Even the threads are hand-spun.* Prices range from 6,800 drs ($52) for a yard of heavy silk to 3,800 drs ($29) for cotton-silk. Made-up items include hand-woven capes from 15,000 drs ($115), and reversible hand-woven handbags with shoulder straps (hand-crocheted finish) for less than 22,500 drs ($173). They'll also make up anything for you, carefully tailored, within two to three days. **Tsantilis,** at 4 Stadiou St., presents a dazzling array of fashion fabrics; also available in ready-made clothing from their boutique at 23 Ermou.

Worry beads are another popular souvenir. The *komboloia,* as they're called in Greek, are Greece's answer to tranquilizers, but try twiddling them yourself and you may find they have just the opposite effect—it's not as easy as it looks. Fortunately, they don't cost a fortune. You'll find selections in most "Greek Art" shops.

Sponges might seem an unlikely purchase, but they're on sale on street corners all over the city. These are natural sponges fetched out of the nearby sea by hardy divers. They come in all sizes, from 300 drs ($2) all the way up to somewhere around

2,300 drs ($18)—but you'd pay several times the amount back home.

DEPARTMENT STORES AND SUPERMARKETS

The three major emporia (at least, those that come closest to the American concept of a department store) are the **Athenee,** halfway along Stadiou Street, at nos. 33-35; Lambropouli, at Aiolou and Lykourgou Streets; and **Minion,** "the Macy's of Greece," at 10 September St., near the National Archeological Museum. The **Pris-Unic-Marionopoulou** stores are a combination department store and supermarket, where you can buy Marks & Spencer's knitwear or pick up some useful inexpensive items and the makings of a great picnic; these stores are identified by a large orange M, and the closest one to Syntagma is at 9 Kanaris St., just off Kolonaki Square. Two supermarket chains with a wide range of European delicacies are Vassilipoulos and Sklaventis.

TAX-FREE SHOPPING

The tax-free shop at the airport is very limited in its choice: don't put off serious shopping until you get there, other than small gifts, perfume, cigarettes, liquor, and souvenirs.

CHAPTER X

THE ABC'S OF ATHENS

□ □ □

This chapter will serve as a reference guide to all the essential miscellany of travel in a strange city. These include the simple things you don't think about back home that can become major when you're away: buying stamps, finding an all-night drugstore, changing money, getting the news. So here is an alphabetical listing covering emergencies, and also some of those "uncategorizable" items I couldn't slip in elsewhere.

AIRPORTS: Plural, please note—there are two airport terminals in Athens. If you're flying a foreign airline, you'll arrive and depart from **Hellinikon East Terminal,** which is for international flights by overseas airlines. If you fly anywhere via Olympic Airways, internationally or to the islands or some other city in Greece, you'll leave from the **Hellinikon West Terminal** (sometimes referred to as the Olympic Terminal). Make sure you tell your taxi driver which one you want. There is a shuttle service between the East Terminal and West Terminal, every 20 minutes from 6 a.m. to midnight. Normally a ten-minute drive, it can take much longer since there's construction work in progress for a new West Terminal.

AIRPORT BUS: There's airport bus service to and from 4 Amalias Ave., near the corner of Syntagma, every 20 minutes from 6 a.m. to 11 p.m. Number 18 Express yellow buses leave for the East Terminal every 20 minutes; the ride takes 30 to 45 minutes, the fare is 80 drs (65¢) each way; there is no charge for luggage. But if you're not on a tight budget, the taxi fare is around 500 drs ($4) including luggage, direct from your hotel (if you're staying around Syntagma) to the airport. Olympic Airways buses leave from the same corner and from the Olympic downtown terminal at 96 Syngrou and go direct to the West Terminal at Hellinikon. The ride takes 30 minutes, leaves every half hour from 4 a.m. to 10 p.m., and is free to Olympic ticket holders.

Note: Some of the deluxe hotels operate shuttle bus service to and from the airport—check out times when you make your reservations.

AIRPORT INFORMATION: East Airport, tel. 9699-466; West Airport, tel. 9814-093; Olympic Airways only, tel. 9892-111.

AMERICAN EMBASSY: 91 Vassilissis Sofias Ave., a few blocks beyond the Athens Hilton (tel. 7212-951), any time of the day or night).

AMERICAN EXPRESS: 2 Ermou Street, just off Constitution Square (tel. 3244-975; Banking Division, tel. 3234-781). For changing money, buying traveler's checks, making travel arrangements, booking sightseeing and escorted tours, receiving mail, meeting people. Open 8 a.m. to 2 p.m. Monday to Friday.

BABYSITTING: Ask your hotel concierge.

BANKS: Open weekdays from 8 a.m. to 1:30 p.m. The National Bank of Greece on Syntagma is open for currency exchange until 9 p.m. weekdays, until 8 p.m. on Saturday and Sunday. There are Athens branches of a number of American and Canadian banks: American Express, Bankers Trust, Chase Manhattan, First National Bank of Chicago, Bank of Nova Scotia, Continental Illinois National Bank, Bank of America, Manufacturers Hanover Trust, and First National City Bank.

BEAUTY PARLORS: No problem. They're all over the place, but you'll probably feel most comfortable in one of the hotel beauty parlors that cater to an international clientele. Try **Costi and Taki** at the Hilton or **Dino & Gino,** behind the Hilton at 11 Vrassida (tel. 7248-292)—wash/cut/blow-dry is 2,600 drs ($20) for women, 1,500 drs ($12) for men.

BUSINESS HOURS: Athenians have a five-day work week. Offices are open Monday through Friday, 9 a.m. to 5 p.m. Most government offices are open from 9 a.m. to 1 p.m. As it was for shops, the two- or three-hour "siesta" break was eliminated as part of pollution-control efforts.

BUSINESS ORGANIZATIONS: Athens Cosmopolitan-Lions Club (tel. 3601-311); **Rotary Club,** 3 Kriezotou St. (tel. 3623-150); **American Hellenic Chamber of Commerce,** 17 Valaoritou St. (tel. 3636-407).

CAMPING: Inquire at **National Tourist Organization** (see below). There are a dozen sites in and around Athens, and more than 100 throughout Greece. You can now rent fully equipped campers for around 61,750 drs ($475) a week in summer. For details, contact **Camper Caravans,** 4 Nikis St., Athens (tel. 3230-552).

CANADIAN EMBASSY: 4 Ioannou Gennadiou St. (tel. 7223-511).

CAR RENTALS: For full information, see Chapter XIII on "Touring the Hinterlands."

CASINOS: There are casinos at Mount Parnes (just north of Athens), and on the islands of Corfu and Rhodes. Roulette, baccarat, chemin de fer, blackjack, and slot machines. Take your passport with you—you have to show it at the door.

CHURCH SERVICES: The main non-Orthodox churches are St. Dennis Roman Catholic Church, on the corner of Panepistimiou Avenue and Omirou Street; St. Paul's Anglican Church, Filellinon Street; St. Andrew's American Church (interdenominational), 66 Sina St.; the Synagogue, 6 Melidoni St.

CIGARETTES: A pack of American regulars (made in Greece) costs around 170 drs ($1.30).

CLIMATE: Summers are dry and hot, hovering around 90°F. It's cooler, of course, along the coasts and in the mountains to the north. In winter, the temperature can go down to 40° in some areas (Athens has an average temperature of 55° in January), and rain can also be expected 12 or 13 days a month from October through April. But the sun shines 300 days a year.

CLOTHING: Specifically, sightseeing garb. For hiking up steep hills and steps (of which there are countless thousands in Greece), women will probably be happier in slacks rather than skirts (which can be too revealing). If you're planning to visit one of the sites where donkeys are the standard method of conveyance, slacks are again recommended to avoid a case of donkey chafe on your knees. For churches, women are expected to wear appropriate clothing. Heavy shoes are essential for all ancient sites—and not such a bad idea for some sidewalks in Athens. In casinos, men must wear jacket and tie, women should wear cocktail dresses or pant suits. For dining, jacket and tie are rarely required, but a jacket or sweater may be useful in some air-conditioned restaurants.

CREDIT CARDS: Diners Club, VISA, MasterCard, and **American Express** are honored in Athens and major tourist centers throughout Greece. Decals identify cooperating merchants, but verify beforehand that the contracts are still in existence.

CURRENCY: The **drachma,** divided into 100 lepta (almost obsolete), is worth less than 1¢ U.S.; 130 drachmas equal $1 U.S. Coins come in 1-, 2-, and 5-drachma denominations, and a 50-lepta piece. Bills are the blue 50-drachma note, the red 100-drachma note, the green 500-drachma note, and the brown 1,000-drachma note, and the blue 5,000-drachma note. *Note:* There are *no* facilities for changing currency in the airport departure halls; change your remaining drachmas *before* going through passport control, $100 per person maximum; the procedure is very slow, so don't leave it until the last minute.

CURRENT: Talk to your concierge before using any U.S. appliances. You will probably need anywhere from one to three adapters, which should be available from reception in the *better* hotels. However, in Athens and most of the mainland the current is 220 volts, A.C. Top hotels also have a 115V outlet for shavers.

CUSTOMS: U.S. and Canadian nationals may travel freely anywhere in Greece for up to three months. On entering the country, you may bring in one liter of alcoholic beverage or two liters of wine, 200 cigarettes or 50 cigars—and five boxes of matches. There is no restriction on the number or value of traveler's checks on either entry or exit. Be very careful about antiques you buy in Greece. The laws protecting Greek antiquities are very strict and no genuine antiquities may be taken out of the country without prior special permission from the Archeological Service, 13 Polygnotou St., Athens.

DOCUMENTS: All you need (as an American or Canadian citizen) is a valid passport. Customs and passport control are fairly quick on arrival; the latter can slow you down on departure—so leave yourself a few extra minutes. Your arrival automatically gives you permission to stay three months; if you want to stay longer, you have to apply for a special permit.

DRINKING WATER: Safe to drink in hotels and restaurants, but beware of well water. If you get bottled mineral water, make sure the cap is tightly fixed.

DRIVING: The **International Drivers' Licence** is officially recommended, but not usually required when renting a car. However, it's useful in emergencies since it may be easier for the local constabulary to understand. For information, contact the **Automobile and Touring Club of Greece** (ELPA), Tower of Athens, 2-4 Messogion St., Athens (tel. 779-1615). For ELPA road assistance, dial 104.

DRUGSTORES: In an emergency, dial 107 for all-night service.

ELECTRIC CURRENT: (See "Current," above.)

ELEVATORS: Greek elevators are reliable, but they don't operate on the same principles as in the U.S. Except in modern places, doors don't open automatically; you have to watch for the elevator arriving at your floor, then quickly pull the door open before someone else presses a button on another floor and the elevator shoots off. Others signal their arrival with a "ping." Also, in many cases the button doesn't register the floor you want to go to until *after* the door is closed tight; so you may have to press your number a second time after the door has closed. Some elevator floors seem to fall out from under you when you step onto them; don't be alarmed—they're simply registering the weight.

EMERGENCIES: For all kinds of emergencies, dial 171 for the Tourist Police; 100 for emergency police service; 104 for help with your car; 107 for all-night drugstores; 150 for ambulance and 166 for first aid; 199 for the fire department; 7212-951 for the American Embassy and 7239-511 for the Canadian Embassy.

EXECUTIVE SERVICES: For the business traveler who needs a temporary office base in Athens, an organization called **Executive Services** will provide telephone, Telex, secretarial, translating, and interpreting services; fully furnished, air-conditioned offices, equipped with phones and Telex lines, can be rented by the day, week, or month. For details, contact Lorraine Batler in the Athens

Tower (tel. 7783-698; Telex 214227 EXSE GR; Fax 7795-509). Executive Services now has a satellite office in the Athens Hilton.

FILM: Expensive. Bring supplies with you.

GUIDES: If you want to hire your personal guide, the rates are 10,000 drs ($77) to 12,000 drs ($92) for a full day plus all expenses. Call the association of tour guides at 3229-705.

HOLIDAYS: Most shops are closed on the following days—New Year's Day, January 6, March 25 (National Day), Shrove Monday, Greek Orthodox Good Friday, Easter Sunday and Monday, May 1, Whit Monday, August 15, October 28, Christmas Day, December 26. In reality, the Orthodox Easter (one or two weeks after Protestant and Catholic Christians celebrate Easter) is a four- or five-day holiday.

HOSTELS: There are two types: youth and student. In Greece, call or apply to the **Greek Youth Hostels Association, 4** Dragatsaniou St., Athens (tel. 3234-107 or 3237-590).

LAUNDERETTES: In the Omonia Square area, the self-service **Maytag** at 46 Didotou (near Zoodochou Pighis, and three blocks back from Akadimias) charges 600 drs ($5), soap included, for a full-service wash. Other launderettes in the Plaka are **Nakopoulos** at 9 Erechtiou and **Golfinopoulos** at 24 Kythathineon, with approximately the same rates.

LIQUOR: You can buy it by the bottle or take your own bottle to the grocery store and get a refill—the cost depends on the amount. Famous brands of scotch whisky cost about 1,300 drs ($10) to 2,000 drs ($15), but you can also buy bottles at supermarkets for around 1,000 drs ($8) to 14,000 drs ($107).

LUGGAGE: Pacific, Ltd., a travel agency at 24 Nikis St. and the East Terminal at the airport, will store excess luggage while you tour the hinterlands or islands. Call 3236-851 for more details.

MASSAGE, SAUNA: The Hilton's resident masseuse charges 3,000 drs ($23) for 30-minute massage; sauna is 1,300 drs ($10). Call 7220-201, ext. 381, from 11 a.m. to 9 p.m. Or try the Inter-Continental (tel. 9023-666), where rates are similar.

MEDICAL ATTENTION: For doctors and dentists trained in the U.S. or fluent in English, contact the **Tourist Police** (tel. 171), the **American Embassy** (tel. 7212-951), or the **State Hospital of Athens** (tel. 7778-901). Dial the Athens emergency medical and ambulance service at 166 (English spoken). Taxis are often faster than ambulances, and they are permitted to function as emergency vehicles by flashing their lights and honking their horns.

MEDICINES AND TOILETRIES: American brands are available in most pharmacy-type stores in Athens and other major tourist centers. But at a price. Bring your own supplies in the interests of economy. European brands are usually less expensive—but reliable. For names of all-night pharmacies, dial 107.

MONEY CHANGING: Best bets are the 8 a.m. to 8 p.m. or 9 p.m. service of the **National Bank of Greece,** 2 Karageorgi tis Servias, right on Syntagma (the tourist office is in the same building), and the **General Hellenic Bank,** also on Syntagma. Most hotels will also offer this service to registered guests, but the rate will be less favorable. And remember—on leaving from Athens Airport, change your drachmas back into dollars *before* going into the departure lounge.

NAMES, SPELLINGS: As you've already learned, several places and streets in Athens have one or more names, and in most cases each name has one or more spellings. Thus Syntagma Square, also Constitution Square; Venizelou Avenue, also Panepistimiou Avenue; Octovriou 28, also Patissiou; Mitropoleos, Metropoleos Street. Outside of Athens, the situation becomes even more confused. So you may have to check every street, restaurant, and town on your maps twice.

NATIONAL TOURIST ORGANIZATION: The **E.O.T.** Information office is at 2 Karageorgi tis Servias St., Athens (tel. 3222-545), right on Syntagma *in the National Bank of Greece*. In the U.S.A., it's at 645 Fifth Ave., New York, NY 10022; 611 W. Sixth St., Los Angeles, CA 90017; 168 N. Michigan Ave., Chicago, IL 60601; and 31 State St., Boston, MA 02109. In Canada, at 2 Place Ville Marie, Montréal, PQ H3B 2C9; and 80 Bloor St., Suite 1403, Toronto, ON M5S 2V1.

NEWSPAPERS: English-language newspapers and magazines can be bought throughout Athens. Check with your kiosk around 6 p.m. for that day's edition of the *International Herald Tribune;*

British papers arrive around 8 p.m. The *Athens News* and *The Athenian* are local papers serving the English and American communities, and are worthwhile for restaurant, concert, and theater listings.

POLICE: For emergencies only, dial 100 on the telephone. The Tourist Police will handle your travel-connected problems. The address is 7 Syngrou, Athens (office number: 9239-224 or 9236-968; and the area code 01 prefix if you're calling from outside Athens). Dial 171 for Tourist Police Information in five languages, 24 hours a day.

POSTAGE: An airmail postcard to the U.S. costs 40 drs (30¢); a letter, 60 drs (46¢) per 20 grams weight. Don't even consider surface mail: it could take up to two months. The central post office is on **Kotzia Square** at 100 Eolou St. (opposite Omonia Square). There are branches at 4 Stadiou St. (only for parcel post, and located in the Spyromilios Arcade), in the lower level of the subway station at Omonia Square, on Syntagma Square at the corner of Mitropoleos Street (open 7 a.m. to 8:30 p.m.). There is also a Central Philatelic Service of the Hellenic Post Office on the first floor above the Central Post Office of Athens at 100 Eolou St., open in the morning, in order better to serve the requirements of stamp collectors. *Note:* Packages should be left unwrapped until they've been inspected at the post office.

PRICES: As I've noted elsewhere in this guide, prices are liable to change. Probably up. Probably 15% to 20%. So please, *please* check the rates of hotels, tours, and meals with your travel agent.

RADIO AND TV: The **American Armed Forces Radio** provides 24 hours of programming each day, including music, hourly newscasts, and excellent sports reporting. In the smaller hotels, **television** usually costs a minimum of 350 drs ($3) additional per night, but features lots of English and American programs and old movies, with Greek subtitles.

SHOESHINE: Shoeshine boys wait on the sidewalks at the thoroughfares with heaviest traffic. The cost is 150 drs ($1.15) including tip and the quality is excellent. For the same price you can flop down in one of the four stools of the shoeshine parlor on

Filellinon Street, corner of Syntagma, where you can also have shoes repaired. Many hotels have free shoeshine service.

STATIONERY: Pallis, on Ermou Street opposite the Electra Hotel, probably has the best selection, but as in all stationery stores in Athens, procedures are antiquated and service is slow. You can also have photocopying done here.

STUDENT DISCOUNTS: Valid student identification will get you discounts: to 50% on state railway travel; at a number of lodging spots (see "Hostels," above); to the Son-et-Lumière shows; at the Herod Atticus Theater; on island tours; on bus and train travel to the rest of Europe; at theaters; at all antiquity sites; in some restaurants; at a number of museums and other entertainment facilities. Two important addresses are: **Vikings's Travel Bureau, 3** Filellinon St., Athens (tel. 3229-383), and **Lotus Student Travel,** 7 Filellinon St. (tel. 3221-680), for information on special travel rates.

SUNBATHING: The Greek sun is hot and piercing. If you overdo it and catch a burn, rub on—*yogurt.*

SWIMMING: There are no public pools in town (you can pay to swim at the Hilton or Caravel and some of the other hotel pools). Your best bet is to head directly for the Apollo Coast and establish a base of operations there. Keep in mind that Piraeus is a very busy port and that at Glyfada and Vouliagmeni you have the problem of aircraft noise. The place you may want to head for along with the Athenians, is **Varkiza,** about an hour from the city by bus (it leaves from Leoforos Olgas, near the Zappeion, but you may be able to join other beachgoers and share a taxi inexpensively). At all the beaches along the shore where you pay an admission fee there are changing facilities and showers, and the beaches themselves are cleaned every morning; most of them also have snackbars and/or restaurants. Rates average 100 drs (75¢); Varkiza is in the top range and costs 170 drs ($1.30). There are often beach cabins available for an additional 500 drs ($4). *Note:* If you swim from rocks rather than sand, beware of sea urchins.

TAXIS: The rates are 25 drs (20¢) to begin, then 20 drs (15¢) per kilometer within the Athens/Piraeus area. Minimum charge is 170 drs (about $1). Extras are 50 drs (40¢) for every piece of baggage, 100 drs (75¢) for any ride between midnight and 7 a.m. There is an additional charge of 100 drs (75¢) when going to or from the airport or harbor, when the per-kilometer charge becomes 35 drs (30¢) beyond the city boundaries. That's the cost of a cab *if* you can find one! Anti-pollution ordinances now have central Athens-bound cabs operating on an alternate-day schedule, depending upon license number. Theoretically, there are taxi stations on or near every major square, but that doesn't necessarily mean there are any taxis at the stations. There is no telephone service for radio-controlled cabs (you have to go all the way up to a limousine for that kind of service); a recent law allows would-be passengers to flag down taxis (be prepared to shout out your destination as soon as the cab slows down near you) that already have passengers and share the trip if they are going in the same general direction. This is supposed to spread the taxis around, but in reality, it makes a taxi more difficult to find than ever. There's no easy answer, other than appearing on the doorstep of a deluxe hotel and tipping the doorman handsomely.

TELEGRAMS: Expensive! But if you must send one, the office at 85 Patission St., Athens, is open 24 hours a day. Another at 15 Stadiou St. has hours from 7 a.m. to midnight. Daily rates to the U.S. are around 677 drs ($5) plus 60 drs (46¢) per word, plus tax. There is a 100% surcharge for urgent messages.

TELEPHONES: Public telephones are attached to the sides of kiosks, for local calls only; the cost is 20 drs (15¢), and you pay the kiosk owner. Phone booths with blue trim are for Athens calls only, those with orange trim for calls outside of Athens; in either case, before dialing, the appropriate coin must be inserted.

TELEPHONE SERVICE FROM GREECE TO U.S.A. (mainland): Via the operator: Station calls (first three minutes) cost 1,072 drs ($8); person-to-person calls (first three minutes) cost 1,929 drs ($15); each additional minute for person and station calls is another 357 drs ($3). The total amount of the call is subject to 8% tax.

Automatic service: From public telephone offices and coin boxes the cost is 357 drs ($3) per minute.

You can place telephone calls at OTE offices—85 Patission St. (open 24 hours a day), Omonia Square (open 24 hours a day), 15 Stadiou St. (open from 8 a.m. to midnight)—or dial 161 from any telephone to get the long-distance operator. When you want to communicate by I.D.D.D. system you have to dial the international prefix (00), then the U.S.A. country code (1), and then the area code and local number.

Please note that when dialing, all digits should be dialed without any pause, and there is no special signal between groups of digits. Dial 169 for recorded instructions for making international calls.

TIME: Athens time is Greenwich Mean Time plus two hours—or seven hours ahead of New York.

TIPPING: Porters at the airport and train station receive a fee of 100 drs (75¢) per bag minimum. Taxi drivers expect you to round off the meter in their favor. Leave chambermaids 100 drs (75¢) per day for an average stay of two or three days. Doormen who hail your cab, 100 drs (75¢) to 200 drs ($2). Tour guides expect 150 drs ($1) or up, but *never* coins, although the tourist authorities say they don't have to be tipped at all. Theater ushers traditionally get 50 drs (40¢) for showing you to your seat. Barbers get from 20% to 30%; public toilet room attendants get 5 to 10 drs (5¢ to 10¢); hatcheck girls get 5 to 10 drs; busboys in restaurants get the loose change.

TOILETS: Most public toilets have symbols on the doors that quite clearly distinguish between the sexes. In case they don't, however, and instead have the appropriate words in Greek, remember—the Greek word for men has six letters, the word for women has eight.

TOURIST POLICE: Dial 171 for information (hotels, shops, sports, nightclubs, etc.) in five languages, 24 hours a day.

TOURS: A great variety of organized tours is offered, from sightseeing in Athens and environs to complete tours of the Greek mainland, to air tours and cruises to the many islands. A few of the leading tour operators are: **American Express,** Constitution Square (tel. 3230-603); **Vikings Tours,** 3 Filellinon St. (tel. 3229-383) and in the U.S., 6 Turkey Hill Rd., S., Westport, CT 06880 (tel. 203/226-7911). **Key Tours,** 2 Ermou St. (tel. 3232-520); **CHAT Tours,** 4 Stadiou St. (tel. 3223-137).

TRAVEL AGENTS: Here are two reliable organizations besides American Express and Viking's: **American Travel,** 11 Patriarchou Ioakim, Kolonaki (tel. 7233-863); **Wagons-Lits/Cooks,** 5 Stadiou St. (tel. 3242-281). **Camel Tours** at 7 Voulis St. (tel. 3234-617) specialize in rail travel.

CHAPTER XI

ATHENS BY THE SEA

□ □ □

Piraeus, Glyfada, Vouliagmeni, Sounion

The Acropolis is five miles from the sea, and in the days of Pericles it was quite a hike across the countryside to reach Phaleron Bay. Now it's a short bus ride, and the suburbs of Athens reach all the way to the edge of the sea. But the entire coast—from Piraeus in the north all the way south past the airport to Glyfada, and even as far as Lagonissi—is virtually an extension of Athens. In summer, the downtown nightclubs move out there, Athenians go to the seaside for dinner, wealthy Athenians flock out to the luxury hotels and beach houses—and stay put until September.

So, you're not really seeing Athens until you see something of its seaside satellites. In fact, if you're planning to be in these parts in midsummer you might even consider checking into a hotel by the sea and making your sightseeing excursions into town from there. Glyfada is only 20 minutes by car from downtown Athens; Vouliagmeni is 30 minutes; Piraeus, about 15 minutes.

PIRAEUS—EVEN ON SUNDAY

The port of Piraeus is about six miles from Syntagma. In 461 B.C. Themistocles linked the two cities by his "Long Walls," but now they're intertwined by their sprawling suburbs.

Two outstanding events have taken place in the history of Piraeus. Themistocles chose the site as the home port for the Athenian fleet he was about to build—the "wooden walls" predicted by the oracle. After the Peloponnesian Wars it slumped back again to a fishing village, and when Greece became independent and Athens became the capital in the 19th century, Piraeus was a ragtag hamlet on the edge of the water.

After the turn of the century it slowly emerged as one of the major ports of the Mediterranean, thus preparing it for its second outstanding event—when Melina Mercouri made a movie called *Never on Sunday,* which has since introduced the waterfront of Piraeus and its boisterous bars to the whole world. The waterfront still looks like the movie here and there, but Piraeus has blossomed in recent years and on your way to or from your cruise ship you may want to spend an hour or two among its flower-decked boulevards and terrace cafés.

The dedicated archeologist can find many remnants of antiquity here, including traces of the Long Walls (the subway track follows roughly the same route). The city's museums of archeology and naval history are worth peeking into.

In the past few years, the city's gung-ho council has pushed ahead a rejuvenation program that included new beaches, new beach facilities, and especially the big new marina at Zea. You may be coming here at some point to catch a small ferry or hydrofoil to some of the islands, but if not, come anyway and take a look at the luxury yachts and three-masted schooners and other toys of the Mediterranean jet-set. There's a new, completely equipped marina here with restaurants, hairdressers, ship brokers, ship chandlers, and other appurtenances of seagoing. The large cruise ships, by the way, leave from the docks around Akti Miaouli and Akti Xaveriou in Piraeus port, over the hill, or around the bend.

On the opposite side of the bay is the hilly peninsula known as **Castella** (which was the site of ancient Munichia and another acropolis). It's mostly residential (very desirable, with views over the harbor and the Royal Hellenic Yacht Club next door), and there are several good restaurants and cafés up here.

Round another bend and you're into another bay and a circular harbor bobbing with more yachts and sailboats, the entire waterfront ringed with blue, yellow, and red awnings of the restaurants across the street. This is **Mikrolimano,** which you read about in an earlier chapter. In the morning it's a typical little fishing village, with the fishermen mending their nets and drying them in the sun; in the evening it's Athens's dining hall. It's one of the most romantic places for dining out along the entire coast (yet only 20 minutes by car from Syntagma, or by subway from Omonia Square to the Neon Phaleron, or New Faliron, stop). There are tables all along the waterfront, their matching restaurants across the street. After dinner you can take a half-hour trip around the harbor with a gnarled old Greek seafarer in his caique. Around midnight you still won't want to head back into town, so take your car or a taxi farther down the coast to one of the night-clubs by the sea.

THE APOLLO COAST: The next spot along the shore, known by the tourist authorities as the Apollo Coast, is **Faliron,** which away back used to be *the* harbor of Athens; then comes **Kalamaki,** which is a continuation of the nightclubs, restaurants, and tavernas of Old Faliron. The blue bus (no. 132), marked Edem, will take you from Syntagma to Faliron, and the no. 103 bus, marked Aghios Cosmas, will take you to Kalamaki, both for less than 30 drs (25¢).

Aghios Cosmas is a new beach development and sports center—two soccer fields, eight basketball courts, eight volleyball courts, two tennis courts, and a beach for 3,000 bathers.

GLYFADA

Glyfada is the first of the big resorts, and it's only ten miles from Athens—you can catch a no. 129 bus from Vassilissis Olgas Avenue, and the fare is only 30 drs (25¢). The main road to Sounion passes through the center of town, but turn off at the big green nightclub, Dionysios, onto the marine drive and you pass an unending stream of cafés, restaurants, tavernas, hotels, and marinas. The café/restaurants on the beach side are mostly modern places where you can have anything from pizzas to freshly caught mullet, and your dinner bill needn't go above 1,910 drs ($15).

One of the most famous restaurants along here is **Psaropoulos** (telephone for a reservation—8945-677), popular with politicians and high society, but rather expensive by Greek standards—say, 2,600 drs ($20) and up per person, with wine.

All the way at the end of this marine drive, you'll come to a restaurant on both sides of the street, with tables right at the edge of the marina. This is **Antonopoulos** (tel. 8945-636). An order of prawns here (big ones, but only three of them) costs about 1,000 drs ($8); mullet is also about the same price. Right next to it, behind the trees and right on the beach, is the **Asteria** nightclub and taverna (tel. 8945-675). It's part of the big Astir Beach development that includes restaurants, snackbars, a bookstore, public beach (130 drs, or about $1 admission) with pedalos and canoes (120 drs, or 95¢ an hour). This area is also the best place to stay in Glyfada.

The **Astir Beach Bungalows** curve around one side of the bay, in groves of lemon, orange, and pine trees. The bungalows have kitchens, refrigerators, showers, closets, beach towels, 24-

hour service, beach chairs, patios for dining or sunning—and all a step from the cool, clear water. In other words, you have your own private little beach house. It's classed as a deluxe hotel, so the rates in summer are 10,743 drs ($83) and up for a double. Come in April, May, September, or October, however, and you can have the same room for two-thirds the price. The complex has 120 one-room bungalows, seven two-room, and seven three-room bungalows, so it's a great place to bring the family, although its proximity to the airport may be a drawback for some people.

There are two more public beaches, with entrance fees of 150 drs (about $1), in the next village, **Voula,** but keep going another five miles to two of the stars of the coast. . . .

KAVOURI AND VOULIAGMENI

These two are the liveliest and loveliest of the resorts within 15 miles and a 30-dr (25¢) bus fare from Athens.

They're on either side of a cape covered with pine trees, separating the bay, one half facing the ocean, the other half on the bay. The ocean beach faces a flotilla of gleaming white yachts (there are still more of them tucked away in a marina farther down the cape); the restaurants are stacked above the beaches with terraces overlooking the sea, and new hotels and apartments are stacked up behind the restaurants. There are so many new hotels going up there's no point in saying which is the best, except for . . .

The **Astir Palace Hotels** complex is one of the grand resort hotels of Europe, the playground of the shipping tycoons. The original Astir Palace Hotel, now known as the **Arion Astor,** has 147 rooms and 34 penthouse suites, all recently refurbished, a palatial glass-and-marble lobby, an enormous terrace overlooking one of three private coves and its 77 relatively secluded bungalows (where the wealthiest of the wealthy Athenians idle away their summers), shaded by trees and cooled by terraced lawns. In 1979 an additional 165 rooms opened in a spectacular new wing, called the **Nafsika Astir Hotel,** built into the hillside, and decorated in a lavish contemporary style. Yet another 165-room wing opened in 1984. This one, called **Aphrodite Astir,** faces out to sea, has a balcony for every room, and comes fully serviced by indoor and outdoor restaurants, boutiques, hairdresser, news ticker, and 100-car garage. In summer (June through September) rooms in the three Astir hotels range from 19,500 drs ($150) to 29,500 drs ($227) with half board. But in April and October you can have the accommodations for 20% to 25% less, and from November through March for 45% to 50% less; the luxury remains, the armies of servants are still there, and even if it's too cold to swim, it's perfect for playing tennis and hiking on the cape. This is certainly class, Greek style.

The restaurants in the Astir complex are international in scope and price; if you want something simpler and more typical, head for the far end of town (en route to Sounion) and the last restaurant on the right, **Taverna Lambros.** It sits amidst a park, on a bluff above the sea, and nobody speaks English but you can go into the kitchen and point—*midia fassolia salata, tzatziki, dolmadakia, barbounia,* and *souvlaki moscharisi,* all that and mineral water for 2,221 drs ($17). The moonlight is free.

SOUTH TO SOUNION: But the best is yet to come. From

Vouliagmeni to Cape Sounion (about 40 miles from Athens) the coastline twists and turns around beaches and rocky coves; a beautiful scenic highway winds alongside, sometimes by the edge of the sea, sometimes up on the cliffs. This is the true Apollo Coast. And from the point of view of sunning and swimming, it's worth the extra miles and minutes from Athens, because here you'll find less pollution and less noise from the aircraft landing at Hellinikon Airport. Try, for example, the town of **Varkiza,** where the beach has small bungalows rentable by the day (about 2,470 drs, or $19, no reservations required), and a good, inexpensive, self-service cafeteria. For a hotel, try the 32-room Class B **Varkiza** or Class A **Glaros.**

South of Varkiza are half a dozen small towns, most of them being spruced up and "resortified," so that you now have a choice of about a dozen hotels in these parts. The most popular of these towns is **Lagonissi,** 25 miles from Athens, where you'll find one of the complete tourist villages set up in recent years by the Greek government—hotels, bungalows, chapel, kindergarten, tavernas, open-air cinema, sauna, beauty parlor, shopping center, beaches, tennis courts—all carefully landscaped to disguise any hint of concrete overkill. You can sunbathe here on any of five beaches, waterski, and snorkel in the clearest of waters. The rate structure at the **Lagonissi** requires a computer to figure out the variations for the complex's 99 rooms, 15 suites, and 243 bungalows (in three sizes). In summer you're obliged to take half board, which will set you back 7,764 drs ($60) or thereabouts in a double room or bungalow; from November through mid-March, rates are about 30% less. *Note:* There's a free, direct service by private coach between Athens and Lagonissi (a taxi or limousine, on the other hand, will cost you about 2,340 drs, or $18).

But the most attractive hostelry along these shores is probably the latest in the government-owned Xenia chain, the **Xenia Ilios**

Hotel in Anavissos—its dun-colored contemporary lines stepping down the hillside. Each of the 102 guest rooms enjoys views of sea, shore, and passing ships. In winter, the Ilios serves as a hotel training school; in summer the students polish their skills on paying guests. The summer service may be better than usual, and the rates are hardly formidable—around 7,800 drs ($60) for two with half board.

But your final goal is Cape Sounion (Sounio on the signposts) —specifically, the romantic Temple of Poseidon, perched high on the cliff above the sea.

CAPE SOUNION

You get your first glimpse of the temple from the coastal road, several twists and bays before you actually get to the cape. First you see it, then you don't. Finally you're there. The **Temple of Poseidon** was built in 444 B.C., probably by the architect who designed the Temple of Theseus in Athens, and only 15 of its original 34 Doric columns remain. But it's still one of the most dramatic sights of Greece. Lord Byron was so carried away by it that he carved his initials on one of the columns (you try that today and *you'll* be carried away). The site is closed on Tuesday. Admission is 300 drs ($2). After you've tramped around this sea-girt acropolis, go down to the bay for a swim (the beach is nothing special but the water and the view are), or lunch at one of the waterfront tavernas.

If you decide to stay overnight, you have a choice of three Class A hotels in Sounion: The 90-room **Belvedere Park** charges 5,682 drs ($44) for two with half board; the 45-room **Egeon** is 5,145 drs ($40) for two with half board; and the 152-room **Cape Sounion Beach Hotel** costs 6,270 drs ($48) for two with half board; the largest resort in the area is the Class B **Surf Beach Club** with rooms and bungalows and great views for over 500 guests, 5,416 drs ($42), for two with half board.

Note: There's an alternative, picturesque route back to Athens from Sounion, following the valleys and wine villages of the interior. It's a tough decision which to take—coastal or inland. Bets are you'll want to enjoy the constantly changing shore, the sparkling water that changes from deep blue to turquoise from bay to bay, the islands and sailboats and fishing boats along the way. In any case, most people want to stay at Sounion until the sun sets beside the Temple of Poseidon, so you may be driving back in the dark anyway. In which case, stop off at the Astir Palace in Vouliagmeni for dinner, or one of the fine seafood restaurants and beachside tavernas along the coast if you're less than impeccably dressed.

CHAPTER XII

DAY TRIPS FROM ATHENS

□ □ □

You'll be amazed how many trips to how many historic sites you can make from Athens. Many of them can be completed in one day—there and back. To get some idea of the choices you have, skim through the catalog of the CHAT tour people: half-day tours to Cape Sounion and the Temple of Poseidon, half-day tours to Ancient Corinth and the Corinth Canal, half-day tours to Attica and Marathon, one-day tours to Mycenae, Nafplion, Epidaurus, Thebes, and Delphi. You can even make one-day mini-odysseys to the Greek islands—and still be back in Athens in time for a night on the Plaka.

You've already read about Cape Sounion and the Apollo Coast in the preceding chapter. Now here's a quick briefing on some of the other sights. Although I have grouped them here as *day* trips, you may decide (wisely) to stay overnight, so I've included some comments, where appropriate, on accommodations.

DAPHNI

Daphni is so close to Athens (five miles to the northwest) it doesn't really merit a tour on its own, so it's often included in the itineraries of other tours, especially during the **Wine Festival** held every summer (July through September). You pay the small admission charge, 250 drs or so ($1.90), then sample as many local wines as you can handle. With a deal like that, your best idea is to take the special bus, no. 864, rather than go by car—the bus fare is only 30 drs (25¢), and the bus leaves from Koumoundouros Square.

The other attraction in Daphni, year round, is the medieval monastery dedicated to the **Dormition of the Virgin Mary.** It was built on the site of an earlier temple, in a grove of laurel trees, dedicated to the laurel-bearing god Apollo. The present church, which dates from the 11th century, is noted for its inlaid mosaics on a golden background, and for its cloisters, cells, and sarcophagi. Opening hours vary with time of the year and day of the week, but as of press time it was temporarily closed—check with the Tourist Organization before you leave **Athens.**

KAISARIANI

A half-hour ride in the opposite direction on bus 234 from downtown Athens and a pleasant half-hour walk from the bus terminal brings you to the delightful 11th-century mini-monastery of Kaisariani, or Caesariani. You can cheat and take a taxi for the last stage rather than walking, but then you won't appreciate the ice-cold water that gushes from the fountain in the monastery wall. In ancient times these waters were believed to cure sterility, and they are still believed to have healthful if not magical qualities. It's quite safe to drink, and you will see many Greeks filling huge containers from the fountain.

You can visit the monastery's mill, bakery, bath house, refectory, and church, all in 20 minutes, if you wish; but it's much better to sit and relax in the peaceful surroundings for a spell before strolling back to the bus terminal. Kaisariani lies almost at the base of Mount Hymettos, so quiet and peaceful it's difficult to believe you're just beyond the suburbs of Athens.

Buses run every 15 minutes, more or less, from Polygonon, but there's also a stop on Kaningos Street, near Omonia. Since there seems to be some doubt about when the monastery closes officially (2, 3, or 5 p.m.), make this a morning excursion.

DELPHI

The famous city of the oracle is in that richly historical part of Greece known as Boeotia. Thermopylae and Thebes are not far off. Delphi itself is 110 miles from Athens, and the combination of ruggedly grand scenery and the haunting quality of the ruins makes it one of the most dramatic sights in all of Greece.

For centuries the story of Delphi was the story of Mediterranean politics. Hardly a decision was reached without consulting the oracles at the Apollo Temple. Evidently, the mountain exuded strange fumes (now considered water vapors or carbon monoxide), which put shepherds and peasant women into trances and led to prophetic pronouncements. In the magnificent setting of Mount Parnassos, with eagles soaring from peak to peak, it was easy to believe that here you stood in the presence of the gods.

Initially the name of the site was Pytho, and the Earth Mother known for her prophetic powers lived here. Later, seafarers from

Knossos introduced the cult of Apollo Delphinius. The story starts with Apollo disguising himself as a dolphin. He jumps into the water and captures a Cretan ship, returning both booty and prisoners to Delphi. The prisoners become "priests" in his sanctuary and Delphi's reputation for wisdom and prophecy is consolidated.

Nearby personages came to consult with the gods. And as was the custom, they brought gifts. From the 8th to the 4th centuries B.C., before an envious Nero looted the temples after Rome's conquest, the gift-giving and advice-seeking rose to such proportions that Delphi became a huge complex of treasuries and temples, all laden with works of art and riches.

Today, Delphi consists mainly of a theater, a sanctuary, an athletic area surrounded by a wall, and an excellent museum. But it is more than a ruins-cum-museum site: it's a total environment. Start your exploration from the main road, which leads both to the town and the ruins. Gaze toward the ruins, noting the distant views, the colors (especially at sunset and sunrise), the sheer valley below. Then amble through the ruins, starting with the **Marmaria** and the **Castalian Spring,** both of which are located below the main road. The ancient Greeks regarded springs as a gift of the gods. Steps leading to the water can be seen carved into the solid rock surface. Then walk up the hill beyond the road, onto the main site.

The **Sacred Way** is a path leading from the entrance to the stadium. Follow it as it zigs and zags between half-columns, perches, stones, and the **Treasury of the Athenians.** The Treasury is easy to recognize: it's almost completely reconstructed, using the original blocks of Parian marble. Look for the inscription written on the marble: "The Athenians dedicate to Apollo the Persian spoils from the Battle of Marathon."

At the top of the ruins site is the **theater,** built for an audience of 5,000, a model of engineering and aesthetic brilliance; and farther up the hill is a 5th-century stadium almost 200 yards long.

Returning from the ruins to town, stop at the **museum** near the entrance to the site and go immediately to the *Charioteer,* the famous bronze sculpture from the 5th century B.C., and one of the great masterpieces of Greek art. The museum's art pieces are mainly from the Mycenaean period (1600–1100 B.C.). Note particularly the Roman *Statue of Antinous,* a column of *Acanthus Dancing Girls,* and the *Wingless Sphinx of the Naxians,* a characteristic work of the 6th century B.C.

For at least six centuries Delphi's priests held most of the known world in thrall. Their ambiguous interpretations of the unintelligible ramblings from the "oracle" changed the course of history many times—and brought riches and incalculable power to a canny bunch of priests in a tiny mountainous village.

How it all began doesn't appear to be on record, but from the 7th century B.C. onward, the god known as Phoebus Apollo was heard to be speaking through the mouth of an old woman known as the Pythia, and her words, after being placed into neat hexameters by the priest-interpreters, made kings tremble and emperors lose their sleep.

Ordinary people consulted the oracle too, of course; the gods were willing to answer the question of anybody who brought money. More often than not, important people brought silver, gold, precious stones, and other gifts, and Delphi soon built up considerable treasure.

There was a set routine for the Pythia to follow on pronouncement days (which at first took place only during February, the month of Apollo's birthday), and it was strictly adhered to by one Pythia after another through the centuries.

First, the woman had to fast for three days and then, on the set day, bathe in the nearby Castalian Spring, burn laurel leaves at the altar, drink some water, and take up her place beside the copper-and-gold tripod which was set up over the fissure in the ground from which came "intoxicating vapors." Working her way into a trance she would then mumble garbled replies to questions asked of her. Sometimes the questions concerned banal personal problems and sometimes they concerned matters of state. But all got answers, usually so cryptic that they could be construed to mean anything at all, and seekers invariably went away happy.

A king, who was told that if he crossed a certain river a great empire would be destroyed, was chagrined to discover that the empire was his own. A man who came to ask about his stammer was instructed to go live in another country. The Roman emperor Nero was warned to "beware 73"—and died well before he reached that age at the hands of Galvus, who was 73.

Naturally there were some skeptics, among them Aesop, but the Delphi city fathers had providentially anticipated that by instituting formal trials for those they charged with sacrilege, and the sentence was usually to be tossed off a high cliff onto the jagged rocks below.

That well-known heretic Socrates may well have been thinking about Delphi when he announced that "the augur should be under the authority of the general and not the general under the authority of the augur."

This advice should have been taken to heart in 480 B.C., when Xerxes prepared to invade Greece with the combination of a massive army and fleet of ships. Athenians consulted the Delphic Oracle to find out what to do. They were told:

> Wretches, why sit ye here? Fly, fly to the ends of creation.
> Nay, not alone shall ye suffer, full many a town shall be
>   leveled;
> Many a shrine of the gods will he give to fiery destruction
> Get ye away from the Temple and brood on the doom that
>   awaits you.

Athens, and most of Greece, was naturally in a panic. The message, for once, hardly seemed ambiguous, and some were ready to take it at face value and flee in panic. But wiser counsels prevailed and the Athenians and their Spartan allies held the northern passes until Themistocles built up the navy (here the Delphic Oracle redeemed itself somewhat with a prediction that the city would be saved by its "wooden walls") and eventually repelled the invasion attempt.

Delphi never entirely recovered from this erroneous taking of sides, however, and although the world rallied with contributions after a earthquake almost destroyed the town in 373 B.C., the oracle's influence continued to decline.

But worse was to come. In 356 B.C. a band of Phocians from the west suddenly invaded the town and captured the shrine along with all its wealth. For a time they terrorized their neighbors by raising an army of mercenaries paid with their new-found treasure, but eventually the shrine was restored to the priests to continue their prognostications for three centuries more.

The coming of the Christian era was the beginning of the end, and in A.D. 381 the emperor Theodosius outlawed "paganism" and Delphi passed into history.

HOW TO GET TO DELPHI: The simplest way is to take a one-day coach tour, in air-conditioned comfort, with a guide to explain the ruins and sights along the way. **Key Tours, American Express,** and **CHAT** operate one-day tours (8:30 a.m. to 6:30 p.m.), costing 5,400 drs ($42) including lunch (4,200 drs, or $32, without lunch), admission fee, and a visit to the nearby monastery of Ossios Lucas. The two-day tour is much better if you can afford the time, because you can spend more time among the magnificent ruins and see them (and photograph them) at sunrise or sunset; this full 34-hour tour costs 10,900 drs ($84), with half board, in air-conditioned hotels.

The cheapest way to reach Delphi is by regular bus service— only 1,840 drs ($14) round trip, with a choice of five departures daily from the bus terminal on Liossion Street, a three-hour trip each way.

The most convenient way to get to Delphi is undoubtedly to rent a car and drive. For the first third of the trip you'll be driving on the relatively fast but tricky Athens-Thessaloniki National Highway; then after an hour you turn off at the Delphi sign and start heading up into the mountains (where the roads are being improved enormously).

This is a tough trip, and you should either leave very early in the morning to get to the site before the museum closes for siesta, or arrive in time for a leisurely lunch, an afternoon visit to the ruins and the museum, lingering there through sunset, then facing the after-dark drive back to Athens (allow four hours in this case). Better still, stay the night in Delphi and drive back the next day, stopping at the quaint hilltop town of Arahova and the monastery of Ossios Lucas along the way.

HOTELS IN DELPHI:
For a tiny town (pop. 800), Delphi certainly offers visitors a vast selection of accommodations, but then it has had a long time to practice being a host. The main street alone has over a dozen hotels, most of them inexpensive; those on the left side as you walk into the town are the most interesting, because they're perched on the edge of a cliff looking all the way across the plain to the Gulf of Corinth. Try the **Iniochos** (Class B, 15 rooms with private baths) or **Hermes** (Class C) for reliable accommodations around 3,000 drs ($23) for a double. The **Castalia,** also on the cliff side of the street, is an elderly Class B hotel with a large dining terrace overlooking the valley. The three most interesting hotels in Delphi are the 61-room **Vouzas** (closest to the ruins), a Class A hotel built in tiers down the side of the cliff; the 50-room Class A **Xenia,** and above all, literally and otherwise, the handsome Class A, 185-room **Amalia,** a spacious affair of granite, marble, polished wood, modern and comfortable furniture, and well-equipped guest rooms that rent for around 8,600 drs ($66) for a double per night, with continental breakfast. The Amalia, Delphi, Vouzas, and Castalia all have attractive dining rooms (the Amalia most of all), but you'll probably want to sample one of Delphi's tavernas with large, sometimes windswept terraces, overlooking the gulf and the plain (all that greenery you see down

there, by the way, is the topside of something like three million olive trees); you can dine on these terraces for less than 1,000 drs ($8).

MARATHON

This, of course, is where the famous battle was fought in 490 B.C., when the Athenians trounced the Persians and the messenger ran the 26 miles back to the city, gasped out the news of victory, and flopped down dead. The site of the battle is now marked by a barrow in which the Greek soldiers were buried, and a white marble column. Buses leave Athens (from the terminal at 29 Mavromateon St.) to the Marathon battlefield approximately every half hour—one hour and 230 drs ($2) each way.

THE PELOPONNESE

The next batch of destinations are all on the peninsula known as the Peloponnese ("the land of Pelops"), the almost-island chunk of land that makes up the southwestern corner of Greece. It's a region of mountain scenery highlighted by an incredible collection of ancient monuments and brightened by flashes of beach and sea.

CORINTH: The first landmark you come to in the Peloponnese is the city of Corinth, or rather the **Corinth Canal.** This channel, 3½ miles long and 75 feet wide, makes the peninsula an island, and chops 185 miles from the voyage between Italy and Piraeus. It was built between 1882 and 1893, but it was originally conceived way back in the days of Nero and Hadrian. In fact, Nero got so far as to dig the first shovelful—with a golden spade. But it didn't get much beyond Nero's first shovelful, and shipowners had to continue hauling their ships overland, over the *diolkos,* a stone-paved track, traces of which you can still see here and there.

This suited the Corinthians fine, because they supplied the hauling power and collected the fees. They also collected tolls on all cargos heading between the peninsula and the mainland, and between the Gulf of Corinth and the Saronic Gulf. Their wealth made them self-indulgent, and at one point the city could boast 1,000 "sacred prostitutes" who plied their trade in the name and to the honor of Aphrodite. No wonder St. Paul came along and gave the Corinthians a tongue-lashing. The tribune where he delivered his sermon is still there in Ancient Corinth. There are now two Corinths. The new city was destroyed by an earthquake in 1928 and an even newer one was built after that. Its main interest for visitors is as a base for excursions to the fascinating surroundings. The more fascinating of the two is **Ancient Corinth.** It too was completely destroyed—by the Romans in 146 B.C.—and most of what you see today dates from 44 B.C. when Caesar set up a colony there. The principal sites are the 6th-century Temple of Apollo, Saint Paul's tribune, the agora, and the Pirene fountain.

Acrocorinth is a mighty citadel towering over the town. This was originally the site of the Temple of Aphrodite. The citadel was built by the Byzantines, and at various stages subtracted from or added to by Crusaders, Venetians, and Turks. Today you get a great view from the top. You can drive to the entrance up a precipitous dirt road, and both the view and the citadel justify the effort. There's a coffeeshop at the top of the hill.

How to Get to Corinth

The full-day sightseeing tours leave Athens at 8:30 a.m. and return at 7 p.m., after stops also at Mycenae, Nafplion, and Epidaurus, and cost 4,200 drs ($32) without lunch, 5,400 drs ($42) with. You can also get there by diesel train, rail, or bus from Athens (check with your hotel concierge for times and fares); or in roughly 1½ hours by car, on the National Highway.

Hotels

The best hotels in the area are all a short drive from town. The new **King Saron** (161 Class A rooms) at Isthmia, the **Kalamaki Beach** (Class A, 66 rooms) at Paleon Kalamaki, and the 48-room Class B **Almyri Beach** at Almyri, for example.

EPIDAURUS: This town, 20 miles from Nafplion, but on the Saronic Gulf, is famed for two things. In the 6th century it was a place of pilgrimage, a sort of Lourdes, where sick people journeyed to find a cure in the **sanctuary of Asclepius,** the god of healing. There was more than faith involved, however, and you can still see inscriptions of prescriptions in the sanctuary, and in the nearby **museum,** as well as the votive offerings brought by the people who had been cured. (*Note:* There's a whole room of the National Archeological Museum in Athens devoted to friezes and statues on this subject—always with an oversize god-doctor seated nonchalantly at his desk, while Hygeia his nurse collects the loot from the patients, who are usually depicted as small and humble. Sound familiar?)

Other sights at Epidaurus include the **Greek Bath** (where the sick washed themselves), the **Abaton** (the so-called portico of incubation), where the sick slept on beds waiting for an apparition of the god who would cure them in their sleep, the **Roman bath, the**

stadium, and **the museum** (admission: 500 drs ($4), but free on Sunday and Thursday; open 8 a.m. to 5 p.m., closed Tuesday).

THE THEATER AT EPIDAURUS. The other great sight of Epidaurus is the ancient theater with its circular "orchestra" and 50 tiers for 14,000 spectators. It was built in the 4th century B.C. by Polycleitus the Younger, who ought to be around today to teach acoustics to his successors: despite its size and its age, the acoustics of Epidaurus are so perfect you can hear the performers' gowns trailing across the stage. Fortunately, you can still enjoy the benefits of these acoustics, because performances are given here every summer during the **Epidaurus Festival** (it's in June and July, and the National Tourist Organization can give you details of dates and plays).

How to Get to Epidaurus

You can get to Epidaurus by regular bus service from Athens via Nafplion, about 780 drs ($6) one way. During the festival, there's a special pullman bus service from Athens direct to Epidaurus on days of the performance only (but you'd better have your hotel concierge make a reservation in advance).

MYCENAE: Identified on some maps, signposts, and guides as Mikines. Either way it's the mountain palace-fortress of Agamemnon, "lord of the many islands and all of Argos" (this part of the Peloponnese, including Nafplion and Epidaurus, is in a region known as the Argolis). This is the place that gave its name to an entire civilization that was cock-of-the-walk in the 14th century B.C., although some of the archeological digs have uncovered evidence that the area was inhabited as early as 3000 B.C. What you see here today are the impressive entrance (the **Lion Gate**), and the remains of granaries, reservoirs, and the **shaft graves** that sheltered the golden treasures of Mycenaean art (Homer's "Golden Mycenae") for all those thousands of years, before they were carted off to the National Archeological Museum in Athens. Just outside the fortress walls, you can see nine **beehive tombs,** one of which is thought to be the tomb of Clytemnestra (who, you'll remember, bumped off her husband, Agamemnon, before she in turn was disposed of by her son, Orestes); one of the others is probably the tomb of Agamemnon himself. Admission to the site is 500 drs ($4); open 8 a.m. to 5 p.m.; closed Tuesday.

How to Get to Mycenae

Take the regular bus from Athens to Nafplion and get off at Argos, where you catch a local bus to Mycenae; there's also a train service from Athens to Fichtia, a couple of miles by bus from the ruins.

Corinth, Mycenae, Nafplion, and Epidaurus are included in one-day (one-crowded-day) sightseeing tours from Athens, leaving at 8:30 a.m. and returning at 7 p.m., and costing 5,400 drs ($42), including lunch at Nafplion.

NAFPLION: I've kept this one to the end of the eastern Peloponnese group because although Nafplion is an easy day trip from Athens, it also makes an ideal tour center if you want to stay overnight (or nights) and do a series of morning and afternoon excursions to Mycenae, Epidaurus, and other attractions such as the ruins of ancient Tiryns, or for longer trips, to Porto Heli and the island of Spetsai.

Depending on your first impression, Nafplion is either a holiday resort, or a medieval fortress town, or a picturesque little port. A walk around town tells you it's all three. Nafplion was also at one time the capital of Greece, right after its liberation from the Turks. The tiny island fortress, **Bourtzi,** out in the bay, was built by Venetians; the **Acronafplion** citadel towering over the town's south side was built on the site of an even more ancient acropolis; and the town's third fortress, **Palamidi,** is actually seven fortresses in one, built by the Franks and added to by several later conquerors. Nafplion is now a pleasant resort, its water-front lined with cafés and tavernas, with steep stairways leading to narrow streets lined with more tavernas, some boutiques, and a few boîtes. If you walk past the cafés, you'll find a narrow pathway by the sea running around the base of the Acronafplion; at the opposite end it leads up to the fortress itself, where you can take the elevator of the deluxe Xenia Palace Hotel back down to town.

How to Get to Nafplion

You can get there by regular hourly bus service from Athens, and it's also included on most of the one-day and two-day coach tours to the Peloponnese.

Hotels

If you decide to stay overnight there's a wider selection of hotels here than in other towns in the region. However, since it's also one of the most popular spots in Greece at any time of the year, you must always make reservations in advance; you may have to pay a half-board rate; and the attitude of the hotel personnel, especially in the two Xenias, tends to be off-hand.

The 54-room deluxe **Xenia Palace** is the most interesting hotel in town, built right on top of the Acronafplion, with all its rooms overlooking the bay and Bourtzi; doubles go for 7,500 drs ($58). Its namesake, the 58-room **Xenia Hotel,** is nearby, on the shoulder of the acropolis with half its rooms facing the bay, half facing the gulf and the fortress of Palimida (possibly the more interesting view of the two); doubles cost 5,000 drs ($39).

In town itself, the top hotel is the Class A **Amphitryon,** with 48 rooms, many overlooking the bay; doubles are 5,700 drs ($44). The 40-room Class B **Agamemnon** is right on the waterfront with a roof taverna for summer dining; doubles run 3,562 drs ($27). And the popular 70-room Class C **Dioscouri** is alongside one of the stepped streets; doubles cost 3,600 drs ($28).

A deluxe **Amalia Hotel** opened in 1983, giving some much-needed competition to the Xenias. The new hotel is in the neoclassical style, near the waterfront, with 175 air-conditioned rooms, pool, and stylish restaurant. Doubles here cost about 7,500 ($58), with half board.

And there you have a cluster of some of the most famous spots in history, and I've covered only one small corner of the Peloponnese; but you'll learn about Arcadia, Sparta, and Olympia in a later chapter, since they're too far from Athens to be accessible on one-day trips (but not too far from Nafplion).

THE $35 MINI-ODYSSEY

Everybody wants to see the Greek islands, but not everyone has the time to be away from Athens for a few days. No problem. You just take the subway down to Piraeus, hop on a ferry, and sail across to an island with pine-clad hills, valleys of vineyards and pistachio trees, and a ruined temple overlooking a bay; or an island with a harbor ringed by restaurants and surrounded by a hillside of small palazzos; or an island with no cars where the only way to get around is by horse-drawn carriage or donkey. Better, call CHAT, Viking Tours, Key Tours, American Express, or some other tour operator, have them pick you up at your hotel, drive you to Paleon Phaleron—and leave everything else to them.

"Everything else" will add up to a memorable day that's part Mediterranean cruise exploration, part sightseeing, part sunning, and wholly relaxing. Say you decide to take the cruise—a bus will collect you, transfer you to a second bus and drive you down to Paleon Phaleron, a new marina at the end of Syngron Avenue, where you'll board your cruise ship and head out of the harbor past the private yachts and the three-masted schooners waiting patiently for busy shipping tycoons to come and take them out for a sail.

There are currently half a dozen ships operating this three-island cruise of the Saronic Gulf—some as big as 3,000 tons, some with cabins you can rent by the day. All of them have swimming pools, plenty of deck space for sunning, as well as dining salons, lounges, bars, hostesses, and boutiques for souvenirs and film.

Your first port of call, 1¼ hours out, is the island of **Aegina.** This is the closest island to Athens, and consequently one of the busiest on weekends. Aegina is a hilly little island, with a precipitous town perched above the dock, with a few cafés, a bakery shop, a souvenir shop or two, and a movie house.

You can go to the beach here, or you can join a tour up through the pistachio plantations and vineyards to the almost mystical **Temple of Aphaea,** "a very ancient local deity," with a hexastyle Doric temple built of local limestone. Back on board it's time to have lunch (a simple tray-lunch). An hour later you come to one of the most interesting parts of the cruise as the ship squeezes through the Strait of Poros.

Poros is a conical island with a tiny village (also called Poros) that's a classic of its kind—a jumble of whitewashed buildings piled above the harbor, which is also the roadway which is also the sidewalk which is also the plaza, and is totally hidden under a mass of awnings and café tables that come right down to the edge of the water. Unfortunately, some of the ships don't stop here, so you may want to mark Poros down in your diary as one of those places you have to come back to some day.

Next stop is **Hydra,** a bleak, rocky, undulating island, until you get into the harbor which you immediately recognize from a thousand photographs. It's unique. The ship sails right into this small bowl-like haven, almost right into the nearest café, next to the fishing boats and the tiny ferries that shuttle cargo and people back and forth to the Peloponnese. Hydra had its heyday in the time of Napoleon, when more than 30,000 people lived here; now the population is down to a little more than 2,000, and most of them are artists or writers or gallivanting jet-setters. The town is different from any other in these parts because it's terraced with a type of house, or rather, mansion, known as the Hydriot palazzo, dating from the 18th century. It's one of the prettiest harbors you'll find anywhere, complete with a cathedral, belfry, the School for Training Merchant Navy Officers, and dozens of stores selling souvenirs and some of the niftiest handcraft bargains in the islands. You have an hour and a half there, so you can either flop into one of the cafés and admire the harbor, or wander around to the rocky cove on the other side of the bay and join the artists, writers, and jet-setters in the unbelievably clear rock-bound sea. (*Note:* Some of the ships reverse this itinerary, giving you longer on Hydra.)

By the time you sail for home the sun is low in the sky and glistening on the sea, and you can enjoy a comfortable cocktail on deck; by the time you get to Piraeus and the waiting buses, the sun has settled behind the mountains of the Peloponnese. You've cruised on the Mediterranean, you've seen three islands, and you've probably had a swim in the "Med." Not a bad day for 4,500 drs ($35) or thereabouts.

INDEPENDENT TRIPS: If you don't feel like following an organized itinerary, you can easily get to any of these islands by ferryboat or hydrofoil. That way you get to go ashore at Poros too, and you'll also be able to visit the fourth and farthest island of the group, **Spetsai** (the one with no cars), and maybe catch a glimpse of Spetsopoula, the private island of Stavros Niarchos, the *other* shipping tycoon. There's plenty to see on all of these islands— ruined temples, monasteries, picturesque fishing villages with almost as many tavernas as houses—but most people come over to find a secluded stretch of beach (and there are hundreds of those).

AEGINA

Perhaps the most interesting, as well as most accessible, of these islands for a one-day excursion is Aegina, mentioned above. To get there independently, you go down to Zea Marina as early as possible in the morning and take the first available regular ferry, express ferry, or hydrofoil (the hydrofoil takes only 35 minutes; the ferry, 75 minutes). When you arrive at the main town of Aegina, find out when the next bus leaves for Aghia Marina; while you're waiting, stroll along the front and have an ouzo with a small platter of freshly grilled octopus. The bus takes you right across the island through fig and pistachio plantations, past vineyards and across the mountains to your first stop, the **Temple of Aphaia,** a 6th-century B.C. marvel in limestone perched at the top of a steep hill above Aghia Marina, a temple which some people rate alongside those at Delphi and Sounion. Pause and marvel. Have a coffee or soft drink, while you decide on your next move. If you opt for sunbathing and swimming, take the bus on down to Aghia Marina (or follow the path down through the fields and vineyards, a 20-minute hike). During the summer months, incidentally, you can catch the boat back to the mainland from Aghia Marina.

If instead you opt for more sightseeing, get on a bus heading back to the town of Aegina and ask the conductor to put you off at Paleochora (if the bus is crowded, sit near the driver and keep reminding him). At Paleochora (rough translation, "old town"; it was once the ancient capital), leave the bus and strike off right, up the hillside, until you come to a hill dotted with numerous tiny churches and monasteries. Right at the top of this hill there's also a ruined castle. Peek inside some of the churches along the way to admire the Byzantine frescoes, some of them barely visible. You should allow yourself a good two hours for this visit (and wear sturdy walking shoes). In springtime the hillside is a riot of red and yellow flowers; in midsummer it's a good idea to take a bottle of water with you as the nearest café is opposite the bus stop, back down by the main road. A word of advice: Before setting off into the hinterland of Aegina, check the times of the last ferries back to Piraeus, but don't wait for the last one, and buy your ticket in advance. All Athens, it seems, heads for Aegina on weekends in summer.

FERRY SERVICES FROM PIRAEUS

To	No. of departures		One-way fares (third class, on deck)
	Weekdays	Weekends	
Aegina	32	48	355 drs ($3)
Poros	12	12	530 drs ($4)
Hydra	4	4	580 drs ($4)
Spetsai	4	4	760 drs ($6)

Fares are subject to change, and may be 20% higher. All will be under 1,950 drs ($15), round trip. For further information, phone 4511-311.

FLYING DOLPHINS: During the summer months (and on calm days in spring and fall) you also have the choice of a **hydrofoil** trip to these islands aboard the Flying Dolphins of Ceres Flying Hydroways. They're Russian-built hydrofoils; they tend to be noisy; there's very little deck space on top and no air conditioning below; the fares are almost double those of the regular ferryboat; and the ride can be unpleasant on choppy seas. Nevertheless, the hydrofoils do get you to the islands quickly (just two hours all the way to Spetsai), so they're popular with Athenians. The Flying Dolphins now also serve four locations on the Peloponnese coast

(Porto Heli, Leonidion, Nafplion, and Monemvassia), getting you there in much less time than by car (but if the sea is rough you may prefer the traffic jams).

   For full details of all schedules to these islands, check with the reception desk of your hotel, or with the National Tourist Organization information services at Syntagma; don't be discouraged if they hedge their answers, because the published schedules don't always tally with reality. In addition, double-check your ticket as soon as you pay for it, to make sure it's for the correct shipping company and correct vessel and correct destination; mistakes have been made, and it's usually impossible to have your money refunded. But don't let these words of caution dissuade you—your trip to the Saronic islands can be one of the highlights of your vacation.

Sample Flying Dolphins fares from Zea Marina

Zea to Aegina	568 drs ($4)
Zea to Hydra	1,447 drs ($11)
Zea to Spetsai	1,615 drs ($12)
Zea to Monemvassia	2,702 drs ($21)

   Fares may be higher in summer and subject to change without notice. For further information, phone the Flying Dolphins at 4527-107.

CHAPTER XIII

TOURING THE HINTERLANDS

□ □ □

Back in Chapter III you read a basic outline of what constitutes the nation known as Greece; now I'll fill in some of the details of the country beyond Athens. You can get to most parts of mainland Greece relatively easily and relatively quickly from Athens by car, bus, train, or plane, and there's certainly plenty to see once you get out there. In fact, there may be too much, and you may find it almost impossible to decide how to fit everything into one short vacation.

THE WESTERN PELOPONNESE

In the chapter on one-day trips from Athens you read about the highlights of the eastern part of this peninsula (Epidaurus, Mycenae, and Corinth); the *western* Peloponnese is a shade too far to be tackled on a one-day round trip—yet the chances are that you will want to visit Sparta, Olympia, and the district known as Arcadia, where Pan and the nymphs frolicked.

Arcadia is a region of rugged mountains rising to 3,500 feet or thereabouts, with many pleasant drives along winding roads through ancient villages and fir forests. Two of the most interesting towns in the western Peloponnese are **Sparta,** which was the seat of the great military power that battled Athens in the Peloponnesian Wars, although not much remains of its former glory; and **Mistras** (or Mystra), where there is more to see—scores of Byzantine monasteries, palaces, and citadels in an extraordinary setting.

The main goal of visitors to this part of Greece is **Olympia,** where you can still see traces of the stadium where the first Olympics were held. Olympia was dedicated to Zeus, and at its peak was an impressive collection of temples, altars, statues, and treasuries. It survived for over ten centuries, until A.D. 426 when Theodosius II commanded that the temples be destroyed. The games, which were also in honor of Zeus, were held for the first time in 776 B.C., and then every fourth year thereafter, from June until September. They were heralded each time by messengers setting off in every direction to announce the start of the sacred truce, during which all warfare and squabbling among the city-states had to be suspended: for four months, the gods and heroes and everyone else in the neighborhood concentrated on running, wrestling, chariot races, horse races, the pentathlon, and, eventually, artistic and literary contests. The names of the victors in each contest were recorded alongside the date of each Olympic Games. You can still see traces of the stadium and temples, the monuments and statues, and the starting block for 20 runners. The museum of Olympia houses many intriguing finds unearthed during excavations, but its most famous exhibit is the famed *Hermes* of Praxiteles, standing nobly in a room all by itself.

There are other virtually unknown spots you might want to include on a tour of the western Peloponnese: **Kyllini,** set among forests of wild oak and eucalyptus, was famous for centuries as a spa and is currently one of the largest holiday complexes in the Peloponnese; **Pylos,** built in tiers at the southern end of the Bay of Navarino, is a historic town in its own right but it is also close to the more famous ruins of the **Palace of Nestor** and the two formidable Venetian fortresses at **Methoni** and **Koroni.**

CENTRAL GREECE

Take the National Highway from Athens to the north and you come to the regions known as Boeotia, Thessaly, and Epirus, none of which means a great deal to the average visitor until they discover that these are the lands of Delphi (which you read about in an earlier chapter), Thermopylae, Meteora, Ioannina, and Missolonghi, all names ringing with myth and history.

North of Delphi, the National Highway follows the outline of the Gulf of Evoikos (which separates the Greek mainland from the island of Evia) and the Gulf of Pagasitikos, past the port of Volos, and across the plain to Larissa. The capital of Thessaly, **Larissa** has several fine hotels, which make it a convenient base for exploring, but the main attraction in these parts is almost 70 km (42 miles) to the west—Meteora.

Long before they reach **Meteora,** visitors can see what the place's fascination is all about—great columns of rock soar almost 2,000 feet into the air, and topping them off are precariously perched monasteries. In all, there are 24 of these aerie-like monasteries at Meteora; only two of them are still functioning as monasteries, but several of them are open to visitors. Inside (once you make it up the hill), you can tour the refectories and cells arranged in rows with balconies and galleries, the chapels with their ikons and frescoes dating from the 14th century.

To the west of Meteora, the magnets for tourists are **Ioannina,** capital of the region known as Epirus, noted for the baronial mansions that dot its narrow streets; **Nikopolis,** which was built by Octavius Caesar to honor his own victory over the combined fleets of Antony and Cleopatra at the Battle of Actium in 31 B.C.; and Missolonghi, which has gone down in the annals of Greek history because of its stubborn resistance to the Turks during the War of Independence—and because Lord Byron died there.

The major landmark between central Greece and the northern provinces is **Mount Olympus** itself, the very aerie of the gods and the highest point (9,793 feet) in Greece. Here you'll see some of the most spectacular, and beautiful, scenery in Greece.

If, on the way north to Meteora or Olympus, you detour to the east, around Pagasitikos Gulf, you come to the port of **Volos** and the ancient land of the Argonauts. Today's Volos is a substantial town and resort, its spacious waterfront lined with cafés and restaurants, and it's hard to conjure up images of Jason and his crew there. The hills beyond Volos are another matter. The wild peninsula that separates the gulf from the Aegean Sea is dominated by the peaks of the Pelion range, their flanks covered by forests of beech and chestnut at the upper levels, with groves of olive, peach, and apple trees on the lower levels. On the eastern shore the mountains dip directly into the sea, dented here and there with tiny bays lined by narrow spits of beach.

There are a few modest one-taverna resorts along this coastline, but the main appeal of the Pelion range is its hill towns— **Portaria, Makrynitsa, Vizitsa, Kissos, Tsagarada**—clinging precariously to the slopes, their mule-wide cobbled streets winding between attractive balconied homes with russet roof tiles and traditional painted woodcarvings. The two hill towns most popular with sightseers are probably **Makrynitsa** and **Vizitsa,** both of which have historic buildings being preserved by the National Tourist Organization. Skiers head for **Hania** in winter. But lovers of solitude head for tiny towns like **Tsagarada,** teetering on its hillside, its town square dominated by an 800-year-old plane tree with church bells hanging from its massive limbs: there's a taverna up the hill behind the church, cobbled goat paths lead up and down and across the hillside (you can spend hours hiking here, but be sure you get back before dark), and the views from almost any outlook are breathtaking. There are Class B **Xenia Hotels** at Tsagarada (fashioned from the local stone and timber) and Portaria. The roadways are well engineered, but winding, narrow, and at times hair-raising; if you're heading for the Aegean side of the mountains, the easiest drive is not the most direct route on the map, but the seemingly longer one along the shores of the Pagasitikos Gulf and then across the mountains where they're narrower and lower. It's a trip of some five hours, and you can drive straight there, since there's little to see along the way—unless you're a devout archeology buff.

NORTHERN GREECE

This is where Alexander the Great was born (in the town of **Pella,** now noted for its recently excavated pebble mosaics, dating from Alexander's time) and where Marc Antony and Octavius defeated Brutus and Cassius in the battle fought at **Philippi** (the ruins of the ancient agora and acropolis can still be visited). At the village of **Vergina,** archeologists have unearthed a fabulous 4th-century royal tomb, believed to be the grave of Philip II of Macedonia, father of Alexander. Many of the gold funerary objects found there are now on display in the Archeological Museum of Thessaloniki.

The capital of ancient Macedonia and Greece's second-largest city, **Thessaloniki** is a bustling modern city, with a sweeping promenade curving around the harbor; the old quarter of the city is built in tiers against the flank of Mount Hortisti, and between the mountain and the sea you can visit a wealth of Byzantine churches, Roman agoras, and triumphal arches.

But perhaps the most dramatic sight up in the north is **Mount Athos,** a mountainous finger of land on a three-pronged peninsula known as **Chalkidiki.** This "Holy Mountain," or Aghios Oros, has long been an isolated monastic community with its own republican government and police force of gowned monks. The flanks of the mountain are lined with spectacular, if sometimes crumbling, medieval monasteries, which can be visited only by men, and then only by special permission. The easiest way to see them is from a sightseeing boat, on a pleasant two- or three-hour cruise along the coast. The Chalkidiki Peninsula is one of the newest "in" spots in Greece, and there are several striking resorts where you can sport and play between serious excursions to Vergina, Pella, Philippi, or Mount Athos. Two of the grandest Class A hotels are the lavish and tastefully handsome 600-room **Athos Palace** on the Kassandra peninsula-within-a-peninsula and the dramatically sited, 166-room **Eagle's Palace** at Ouranoupoulis (near the entry point for Mount Athos).

GETTING AROUND BY BUS AND TRAIN

There's now an efficient network of bus routes fanning out from Athens through the country to 66 cities and towns. The

THE AMAZING PORTO CARRAS RESORT. The most spectacular resort up here is the 12-year-old Porto Carras development, a self-contained 4,500 acres that produces its own wines (some of them highly regarded in Athens), olive oil, feta cheese, and fruit. The resort's three hotels—Meliton (deluxe), Sithonia (Class A), and Village Inn (Class B)—have hosted princes, presidents, and ballet superstar Rudolf Nureyev; Zubin Mehta and the Los Angeles Philharmonic once regaled guests in the resort's open-air theater. There's also an indoor theater, plus two discos, a range of restaurants, and cafés. Its sports facilities include lighted tennis courts, a pro shop, a golf course, a stable with 35 horses, a marina for 100 yachts, and all water sports from day-sailing to para-sailing. If it all sounds rather crowded, it isn't: the Porto Carras shoreline runs for eight miles, and beyond the marina guests can bicycle along a dirt track to their choice of 34 secluded sandy coves.

Perhaps the resort's most attractive feature is its rates: *the deluxe Meliton costs roughly half what you'd pay in a comparable hotel elsewhere in Greece.* Porto Carras is 65 miles from Thessaloniki and the resort's motorcoach will drive you from and to the airport. (*Note:* Your air fare to Athens on Olympic will probably include the jet flight to Thessaloniki, if you let the airline know in advance, and if you continue north within 24 hours of arriving in Athens.) For information, call 0375-713810.

buses are big, comfortable, mostly pullman-type, and the fares are remarkably low. Athens to Thessaloniki in the north is less than 5,300 drs ($41) round trip. Athens to Corinth is less than 920 drs ($7) round trip. The services operate several times a day —for example, 13 departures daily to Missolonghi, eight a day to Pyrgos (for Olympia), six a day to four different towns in Thessaly.

Greek State Railways operates diesel trains to the Peloponnese and the north, and supplements them with pullman coaches into the smaller towns. There are five trains daily to Pyrgos and Patras (1,723 drs, $13, round trip) and to Thessaloniki (2,736 drs, $21, round trip). These are the least expensive ways of getting around in Greece.

SIGHTSEEING TOURS BY COACH

Most of the tour companies in Athens also offer a choice of conducted tours of the hinterlands lasting for anywhere from three to nine days. Check with your hotel concierge for details of tours by CHAT, American Express, and Key Tours, and by Viking's for budget-priced tours. Meantime, here are some samples of the range of tours and typical prices available.

Four-Day Classical Tour: Corinth, Mycenae (lunch), Epidaurus, Nafplion (overnight), Tripolis, Vytina, Olympia (lunch, dinner, overnight), Patras, ferry ride from Aegion to Itea, Delphi (lunch, dinner, overnight), Ossios Lucas. Cost: 36,010 drs ($277), with half board.

Five-Day Archeological Tour: Corinth, Mycenae (lunch), Epidaurus, Nafplion (dinner, overnight), Tripolis, Sparta (lunch), Mystra, Sparta or Tripolis (dinner, overnight), Vytina, Olympia (lunch, dinner, overnight), Patras, ferry ride Aegion to Itea, Delphi (lunch, dinner, overnight), Ossios Lucas. Cost: 44,980 drs ($346), with full board (CHAT only).

Five-Day Classical Tour plus Meteora: Same itinerary as Classical Tour (above) with an additional day spent in Meteora, Kalambaka, Trikala, and Thermopylae. Cost: 49,920 drs ($384), with half board.

Six-Day Northern Greece Tour: Thebes, Arakhova, Delphi (lunch, dinner, overnight), Amphissa, Lamia, Trikala, Kalambaka (dinner, overnight), Meteora, Larissa, Valley of Tempi, Platamon, Thessaloniki (dinner, overnight), Amphipolis, Philippi, Kavala (dinner, overnight), Thassos (lunch), Kavala, Thessaloniki (dinner, overnight), Pella, Larissa (lunch), Thermopylae, Kammena, Vourla. Cost: 56,940 drs ($438), with full board (CHAT only).

Nine-Day Grand Tour of Greece: Corinth, Mycenae (lunch), Epidaurus, Nafplion (dinner, overnight), Tripolis, Sparta (lunch), Mystra, Sparta or Tripolis (dinner, overnight), Olympia (lunch, dinner, overnight), Patras, ferry ride from Aegion to Itea, Delphi (lunch, dinner, overnight), Amphissa, Lamia, Trikala, Kalambaka (dinner, overnight), Meteora, Kalambaka (lunch), Larissa, Valley of Tempi, Platamon, Thessaloniki (dinner, overnight), Amphipolis, Philippi, Kavala (dinner, overnight), Thassos (lunch), Kavala, Thessaloniki (dinner, overnight), Pella, Larissa (lunch), Thermopylae. Cost: 83,980 drs ($646), with full board (CHAT only).

Note: Not all of these tours leave every day of the week, and not all of them operate year round; your travel agent can find the tour and operator that best suit your schedule.

TOURING GREECE BY CAR

In the end, if you have the time, the cash, and the inclination, the best way to tour Greece is by car. The Greek government has been forging ahead with its road-building program, and although there are only limited stretches of expressway, there are now good, comfortable, roads linking all the major tourist areas.

There's an expressway of sorts, National Highway 1, all the way from Athens, along the eastern shores of Attica, through Lamia, Larissa, and Kateria to Thessaloniki—a distance of just over 300 miles. And another from Athens, around the Gulf of Saronica to Corinth, and along the northern shore of the Peloponnese to Patras (where you can catch a ferryboat to Italy). There's also a new extension of the expressway that goes from Corinth south to the city of Epidaurus. These highways are considered expressways in Greece, and you have to pay tolls (trifling amounts) on some stretches, but don't zoom onto them expecting an interstate highway or you'll be disappointed—in addition to which you'll have your timetable thrown for a loop. The stretch of National Hwy. 1 from Athens to Thebes (the turnoff for Delphi) is a four-lane highway, without dividers and with an unmarked shoulder on the right, so that most drivers seem to position themselves halfway between the right lane and the passing lane. Also, the standard of driving in Greece is probably the most immature this side of the Middle East. This doesn't mean that you shouldn't drive in Greece—it's simply a warning to drive with extra care, and not to plan on averaging more than 40 miles an hour.

But you don't need an expressway to enjoy some pleasurable driving. The coastal road from Athens to Sounion, for example, is a well-engineered corniche-type highway with many bends but no tricky corners, and there are some fine, scenic roads in the mountains of Arcadia and around Olympia.

Distances in Greece are manageable, and you can cover a lot of territory even with leisurely driving. Here are three suggestions for car tours from Athens:

1. A three- to five-day tour could include Corinth, Epidaurus, Nafplion, Mycenae, Arcadia, Sparta, Kalamata, Pyrgos, Olympia, Patras (from which you can head across to Italy or return to Athens). How long you spend on that tour will depend on how much time you spend snooping around the ruins, or nipping off to the beach for a dip.

2. A five- to seven-day tour could take you up through Delphi and Amphissa to Missolonghi, Agrinion, and Arta to Ioannina in Epirus, then back via Trikala and Karditsa to Lamia, where you pick up the expressway to Athens. That itinerary gives you a nice mixture of antiquity, resorts, and scenery.

3. Another three- to five-day itinerary would take you along the old scenic road through Boeotia to Delphi and Lamia, then to Karditsa and Trikala, over a stretch of less than first-rate highway to Grevena and Kozana, with a side trip to Naoussa on the way to Thessaloniki, and returning via Alexandria, Katerina, and Larissa, to Lamia and Athens—on expressway all the way back. Again, a mixture of antiquity, scenery, and resorts.

CAR RENTALS

Greece may well be the most expensive country in Europe for both car rentals and gas. It always seems to cost more to rent than you think it will, so the following tips may help.

There are several reliable companies renting cars and you'll have a fairly wide choice of cars—German, French, Italian, and Japanese, from Ford Fiestas and Volkswagens to a luxury Mercedes with air conditioning and automatic transmission. You'll recognize a few old faithfuls among the list of companies, such as Avis and Hertz, both of which have desks at the arrivals hall in the airport, but there are also several local European or Greek organizations. Rates vary considerably; for a Subaru 600, for instance, they fluctuate between 1,950 drs ($15) a day and 2,600 drs ($20) a day, with kilometer charges from 23 to 30 drs (18¢ to 25¢), and for a Mercedes 200 between 11,960 to 18,200 drs ($92 to $140) a day. Check out possible extra charges for air conditioning, too. Your best bet is to pick out a selection of the rate sheets that seem to be stacked in most hotel lobbies, make a few calculations, and then choose the price that comes closest to your budget. My experience is that most of the local companies are reliable.

SOME SAMPLE CAR-RENTAL RATES*

| | Peak season | | Off-Season |
	Per Day	Per kilometer	Unlimited mileage, per week
Subaru 600	2,500 drs	35 drs	46.500 drs
(Category A)	($19)	(27¢)	($357)
Nissan Sunny	4,300 drs	43 drs	60,200 drs
(Category C)	($26)	(33¢)	($463)
Honda Civic Automatic	5,000 drs	52 drs	78,400 drs
(Category D)	($38)	(40¢)	($603)

*These are average rates among reputable rental companies (local and international). The rates are those in effect during 1988 and are therefore likely to increase. Peak season for most companies is July 1 through October 15, or thereabouts. *Note: All rates are subject to a tax of 16%.*

If you are unfamiliar with European cars and wonder which

one to select, several rental brochures include photographs and descriptions of the cars; but in my experience, the Subaru 600 is a reliable workhorse for the type of driving you'll be doing in Greece—it accommodates four people comfortably (provided they don't have too much luggage), and it is light on gas, which can cost as much as 325 drs ($3) a gallon.

Some additional tips: Read through the insurance information included in each brochure; considering the general standard of driving in Greece, it is recommended that you take full insurance coverage. If you pay with cash, you may be able to get a discount of 6% or 10%. When you return the car, stop into a gas station near the rental depot and fill up the tank; otherwise you will pay (a) a higher rate for the gas, and (b) the 16% tax on the cost of gas, since the tax applies to every item on the rental bill—including insurance and gas.

TOP CAR-RENTAL COMPANIES IN ATHENS: The following six car-rental companies are all reliable and easy to locate:

> **Avis,** 48 Amalias Sofias Ave. (tel. 3224-951)
> and several other locations
> **Hertz,** 12 Syngrou Ave. (tel. 9220-102)
> and several other locations
> **Batek,** 43 Syngrou Ave. (tel. 9215-795)
> and several other locations
> **Autorent,** 94 Syngrou Ave. (tel. 9232-514)
> **Kosmos,** 9 Syngrou Ave. (tel. 9234-698)
> **Hellascars-europcar** 7 Stadiou St. (tel. 9235-353)
> and several other locations

DISTANCE BY ROAD FROM ATHENS TO VARIOUS POINTS IN GREECE

The figures below are in kilometers, the measurement used on Greek maps and road signs. A kilometer equals five-eighths of a mile, but the simplest way to translate kilometers into miles is to multiply by 6 and divide by 10. It's not a precise figure, but close enough for most purposes.

From Athens to:	Kilometers
Corinth	84
Ioannina	444
Kalamata	283
Karditsa	302
Katerina	440

From Athens to:	Kilometers
Lamia	215
Larissa	356
Missolonghi	248
Nauplia	145
Naoussa	533
Patras	217
Thessaloniki	539

SOME GENERAL COMMENTS ON DRIVING IN GREECE:

The wearing of seatbelts is now compulsory throughout Greece, for both the driver and front-seat passenger. The police conduct frequent spot checks, and the fine for nonuse is 4,000 drs ($31), payable at the local public treasury office.

When parking in Greek cities, make doubly sure you're not infringing regulations; if you park illegally the police may remove your license plates (rental cars are not exempted), in which case you have to trot off to the police station (in Athens, on Aghiou Constantinou Street, near Omonia Square), to fight your way through layers of bureaucracy to retrieve your own plates and pay a 5,000 drs ($38) fine (remember to take along your parking ticket). If you happen to arrive at your car as the plates are being removed, under no circumstances try to talk your way out of the dilemma with offers of money or you'll be in real trouble. If you park somewhere really dumb and block other traffic, your car will be towed away.

The speed limit in Greece is 100 kmh (62 mph), and you would be well advised to stay well within that limit. Signs are in Greek with phonetic English.

Outside of Athens, the majority of accidents are head-on collisions caused by careless or foolhardy overtaking on bends or on two- and three-lane highways. When it's time for you to pass, always alert the driver in front by signaling, honking your horn, and/or flashing your lights. *Never* rely on the driver to look in his rear-view mirror to see what other cars are doing. On narrow roadways you may drive temporarily on the hard shoulder to allow other cars to pass. Be doubly alert for mammoth coaches and trucks.

Traffic on main roads has priority over traffic on side roads; except that there is also the basic principle of "priority on the right." Most of the time this is not a problem, since most main highways are clearly defined—but never take it for granted. *Always observe traffic on your right with extra caution.*

Never let your tank get too low since gas stations can be few and far between out in the country, and most of them close around 7 p.m. If you do get into a tight spot out in the country, head for the nearest village café, which frequently keeps a can or two in reserve for forgetful locals.

All these dire warnings apart, Greece offers some of the most pleasant and interesting driving in Europe, especially off the beaten track. But take along a reliable map. Your car-rental company will probably offer you a basic map, but it may not be completely up-to-date. The most reliable map is considered to be the one published locally by Efstathiadis.

CHAPTER XIV

THE ISLANDS

□ □ □

And How to Reach Them from Athens

Go down to Piraeus any day of the week and you can take your pick of a score of cruise ships or ferryboats waiting to take you to some offshore Elysium. Or go to the airport and hop on a jet to any of a dozen islands. In some cases, you can fly over and back in the same day. So your vacation in Athens can easily include a day or two on the Greek islands as well. The question is: Which one? That's an impossible question to answer. Start with the numbers.

There are 1,425 Greek islands. Of these, 166 are inhabited, including the privately owned islets such as the Niarchos family's Spetsopoulos and the Onassis family's Skorpios, but only about three dozen are visited regularly by tourists from abroad.

Within that three dozen you have a choice of highly sophisticated, swinging resorts or unspoiled one-taverna-one-guest-house-and-a-handful-of-fishermen islands.

The islands all have a few things in common. Sun. Torrential sun. About 300 days of sunshine a year, and many of the islands are warm enough for sunbathing or swimming in January. They all have their typically Greek villages, with whitewashed houses huddling around narrow alleyways leading to a tiny harbor confettied with the red, blue, and yellow awnings of cafés and tavernas. Many are dotted with remnants of antiquity—temple columns, Byzantine churches, Crusader fortresses—others have little besides secluded coves and beaches, and valleys filled with olives, lemon trees, and vineyards.

Whatever type of island you choose, they're all great places to be . . . day or night.

GETTING YOUR BEARINGS

It's no easy matter charting your way through all these islands, even on paper. Begin by breaking them down into groups.

There are eight groups—from west to east (more or less). They are the Ionians, the Saronics, the Sporades, the Cyclades, the North Aegeans, the Eastern Aegeans, the Dodecanese and Rhodes, and Crete (which is one island, but large enough to be ranked with the groups).

The Saronic Islands are in the Gulf of Saronica, just off Piraeus, and you've already read all about them in the chapter on one-day tours from Athens—Aegina, Poros, Hydra, and Spetsai.

Now here's a brief preview of the others. Very brief, because this is a book about Athens, and the islands really deserve a volume all to themselves, but you'll read about half a dozen island highlights in the next chapter.

THE IONIAN ISLANDS: Greece's seven islands in the Ionian Sea (at the southern end of the Adriatic Sea) are Corfu (or Kerkyra), Paxi, Lefkas, Kefalonia, Ithaca, Zakynthos, and Kythera (or Cerigo). **Ithaca** was the birthplace and kingdom of Odysseus, and **Lefkas** is the closest island to Skorpios.

But the island most visitors flock to is the largest in the group, **Corfu.** It's one of the most beautiful (unlike the Aegean islands, Corfu has lots of greenery), and one of the most interesting (it has been held variously by the French, the Venetians, the British, and the Greeks, and it's only a few miles from Albania). Turn to the next chapter for more details on Corfu.

THE SPORADES AND EVIA (OR EUBOEA): The islands known as the Sporades—Skiathos, Skopelos, Alonissos, and Skyros—lie to the northeast of **Evia** (or **Euboea**), which looks like a peninsula off the eastern shore of central Greece but is, in fact, the second-largest Greek island after Crete. It's joined to the mainland by a swing bridge over the Straits of Euripos, which are famous for an unusual tidal current that zips through in alternate directions roughly every six hours, at speeds that vary from four to six knots, depending on the moon. If you don't see it, you'll hear it.

Skyros is the island where Odysseus discovered Achilles, who had been hidden there, disguised as a girl by his mother to protect him from the ravages of the Trojan War; you can also see the tomb of Rupert Brooke, another of those English poets who died unheroically of fever or blood poisoning in Greece. There's nothing you really must see on these islands—you simply go there to lounge on the beach by day and live it up in the tavernas by night.

All of them are acquiring new hotels and resorts at a rate to match that tidal current. Evia now has six Class A hotels. For more information on Skiathos, turn to the following chapter.

THE CYCLADES (OR KYKLADES) ISLANDS: Next to the Saronics these are the islands closest to Athens, and therefore the most popular and the most developed. Some of their names are probably familiar—Mykonos, Delos, Kea, Serifos, Kimolos, Milos, Paros, Naxos, Kythnos, Sifnos, Ios, Sikinos, Andros, Tinos, Syros, Antiparos, Anafi, Santorini, Amorgos, Pholegendros. They get their collective name from an ancient Greek word meaning "wheeling ones," because they seem to whirl, like one of the islands' famous white windmills, around Delos.

Delos is accessible only by caique, or fishing boat, from Mykonos (unless it's included on a cruise itinerary); it was the birthplace of Apollo, the god of the sun, among other things, and was, therefore, a sacred island. Its most famous features are a line of marble lions, and three temples dedicated to Apollo and his twin sister, Artemis. The island is now uninhabited—and because of a pronouncement from Delphi, no one has been born there or died there since the 6th century B.C.

Kea is the Cyclade closest to the mainland (a mere 13 miles from Cape Sounion), but because tourists have to catch the ferryboat from Lavrion, near Sounion, rather than convenient Piraeus, it's almost totally unspoiled, the way Mykonos was until it was discovered. Unspoiled maybe, but it can offer you fine accommodations in three Class B hotels; otherwise you can enjoy the beaches, the snorkeling, the walks, and the tavernas without being crowded out by tourists, Greek or otherwise.

Tinos was the legendary abode of Poseidon, the god of the sea, but in more recent years it has acquired a reputation as the island of the Virgin Mary, and Greeks come from all over the country on her feast day, August 15 (an interesting day to visit the island, but no time to turn up without a hotel reservation).

Syros was an old shipbuilding center, and is now the home for wealthy shipowners who can't quite afford a Skorpios or Spetsopoulos. **Andros, Naxos,** and **Paros** are all dreamy and idyllic, the way Greek islands are supposed to look, and still relatively undiscovered. **Santorini** (or Thira, for the main village) is, in many ways, the most fascinating of the Cyclades, and you'll read more about it, and Mykonos, in the highlights chapter that follows.

Santorini still has no more than half a dozen hotels, which is about par for most of the Cyclade islands—except Mykonos and

Tinos, which are well endowed with accommodations up to Class A hotels.

THE NORTHERN AEGEAN ISLANDS: These are sometimes called the Thracian Islands because they're way up north off the coast of Thrace: Samothraki, Thassos, and Limnos. **Samothraki** (Samothrace) is a mountainous island (5,000 feet and more) that was the home of the *Winged Victory;* most of the island's hotels are now booked by archeologists who're busy digging up all sorts of fascinating relics from B.C. eras.

Thassos is just off the coast of Macedonia; this is where the Phoenicians got their gold, and where modern Greeks now spend their vacations (it's one of the up-and-coming resort areas). **Limnos** is the island where Hephaestus, goldsmith of the gods, landed when his old man, Zeus, tossed him off Olympus, and where Jason and the Argonauts came searching for the Golden Fleece and found an island populated only by women who had killed all their men. The Argonauts stayed a year. You'll probably want to stick around too. Especially if you're staying in the island's sole deluxe-class hotel—the serene, 125-room **Akti Myrina.** Thassos is well supplied with budget-priced hotels; Samothraki has only a small number of beds for visitors.

THE EASTERN AEGEANS: There are four of them, all tucked in close to the coast of Turkey—Samos, Ikaria, Chios, and Lesvos (sometimes spelled Lesbos, and sometimes called Mytilene after its biggest village). Sappho, the greatest poetess of antiquity, and Aesop, the greatest yarnspinner of antiquity, were both born on **Lesvos;** there are various ruins, galleries, and museums there, but it's really a place to go to lie on the beach and read Sappho and Aesop.

Chios (sometimes spelled Hios) is one of the larger Greek islands, with a population of 60,000, most of them descendants of generations of seafarers. Both **Samos** and **Ikaria** have been bypassed by history—ancient and modern. All four islands have a range of budget-priced hotels.

THE DODECANESE ISLANDS AND RHODES: Rhodes is the largest, and the others include Patmos, Leros, Astypalaea, Karpathos, Kassos, Nisyros, Castellorizo, Kalymnos, Kos, and Symi. **Kos,** the second largest, is the island of Hippocrates, the father of medicine, and you can still see the ruins of his school and the temple to Asclepius. This is another relatively lush island, plump with figs, pomegranates, bananas, mulberries, cherries, oranges, and lemons—and, of course, grapes. **Patmos** is sometimes

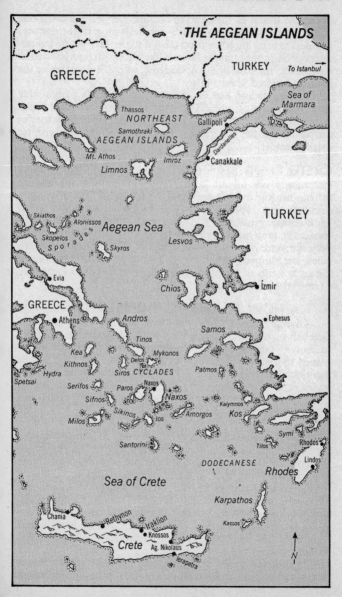

THE AEGEAN ISLANDS

GREECE

TURKEY

To Istanbul →

Sea of Marmara

Thassos
NORTHEAST
Samothraki
AEGEAN ISLANDS

Gallipoli

Mt. Athos

Imroz

Dardanelles

Canakkale

Limnos

TURKEY

Skiathos
Alonissos
Skopelos
Sporades

Aegean Sea

Skyros

Lesvos

Evia

Izmir

GREECE

Athens

Andros

Chios

Ephesus

Samos

Tinos

Kea

Mykonos

Kithnos

Delos

Siros CYCLADES

Patmos

Hydra

Spetsai

Serifos

Paros Naxos

Sifnos

Naxos

Kalymnos

Sikinos

Milos

Ios

Amorgos

Kos

Santorini

Symi

Tilos

Rhodos

DODECANESE

Lindos

Rhodes

Sea of Crete

Karpathos

Chania

Rethymon

Iraklion

Kassos

Knossos

Crete

Ag. Nikolaus

Ierapetra

N

called the Island of the Donkey because every family owns one (there are even some two-donkey families); most of the donkeys are used to carrying tourists up the hill to the 11th-century monastery of St. John, a unique fortress-like place with priceless manuscripts, and the Cave of the Apocalypse, where St. John wrote the divinely inspired Revelations.

Kalymnos and **Kos** are the only other islands with a wide range of accommodations. The others have hotels or rooms in private homes—but only in limited quantities. That's why they're unspoiled. **Rhodes** is featured in the "Islands Highlights" chapter that follows.

CRETE: Crete is the fourth-largest island in the Mediterranean (technically, it's surrounded by its own sea, the Cretan), and it's full of ruins and historic sites from the days of the Minoan civilization right up to World War II. The main town is **Heraklion,** which has interesting museums and churches, but the goal of most visitors is the great palace at **Knossos** to see the royal apartments, drainage system, terraces, and traces of the dreaded Labyrinth where the Minotaur gobbled up its human prey. Knossos is one of the great sights of the Mediterranean, so you'll read more about Crete in the next chapter.

HOW TO GET TO THE ISLANDS

Olympic Airways, its subsidiary Olympic Aviation, and Greek shipping companies operate "bus" services by plane or ferry to many of the islands, and between them they cover most of the islands tourists are likely to visit. However, some of the islands mentioned in the previous pages cannot be reached directly, either by sea or air from Athens, and if you have an urge to visit any of those spots, check out possible transportation with the National Tourist Organization.

BY SEA: In an area of the world where so much history was written by seafarers for so many centuries you'll probably want to sail from the mainland to the islands. That's no problem, as you'll see from the following table. There are plenty of boats, lots of departures, accommodations to suit every budget. An island like Mykonos, for example, is only six or seven hours away by sea, and you can get to the farthest islands, such as Rhodes, within 24 hours. Mykonos and neighboring Cyclades islands, and Rhodes and *its* neighbors, are now linked by regular hydrofoil service.

The ferryboats and ships that carry passengers from Piraeus to the islands vary considerably (some of them have been around for a long time), and it's not possible in these few pages to give you a listing of the best craft—you'll have to get that information from your travel agent, or the National Tourist Organization, or from someone standing in line at the American Express office on Syntagma. Generally speaking, you'll be able to choose between private cabins, shared cabins, bunks, lounges, or deck class (which may be rugged but in some ways is the most fun). Most ferryboats have some kind of snackbar on board, but to be on the safe side take along some kind of simple picnic.

Theoretically, the boats operate on a fixed schedule but since so many indirect factors may affect their performance (weather and cargo, to name two), you should never rely on precise timing. Getting around *between* the islands is strictly for people with time to spare.

There's a more reliable (and more comfortable) way of seeing the islands by boat, and that's by taking one of the dozens of cruise ships on three-day, four-day, or longer voyages, which you'll read about later. But the great advantages of ferryboats and inter-island boats are frequency of schedules and *economy,* as you can see from the chart below.

FERRYBOAT SERVICES FROM PIRAEUS

To	No. of sailings per week	Duration of trip (hours)	One-Way fares (drachmas)* Second	Tourist
Crete				
(Heraklion)	15	12	3,436	2,560
Hios (Chios)	7	10	2,811	2,064
Ios	9	8-10	2,548	2,039
Kos	11	15	4,044	2,686
Mykonos	15	5-7	2,063	1,625
Rhodes	9	12-19½	4,409	3,380
Santorini				
(Thira)	11	12	2,548	2,039

*The Tourist Class fare is for the young and adventurous; you get a chair on the deck if you're lucky, the deck itself if you're not. Most travelers will prefer the comfort of the more expensive class of accommodations—"expensive" in this case being a mere 2,063 drs ($16) for the trip to magical Mykonos; first-class fares vary from vessel to vessel and they are usually 25% to 30% more expensive than second-class fares.

Again, always check details of shipping company, name of vessel, and destination before you leave the ticket office; otherwise you may have to pay again to get to where you really want to go.

BY AIR: Internal air service within Greece is operated by Olympic Airways and a subsidiary, Olympic Aviation S.A., the latter handling those domestic services involving light aircraft. However, all the services are listed together in the Olympic timetable, individual flights use Olympic codes, and all reservations are handled by Olympic Airways offices throughout the world.

On its domestic routes, Olympic Airways flies Boeing 707s, Boeing 720s, and a few Nihon YS-11As; Olympic Aviation now has a versatile fleet of Piper Aztecs, Britten-Norman Islanders, Alouette helicopters for rich Swiss who can't wait to get to their yachts, Skyvan SC-7s, and, latest addition to the fleet, the 30-seat Short SD-3-30. For island-hopping vacationers, the best news is that this augmented fleet offers service within the islands, so that travelers no longer have to double back to Athens to get from one island to the other. Olympic Aviation operates several times a week between Rhodes, Santorini, and Crete; between Rhodes and Kos; between Rhodes and Kabathos; there are also additional services to and from Skiathos, Limnos, Mytilene, and Kastoria, and between Athens and Volos, to name just a few. These new services make life much simpler for travelers with limited time; when it's time to plan your trip, ask your travel agent for the latest details of these and other new domestic services.

FLIGHTS TO THE ISLANDS (SUMMER SCHEDULES)

From Athens to:	No. of flights weekly	Duration of flight	One-way fare in drachmas (dollars)*
Chios (Hios)	23	50 mins.	4,500 (35)
Corfu (Kerkyra)	32	1 hr. 20 mins.	7,700 (59)
Crete (Heraklion)	54	1 hr. 10 mins.	6,600 (51)
Kos	21	1 hr. 10 mins.	6,400 (49)
Limnos	10	1 hr. 5 mins.	4,800 (37)
Lesvos (Mytilene)	35	1 hr. 5 mins.	5,300 (41)
Mykonos	22	55 mins.	5,100 (39)
Rhodes	49	55 mins.	8,500 (65)
Samos	21	1 hr. 5 mins.	5,300 (41)
Skiathos	21	40 mins.	5,100 (39)

*Subject to change (probably 20% higher in summer 1989); check with your travel agent.

CHAPTER XV

ISLAND HIGHLIGHTS

□ □ □

As I mentioned earlier, choosing which island to visit is a ticklish problem. They all have something to offer—antiquity, glamour, beaches, or in some cases, just plain isolation. If you're having trouble making a decision, here are some notes on half a dozen islands.

CORFU

This is the green Greek island. Because of its location in the Ionian Sea, a few miles from the coast of Albania, Corfu has much more foliage than most of the other islands. (It also rains more often here, but that still adds up to only a few showers in winter.)

The main town of Corfu, also called Corfu (or **Kerkyra** to the Greeks), has arcaded streets modeled on the Rue de Rivoli, palazzos in the style of Venice, and cricket fields in the style of Eton—all holdovers from the centuries of conquerors from different parts of Europe.

It's an old town, relatively unchanged through the ages, and to this day its cobbled back alleys, or cantounias, are accessible only to pedestrians. It's a great place for walking and exploring (houses built in the style of Naples or Paris or London, Byzantine churches and fortresses), but once you get beyond the cantounias there's a lot to see on the island.

Corfu has its own patron saint, St. Spyridon, who lies in a richly decorated sarcophagus with his mummified, slippered feet sticking out; four times a year (Palm Sunday, Easter, August 11, and the first Sunday in November) his body is carried through the streets, and anyone who has a favor to ask whispers it to his slippered feet. St. Spyridon is credited with several miracles.

At **Gastori,** a few miles from the town of Corfu, you can see the remains of the Kaiser's Bridge, which crosses the main road and allowed Kaiser Wilhelm to walk from his royal yacht directly to Achilleion Palace; this sumptuous palace, which was built by Empress Elizabeth of Austria in 1890, is now a gambling casino. Mon Repos, a more modest villa built by a British governor in the 19th century, was the birthplace of Prince Philip, duke of Edinburgh.

But in the end, it's the natural beauty of the island that will probably make the most lasting impression on you. A spectacular spiral road will bring you to **Aghios Gordis,** one of the island's most beautiful beaches, surrounded by rugged, almost spooky nature; readers of Henry Miller will know about **Paleokastritsa** even before they reach its beautiful beach—small tavernas where you can select a meal from tanks of live lobsters, the 13th-century fortress of Angelokastio, and the panoramic view from "Bella Vista," a natural balcony overlooking the town and the sea. The island has lots of seafood restaurants, of course, besides the tavernas of Paleokastritsa. One of the most famous is **Giannis,** which hangs over the edge of a cliff, in the aristocratic quarter of the island, Perama, about five miles from the town.

Before you go exploring the island, check out your plans with the tourist office in the new Government Building next door to the post office on Samara Street. They'll give you information on how to get around the island by scheduled bus, or by tourist boats to the various coves along the west coast. You can also rent a car and try to find your own way—no easy matter because the signposting is unreliable or nonexistent, and out in the countryside you won't find too many people who speak English.

HOTELS ON CORFU: When it comes to a place to stay, your only problem will be choosing among several attractive locations and hotels. You can stay in the town itself, or at some of the new hotels and resorts out on the island. In town, the top choices are the deluxe **Corfu Palace,** where the management is Swiss and most of the 106 rooms look out to the sea; swimmers have a choice of the hotel pool or the beach at the Miramare Beach Hotel (12 miles away but linked by free shuttle bus). Summer rates are 14,550 drs ($112) to 19,550 drs ($150) for a double. One of the loveliest hotels in town is the 48-room Class A **Cavalieri,** converted from a 17th-century nobleman's mansion (or what remained of it after it was hit by a bomb in World War II). Rates were unavailable at press time but should be in the 6,000 drs ($46) range, double without meals, in season. The **Corfu Hilton International Hotel** is located in Kanoni a few kilometers south of the town; each of its 274 rooms and bungalows has balcony, well-equipped bathroom, telephone, individual controls for heating and air con-

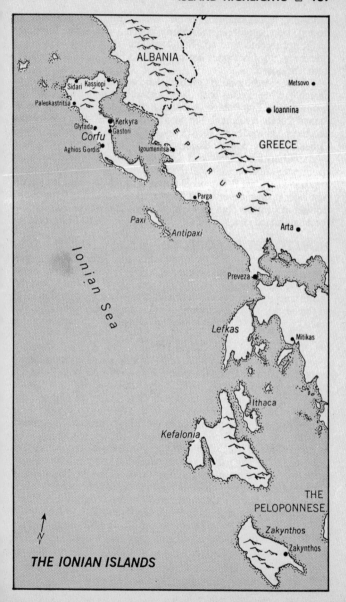

THE IONIAN ISLANDS

ditioning; resort facilities include two swimming pools (one indoors), bowling alleys, two tennis courts (with lights for night play), health club, and an 18-hole golf course a short shuttle-bus ride away. Summer rates are around 17,974 drs ($138) double, with half board.

Other leading hotels on the island are the deluxe **Miramare Beach** (at Moraitike) with 149 beachside bungalows; the 174-room deluxe **Eva Palace** at Dafnila; the 308-room deluxe **Astir Palace Corfu** in Komeno Bay; and the deluxe 260-room **Marbella Beach** at Aghios Ioanis Peristeron, about 12 miles south of town. Other Class A accommodations include a pair of Chandris hotels —the **Chandris Corfu** and **Chandris Dassia,** where summer room rates are around 9,000 drs ($69) double. In addition, there are scores of Class B, C, and D hotels throughout the island, with new ones opening every year. *Room* rates are from 4,600 drs ($35) double in summer, but in most cases you'll be expected to settle for a half-board rate.

HOW TO GET TO CORFU: The quickest way, of course, is by Olympic Airways—half a dozen flights from Athens every day in summer, the first one leaving very early in the morning to give you a full day on the beach. The slowest way is by car or bus across the mountains to Igoumenitsa, where you board a ferry for a short trip to the island. There is also ferryboat service once a week from Patras.

SKIATHOS

Think of a tiny island covered with wild strawberries and pine trees and rimmed with—wait for it—66 beaches. Beautiful beaches, most of them, particularly Koukounaries, a half-mile combination of dazzling sand and clear water, named for the stone pines which separate the sea from a freshwater lagoon. And so that you can enjoy this beach to the fullest, fortune has perched two luxury hotels there—one at each end of the beach. The **Skiathos Palace** has 208 rooms and 15 suites, heated swimming pool, disco, beauty parlor, and sauna. Guest rooms are decorated in white with cinnamon and turquoise highlights, and come equipped with two-channel radio, telephone, refrigerator stocked with everything from ice and beer to cognac and crème de menthe miniatures. It's open all year. Rates are 5,250 drs ($40) to 7,000 drs ($54) for a double, in season. The 32-room, Class B **Xenia** is open only during the summer, when doubles cost 2,400 drs ($18). There are another half a dozen hotels in town, offering double rooms for less than 2,600 drs ($20) for a double in-season, with half board.

Nightlife on Skiathos consists of a couple of clubs, a couple of tavernas with bouzouki, and lots of waterfront cafés where you can watch the fishing boats in the harbor and the brightly colored nets hanging in the trees to dry.

MYKONOS

Everyone has heard of Mykonos—and when you get there, you won't be disappointed—it's everything you've hoped for . . . maybe even more: whitewashed waterfront, disappearing in whitewashed cobblestoned alleys, lined with whitewashed houses and balconies with blue or yellow trim; tiny cobblestoned squares with whitewashed churches. There are no cars in this part of town, just hundreds of spindly tables and chairs, sun umbrellas, little old ladies in long black dresses, and tourists in next to nothing; take a bus and a boat to Paradise Beach (about 78 drs (60¢) or Super Paradise Beach 130 drs ($1) and you'll find yourself among tourists in nothing at all. Or wander around the island and admire its famed windmills (whitewashed, of course), or some of its 300-odd churches and chapels.

Where to stay? When you set foot on the island you'll probably be surrounded by dozens of those little old ladies in black offering rooms in their cottages, most of which are simply furnished but spotlessly clean and inexpensive; if you want to play it safe, go first to the Tourist Police office, right on the harbor, and ask them to recommend some rooms. Otherwise, you have a choice, at least from April through October, of every class of accommodation—including, finally, a luxury hideaway that opened in the summer of 1988. It's called **Santa Marina,** located on a rise above Ornos Bay, a cluster of white-walled villas and a replica windmill housing 22 one- or two-bedroom suites; sports facilities include tennis, a pool, private beach (white pebbles), waterskiing, windsurfing, and a native caïque for fishing. Rates are 22,500 drs ($173) to 27,500 drs ($212), including breakfast. Elsewhere on the island, best buys include three small hotels just outside of town—the Class B **Cavo Tagou** (40 rooms, 15,700 drs—$120—for two with half board); the Class A **Ano Mera** (67 rooms, 14,900 drs—$115—for two with half board); and the Class B **Hotel Petassos** (16 rooms, 6,760 drs—$52—for two with breakfast).

Try to avoid half-board rates if you can, because there are so many delightful little restaurants on the island. Many visitors simply stroll along the waterfront or among the alleyways until their eyes (or noses) find something appealing. However, if you're there in the busy season, you might want to stop off and make reservations at the pricey **Philippi Edem** or **Chez Katrin,** or the more modest **Skarpa** or **Alefkandra.**

Some of Greece's finest jewelry (**Galatis** and **Lalaounis**) and fashion shops have places on Mykonos, but two of the most popular events for insiders are visits to the hand-weaving workshops of **Vienoula** in Three Wells and **Panos** on Adronikou-Matoyanni.

HOW TO GET TO MYKONOS: Two or three flights daily in summer (45 minutes flying time), or 15 crossings a week by boat from Piraeus (six to seven hours).

SANTORINI

Alias Thira (for the main town). Alias, perhaps, Atlantis. No island in the Mediterranean offers a more dramatic landfall than this one: you sail into what remains of the crater of the volcano created when, as you read back in the chapter on museums, "Enkeladus in the bowels of the Earth was roused with undescribable fury," past a flat island of brown-black lava to the towering cliffs of Santorini itself, topped by the gleaming, whitewashed churches and homes of the village. Most visitors to Santorini probably arrive (at least the first time around) aboard a cruise ship, in which case they sail into the very crater of the volcano, a setting of black lava islets crowned with white villages, like icing on a Christmas cake. When you go ashore by tender, you still haven't arrived, because you still have to surmount that almost vertical 600-foot cliff. There's a zigzag path to the top and an army of 100-odd donkeys to cart you up its slippery steps, and until recently that was the only way to get up (except for some foolhardy people like myself who *walked*, a hike of about half-an-hour). Now, however, there's an efficient Swiss-built funicular that gets you to the top in a few wobbly minutes for a fee of 300 drs ($2). It's an awesome ride. And once you get to the top, it's an awesome sight.

Scientists speculate that Santorini/Thira was destroyed by a gigantic earthquake, volcanic explosion, *and* tidal wave, which left only the tips of the volcanic cone behind. That became Santorini and its satellite islands. The tidal wave, according to some estimates, may have been as high as 600 feet, which would make it the largest natural convulsion in the recorded history of mankind; some scientists and archeologists speculate that this same convulsion wiped out the civilization of Knossos on Crete, caused the parting of the Red Sea (the same one recorded in the Bible), and sent that giant wave all the way to the Sahara where it gathered up some desert sands before sweeping all the way back to deposit the sands on Crete. (If this seems far-fetched, compare it with history's most recent counterpart, the eruption of Java's Krakatoa in 1883, when so much red-hot pumice was forced into the air that skies turned red in *North America* . . . so red that fire departments in

Poughkeepsie, New York, and New Haven, Connecticut, were called out twice because people thought those towns were on fire, and a Dutch ocean-going freighter was carried off by the tidal wave and dumped intact in the jungle *two miles away*.) Anyway, it's romantic to speculate that somewhere far beneath this gleaming, white clifftop village there may rest the lost continent of Atlantis.

As it happens, **Atlantis** is the name of Thira's most prominent hotel, though not best despite its Category A classification. Two unusual small inns opened here in recent years and they're worth checking into, both located part way down the precipitous hill, with stunning views across the caldera: the **Hotel Porto Fira** (note the alternate spelling of Thira) with 20 rooms, each with private bathroom/shower and refrigerator, eight of them fashioned from the traditional arched rock homes (10,000 drs to 12,000 drs for two, $77 to $92, including breakfast); and the five-year-old **Hotel Villa Renos** with six rooms, again with private bathroom/shower and refrigerator (7,090 drs, or $55, including breakfast).

Elsewhere on the island, visitors can check into hotels or villas beside the beach (black-sand Kamari Beach is the most popular) or in restored "habitats" in some of the hillside villages.

If you come to Santorini on one of the cruise ships, you won't be able to see much more than the whitewashed village at the edge of the crater—which for most people may be experience enough for one day, since it *is* such an extraordinary place. Visitors who stay for a few days may want to explore some of the quiet coves and beaches on the opposite side of the island, linger in the tavernas (Franco's Bar, for example) drinking the local wines, or explore the site of Ancient Thira—the agora, theater, temples, and shrines. On July 20, the feast day of the Prophet Elijah, the islanders celebrate at the monastery of the same name, and the evening is given over to the local dances—the syrtos and the repati. Join them. You'll soon learn the syrtos and repati. In September, there is a modest festival of classical music.

HOW TO GET TO SANTORINI: There are daily flights (55 minutes) on Olympic from Athens, one or two a week from Rhodes or Crete, but really the only way to arrive in Santorini is by boat—either ferryboat (once a day from Piraeus) or cruise ship.

CRETE

Zorba's island is the largest of the Greek islands, with half a million people. Its 3,000 square miles are mostly mountains, which rise to 7,500 feet at their highest peak. Crete lies equidistant from Europe, Asia, and Africa (which is only 200 miles to the south), another of those islands with a mishmash history—except that this one goes back farther than the others. As Cretans will constantly remind you, the *first* civilization in Europe was on Crete—the legendary Minoan kingdom with its bull-oriented culture that flourished here 3,000 years before the birth of Christ.

All that remains of this culture are the ruins of the **Palace of Knossos,** one of the outstanding archeological sites of Europe—what was once a five-story structure (4,000 years ago!), with private bathrooms and flushing toilets (4,000 years ago!). The most striking remnant of the civilization is the modest throne of the king, which still stands against the wall of the throne room after all these centuries, and which Cretans claim is the oldest throne in existence. The palace is only 20 minutes by bus from the town of Heraklion (where you'll probably arrive, whether you come by air or sea), but before you dash over to check out the ruins and the labyrinths, pay a visit to the downtown **Archeological Museum** first, because after you've inspected its exhibits (frescoes, artifacts, and models visualizing the original palace) you'll appreciate the ruins even more. The Palace of Knossos is open weekdays from 8 a.m. to 5 p.m., and on Sunday and holidays from 9 a.m. to 5 p.m. later in the summer; admission is 500 drs ($4). The museum is open from 8 a.m. to 5 p.m. daily (except Monday, to 11 a.m.), on Sunday and holidays from 9 a.m. to 5 p.m. (also has extended summer hours); admission is 500 drs ($4), which includes entry fees to other archeological sites (including the Palace of Knossos). Sightseeing tours to the museum and palace, with English-speaking guides, cost about 850 drs ($6), including admissions.

There are several other Minoan sites on Crete, most notably the secondary palace of **Phaestos;** otherwise the things to see are the natural beauties of the island, wild headlands and rugged mountains, valleys filled with olive trees and cypresses, a plain filled with windmills, and the whitewashed villages. Crete is the island of El Greco, who was born Domenico Theotokopoulos in the village of Fodele, before heading off for Italy, Spain, and immortality. Its second most famous son is Nikos Kazantizakis, who wrote many distinguished novels before one of them, *Zorba the Greek,* was made into a movie earning him international fame.

WHERE TO STAY: If you're coming to Crete mainly to tramp around Knossos and wallow in the Minoan civilization, you'll probably want to stay in Heraklion (where you'll have a choice of several modern Class A and B hotels) or in one of the Class A resorts nearby: the 250-room **Apollonion** and 399-room **Akti Zeus** about four miles from town, or the 490-room full-scale **Capsis Beach Resort** on a peninsula 15 miles from town. Double rates, half board, at these Class A resorts range from 8,000 ($62) to 16,700 drs ($128).

But if your Cretan quest is sea and sand and sun with occasional diversions into the world of culture and history, you may want to make your base one of the island's resorts, mostly along the northern coast, from Chania in the west to Aghios Nikolaos in the east. A few miles west of Heraklion at Rethimno (also spelled Rethymnon and Rithymna), the top choices are the 307-room **El Greco** and the mammoth (556 rooms and bungalows) **Rithymna Beach**—both Class A, with peak-season rates in 1988 of 9,434 drs ($73) to 13,632 drs ($105) for two.

The island's deluxe resorts are clustered around Aghios Nikolaos and Elounda Beach in the east. At Aghios Nikolaos, a small fishing town built around the harbor and a small lake, the largest of the deluxe resorts are the 140-room **Minos Palace** and the 130-room **Mirabella Village;** the smallest are the 108-room **Minos Beach** and the 89-room **Istron Beach**. At Elounda, about ten miles along the coast, the **Elounda Mare,** which has only 81 rooms and bungalows, is the only hotel in Greece that is part of the Relais-Châteaux group; both the **Astir Palace Elounda** and the **Elounda Beach** have 300 rooms and bungalows each. Peak-season rates for these deluxe hotels are in the 15,347-dr ($118) to 16,250-dr ($125) range—but you can enjoy the same comfort and amenities for almost half that price in early spring or late fall, when the climate is still balmy.

HOW TO GET TO CRETE: Olympic Airways has seven or eight flights every day during the summer months between Athens and Iraklion (mostly Boeing 737s; flight time is 50 minutes and the fare is around 13,260 drs ($102) round trip); seafarers have a choice of two boats daily from Piraeus.

RHODES

If you go to Rhodes by sea, so much the better, because that way you can more readily capture the flavor of this, one of the great crossroads of history. You sail into another dramatic harbor, past the 15th-century fortress/lighthouse of St. Nicholas, past three small stone windmills guarding the old harbor, almost right up to the turreted walls of the old city, which at this point is virtually concealed behind its battlements, except for its minarets and the magnificent **Palace of the Grand Masters.** The Grand Masters, that is, of the Knights of St. John, who built these fortifications so thoroughly that they were able to rule the island, behind those walls, for two centuries.

Rhodes is half a dozen Mediterraneans rolled into one—Saracen, Crusader, Turkish, Venetian, Ancient Greek, Modern European. It's the largest of the Dodecanese, and its recorded history goes back all the way to the 11th century B.C. It has one of the most pleasant climates in Europe, with warm days ten months of the year, which makes it a favorite winter resort for Europeans living in northern climes. Fortunately, it's a simple matter to enjoy both the historic and the resort side of the island. The old city of Rhodes is a delightful experience (alleys and courtyards, bazaars, tavernas, fountains, squares, wrought-iron balconies, ornate doorways, mosques, churches, mansions), with a couple of interesting museums, but it won't take you long to complete your tour. The only other major sight on the island (but some sight) is **Lindos**—a circular harbor and a whitewashed village, topped by a Crusader fortress and an even more ancient acropolis which is today not much more than a few toppled columns and some well-trodden steps. You get to the acropolis either by donkey along a special path, or on foot (the best way) up through cobbled streets not much wider than your shoulders, and lined with a phalanx of handcraft and souvenir shops. It's quite a hike, but the view from the top is breathtaking—the town and the harbor on one side, an even tinier harbor on the other, with a pair of fishing boats and a toy-size chapel marking the spot where St. Paul came ashore to preach to the Rhodians.

WHERE TO STAY: In old Lindos, the only accommodations are rooms in private homes, but down by the beach and lagoon there are two attractive small hotels, both Class A: the **Lindos Bay** and the **Steps of Lindos,** both in the 12,000-dr ($92) to 16,000-dr ($123) range for two with half board.

The three main clusters of hotels are to be found in and around the city of Rhodes itself and in two beachside resorts a few miles out of town—Ixia on the west coast, Faliraki on the east coast (where the best beaches are). The best hotel on the island is now the deluxe **Rodos Palace** in Ixia—a self-contained resort on 30 acres, complete with 610 guest accommodations (rooms, studios, apartments, bungalows), three swimming pools (including one larger than Olympic size beneath a soaring geodesic dome), lighted tennis courts, mini-golf, watersports, four restaurants, four bars, a disco, and a shopping arcade. Peak season rates are 7,024 drs ($54) to 10,698 drs ($82), room only.

Elsewhere along Ialisson Avenue, the beachfront promenade of Ixia, there are dozens of A and B category hotels; but for the best beaches, the place to go is Faliraki, where you have a choice of a dozen category A hotels, priced from about 7,800 drs ($60) to

9,750 drs ($75) double. On the outskirts of Rhodes city, the **Grand Hotel Astir Palace** is a popular year-round resort mainly because of its casino (rates are 18,000 drs, or $138, half board for two).

HOW TO GET TO RHODES: Six flights every day from Athens in summer (60 minutes each way, about 6,890 drs, or $53, round trip); five companies operate regular sea service to the island all year round (trips take 20 hours nonstop, up to 28 hours with intermediate stops).

CHAPTER XVI

CRUISES THROUGH THE GREEK ISLANDS

□ □ □

In the previous two chapters you learned about the various Greek islands and how to get to them by scheduled ferryboat and plane, but there are two other ways of seeing these gleaming sunny islands . . . on island cruises by cruise ship or charter yacht. You board a luxury cruise ship in Piraeus and set off for a few days of relaxed island-hopping—without having to pack and unpack more than once, without having to dash out to airports to catch flights. These island cruises are a happy combination of touring and vacationing—you have a chance to see the sights, but you also get to lounge around the pool or sunbathe on the deck between ports of call.

Usually the longer stretches between islands are covered during the night, when you can't really do much sightseeing anyway, and the time you do have to spend on shore varies, depending on all sorts of factors—time of departure from Piraeus, availability of berths on tenders, arrangement of itinerary. Some stops you'll find too short—obviously on a three-day cruise, for example, you can't include everything. However, a stop on Crete will always allow you time at least to visit the Minoan ruins at Knossos, and in Rhodes you'll be able to visit the old walled city and its museums, and you'll probably have time also to take the four-hour coach tour to Lindos.

Here are some sample cruise itineraries:

3-Day Cruise

Friday	Piraeus		dep. noon
	Mykonos	arr. 7 p.m.	dep. 10 p.m.
Saturday	Rhodes	arr. 10:30 a.m.	dep. 6:30 p.m.
Sunday	Crete	arr. 8 a.m.	dep. noon
	Santorini	arr. 5 p.m.	dep. 8 p.m.
Monday	Piraeus	arr. 7 a.m.	

4-Day Cruise

Monday	Piraeus		dep. noon
	Mykonos	arr. 7 p.m.	dep. 11 p.m.
Tuesday	Patmos	arr. 7 a.m.	dep. 10:30 a.m.
	Ephesus	arr. 3 p.m.	dep. 8 p.m.
Wednesday	Rhodes	arr. 8 a.m.	dep. 6:30 p.m.
Thursday	Crete	arr. 8 a.m.	dep. noon
	Santorini	arr. 5 p.m.	dep. 8 p.m.
Friday	Piraeus	arr. 7 a.m.	

7-Day Cruise

Wednesday	Piraeus		dep. 6 p.m.
Thursday	Crete	arr. 8 a.m.	dep. noon
	Santorini	arr. 5 p.m.	dep. 8 p.m.
Friday	Rhodes	arr. 7 a.m.	dep. 9 p.m.
Saturday	Ephesus	arr. 7 a.m.	dep. noon
Sunday	Istanbul	arr. 2 p.m.	(overnight)
Monday	Istanbul		dep. noon
Tuesday	Delos	arr. 10 a.m.	dep. 1:30 p.m.
	Mykonos	arr. 3 p.m.	dep. 11 p.m.
Wednesday	Piraeus	arr. 7 a.m.	

Other seven-day itineraries include Santorini, Crete, Rhodes, Kos, Patmos, Samos, Kusadasi, Mount Athos, Chalkidiki, Delos, Mykonos; and Istanbul, Izmir, Ephesus, Delos, Mykonos, Rhodes, Crete, and Santorini. Some lines also feature regular cruises to the northern islands—Skiathos, Skopelos—and Thessaloniki. The cruise season is from early April through November.

THE CRUISE SHIPS

There are half a dozen shipping companies operating cruises through the Greek islands on a regular basis, and one in six visitors to Greece takes a cruise—or, put another way, a total of more than a dozen ships transport a million passengers every year. The leading cruise lines with dependable track records are Sun, Epirotiki, Hellenic Mediterranean, "K," and Chandris. In addition, you can also board other cruise ships making stops in Piraeus on longer voyages through the eastern or western Mediterranean—ships like the *Orient Express* (operating regular service between Venice and Istanbul), one of the superluxurious *Sea Goddess* liner / yachts (from the French or Italian Riviera), or even superliners like the *QE2* or *Vistafjord* of Cunard Lines.

A recent arrival in these waters is the *Betsy Ross,* of American Star Lines, a 10,000-tonner offering "Great American lifestyle cruises in the Greek Isles."

Many of the cruise ships operating short cruises through the Greek islands, such as the five-star *Stella Solaris,* the *Atlas,* and the *Azur,* are full-scale ocean liners; all of them are equipped with the full range of facilities you would expect to find in a resort hotel—swimming pool, air conditioning, nightclub, disco, bars, mini-casinos, beauty salon—everything except a beach (and even there they invariably put you ashore near one). Most of their cabins are equipped with wall-to-wall carpeting, private toilet and shower (in larger cabins, full bathtub), telephone, two-channel radio. Stewards, cruise directors, tour guides, and most other members of the crew who come in contact with passengers speak fluent English.

Some of these island cruisers may already be familiar from their winter assignments in the Caribbean. The Sun Lines' *Stella Solaris* and *Stella Oceanis,* for example, may spend the months from December through March plowing through the Caribbean or the seas off South America, but come spring they head east to their homeland. There they set sail each week on cruises lasting three, four, or seven days, combining seagoing fun (deck buffets, bingo, dancing, floor shows, movies, fine dining) with enlightening visits to historic sites such as the Minoans' Palace of Knossos in Crete, ancient Lindos in Rhodes, the spectacular ruins of Ephesus in Turkey, as well as island playgrounds like Mykonos and Hydra. Without the bother of unpacking and repacking every day, without having to stand in line for check-ins and boarding passes, these cruises offer a variety of sights and experiences in a carefree, congenial way. Even when you visit additional *countries,* as you do on, say, the *Stella Solaris*'s cruises to Egypt, Israel, Russia, and Turkey, you never have to worry about passports and immigration—the crew takes care of all that.

WHAT IT WILL COST: Rates vary enormously, of course, depending on the duration of the cruise, the size and facilities of the ship, the type of cabin accommodations. An average cost runs something like $125 to $150 per day per person. Your travel agent will be able to show you deck plans when you get around to choosing a specific cruise and a specific ship, at the same time giving you up-to-date details of the fares. Meantime, here are some guidelines.

Fares per person for a three-day cruise:
   with three or four passengers in a cabin, from $450
   with two in stateroom with private shower, from $600
Fares for a seven-day cruise:
   with three or four in a cabin, from $1,250
   with two in a stateroom with private shower, from $1,250

On a deluxe ship like the Sun Lines' *Stella Solaris*, of course, rates are higher—seven-day cruises cost from $1,230 per person to $2,540 per person for deluxe suites. The *average* prices on four-day cruises are around $880 per person, or roughly $220 a day for all meals, accommodations, and transportation. On a seven-day cruise, the average rates work out at as little as $270 a day for meals, accommodations, and transportation.

When deciding how much you ought to pay, keep these points in mind: you spend most of your time on deck or ashore, so the size and luxury of your cabin is of secondary importance; most of these ships are modern and air-conditioned so you don't have to be on an upper deck, and you don't need an outside cabin (in most cases, you can't open the portholes anyway because of the air conditioning); even the least expensive accommodations have private shower and toilet. So don't think that you can't afford to take one of these cruises unless you can afford the most expensive cabins. In fact, in some cases cabins on lower decks are a better value than cabins on the top deck because that part of the ship is wider and the cabins have more space—but they may cost $30 or $40 less.

Remember also that these fares include all your meals for three or four days—a total of 15 meals, for example, on a three-day cruise. The food is usually international fare, with a touch of Greek at most meals; at least one poolside buffet; and usually one Greek evening when the entire meal is Greek and the crew entertains you with folk music and dancing.

Think about it. A cruise is a great way to see several islands on a short vacation. It's a great way to get some sun. The sea is usually calm—*usually*. You see the sights. You make new friends.

You eat heartily. Chances are, you'll probably find the three-day cruise too short and wish you had opted for four days, at least.

Shore excursions are extra but if keeping costs down is a prime consideration, check the prices: you may be able to arrange a better deal with a local taxi driver or tour operator, but, of course, you may lose valuable time ashore if you have to negotiate a trip or find someone who can take you.

The other extra on cruises is tipping—another $6 to $8 per day per person. The crew usually has a system for reminding passengers about tips, suggesting appropriate figures and collecting the currency—but tipping is, of course, optional.

SEVEN-DAY YACHT CRUISE: There's another way to cruise the Greek islands, more in the spirit of the Argonauts but with much less effort—on one of the trips put together by **Viking Tours.** These cruises are on "private yachts" rather than cruise ships: the classic 118-foot, 36-passenger motor yacht *Viking Star.* On the former, accommodations are all in two-berth cabins—on the latter, in two- or four-berth cabins—all with private toilet/shower. There's ample deck space for sunning and lounging, and each vessel carries facilities for water sports; breakfast and lunch are served on board, dinner ashore (the multilingual, cosmopolitan, and in some cases, highly cultivated tour guides will make recommendations, if asked). Because of the limited number of passengers on each cruise, the atmosphere tends to be more congenial, more casual than on larger ships—almost like being, indeed, a select guest (often lawyers, teachers, brokers) on a private yacht. Seven-day itineraries usually include Serifos, Ios, Santorini, Paros, Naxos, Delos, Mykonos, and Tinos, returning to Athens (or, if you reverse the itinerary, beginning the trip) by scheduled ferryboat. Rates range from $795 to $945 per person on the *Viking Star,* including breakfast, lunch with wine, taxes, port charges, and passage between Piraeus/Tinos. For information, contact Viking Travel, 3 Filellinon St., Athens; 6 Turkey Hill Rd. S. Westport, CT 06880.

CRUISING BY CHARTER YACHT

You've seen it so many times in movies—jet-setters taking their ease, bronze bodies in skimpy bikinis, stewards in white, fetching drinks and serving sumptuous dinners by candlelight on the after deck. Maybe this is everyone's dream way of seeing the Greek islands, but for some people it's actually being lived every summer somewhere in the Aegean and Ionian Seas. (And not just by jet-setters either!)

In some ways this *is* the perfect way to see the islands. You set your own pace. You join the crowds or avoid them. You float past headlands with ancient temples, moor beside ancient monasteries, go ashore to mingle with the crowds, then escape when you feel like it. No packing and unpacking, no standing in line waiting for luggage or waiting to board. More and more vacationers are discovering the advantages of cruising by charter yacht, yet there's no feeling of crowded anchorages (how could there be, with 2,000 islands to chose from); the sailing is easy too, with islands rarely more than two or three hours apart. And these days there's a wider choice of charter yachts than ever—everything from 25-foot sailboats without crew ("bare boat") to 200-foot luxury yachts with a crew of 20. You can charter yachts that once belonged to Mussolini or Prince Rainier—even, for $10,000 a day, the floating palace that appeared in the movie *The Greek Tycoon*. But don't get the idea that charter yachts are the special privilege of the rich—that 25-foot sailboat, sleeping six, is yours for around $160 a day, or less than $30 a head for accommodations *and* transportation.

Between those two extremes, there are charter boats for every taste and budget—with or without private facilities, with or without air conditioning, with or without wall-to-wall carpeting and wall-to-wall stereo. Charter boats all have certain things in common: by law they must carry adequate navigational and radio telephone equipment; they must be drydocked once a year and inspected by representatives of the Ministry of Merchant Marine; with the exception of boats based in Rhodes, they must be Greek registered and carry a Greek skipper; and their skippers must qualify for a Merchant Mariner's license.

I've checked out a selection of the charter yachts based at Zea Marina, and without exception they were in first-class condition, the crews obviously took a pride in them, and there seemed to be little reason to suspect any language problem under normal circumstances. Nevertheless misunderstandings could arise, as they could even with an English-speaking crew, and the charterers should determine in advance exactly the kind of trip they anticipate—whether or not they want to do a lot of sailing or whether they'd prefer to motor from island to island; whether or not they want to go ashore for dinner or dine aboard; whether or not they want to spend evenings in harbors and marinas or in some secluded cove; whether or not they want to do a lot of sightseeing ashore, which will affect the way the skipper plans the itinerary, and so forth. Above all, the charterers should know clearly in advance exactly what size of boat they need, what kind of facilities they expect (such as a dinghy for waterskiing, and how much extra that will cost). The people to give you this information are yacht brokers specializing in charters: several of the leading brokers in the U.S. handle bookings for the Greek islands, and many of them (such as Sparkman and Stevens or World Yacht Enterprises in New York, and Nicholsons in Cambridge, Massachusetts) have personal experience of individual yachts.

In Greece, charters are handled by some 40 brokers, most of whom are members of the Hellenic Professional Yachting Association (at 64 Akti Themistokleous, Piraeus) which will send you a list of members. In the meantime, you might want to consider three typical organizations and some of the services they offer. The largest of these brokers (and indeed the largest owner and operator of charter yachts in Europe) is a company called **Valef Yachts** at 22 Akti Themistokleous in Piraeus. Their office is right at the marina in Zea Marina, and the rates of their 200-odd boats range from $160 a day to $7,500 a day, from 25 feet to 188 feet overall. Bill Lefakinis, the owner, is a Greek-American applying Yankee ideas of marketing to the sometimes confusing business of chartering. He has a distinguished roster of clients, 80% of whom are Americans, and he now has an office in the U.S. to spread the gospel stateside—at 7254 Fir Rd., Ambler, PA 19002 (tel. 215/641-1624)—and to answer any questions you may have about what boats are available and how much they cost.

Another major broker is **Hellenic Marine Consultants** (tel. 9593-712), which specializes in charters in the eastern Mediterranean as well as out of Zea Marina. Their yachts, from $200 a day bare boat to $10,000 a-day with crew (but mostly in the $3,500- to $4,500-a-day category), are popular with experienced charters who want to get off the beaten track and sail out of Rhodes to explore places like Izmir and Kusadasi on the Turkish coast.

Both of these companies list a selection of bare boats, but their main business is crewed vessels: a company that specializes in bare boats is **SeaHorse** (tel. 8952-212), which was founded 20 years ago by two Dutch brothers called van Seggelen. Their roster of 100 yachts ranges from a 32-foot Beneteau at $230 a day to a 76-foot Swan for around $2,000 a day. They're really interested in chartering to serious sailors (who must prove their ability before they hoist sail), but they can also arrange to have a skipper aboard for $80 a day, and a cook for $50 a day. Unlike most brokers, SeaHorse offers discounts in the off-season.

Please note that all these rates are subject to change. Food, liquor, and fuel are extra, and there's an additional tax of 2½%. Even so, a charter yacht can be a relatively inexpensive way for four, six, or eight people (even more, since many yachts are chartered to corporations for seminars), when you consider how much it would cost to fly four, six, or eight people around the islands, to say nothing of their hotel bills.

How much can you see, how far can you travel? That depends on all sorts of factors, of course, not the least being the wind, but a couple of sample itineraries, based on average cruising times by sail or power, will give you some idea of the opportunities. On a five-to six-day odyssey (in most cases seven days is the minimum rental, but you may not be able, or want, to travel each of the seven days) you could cruise from Piraeus to Hydra, Monemvassia, Spetsai, Poros, or Aegina and back to Piraeus, a total of 185 to 190 miles. In seven days you could cover almost 300 miles, visiting Mykonos, Naxos, Ios, Santorini, Sifnos, and Kythnos, depending on how long you plan to stay in each.

The National Tourist Organization of Greece publishes a useful 54-page booklet called "Greece for the Yachtsman" which lists and describes a range of itineraries; copies may be available from the NTOG in New York: 645 Fifth Ave., New York, NY 10022 (tel. 212/421-5777).

When is the best time to go? The most popular time is June, July, and August, when it may be blisteringly hot ashore but pleasantly cool among the sea breezes. Many Greek yachtsmen consider September the best month for cruising; May, June, and possibly October are good for *sailing,* if you don't want to do much sunbathing or waterskiing. The remainder of the year is really for enthusiasts.

CAPSULE VOCABULARY —AND CALENDAR OF EVENTS

□ □ □

Learn a few basic words and phrases in Greek before you go (you could memorize the following list, for example, on the flight over.) You'll be amazed how much difference this will make to your reception in shops, restaurants, and hotels. Greeks *really* appreciate it when foreigners make an effort to speak a few words of their language. When you go into a shop, for example, say *"kah-lee-MEH-ra"*—good day (you can use it any time up to, say, 4 o'clock). Good evening is *"kah-lee-SPEH-ra."* When you are introduced to someone, say *"HEE-ro po-LEE,"* and at the end of that first meeting you say *"HAH-ree-kah,"* which means "pleased to have met you." Greeks are much more formal about such basic courtesies, as you can see.

Because the Greek alphabet is different from our own, I am including in this guide a phonetic vocabulary of useful expressions to assist you in your everyday dealings.

To aid your **pronunciation,** I have written the *accented syllable in capital letters,* the rest of the word in lowercase. As a general rule, in modern Greek the *accent* of the word is *on the middle or last syllable,* unlike English, where you usually find the accent on the first syllable of a word. This simple difference in pronunciation often determines whether or not you will be understood. Don't worry too much, though. So many people in Athens learn English in school that you may find you need this handy vocabulary only for courtesy or fun.

EVERYDAY EXPRESSIONS

Good morning
   kah-lee-MEH-ra
Good evening
   kah-lee-SPEH-ra
Hello or good-bye (informal)
   YAH-sahs!
Hello or good-bye (formal)
   HEH-re-te
What is your name?
   POSS-ssas LEH-neh?
**I have enjoyed myself very
  much** HAH-ree-kah
   po-LEE
Yes neh
No O-nee
Excuse me sig-NO-mee
Does anyone speak English?
   mi-LEYE kan-EES
   on-glee-KAH?
Thank you (very much)
   eh-hah-ree-STOH
   (PAH-rah-po-lee)
Please pah-rah-kah-LO
You're welcome
   pah-rah-kah-LO
Good health! (Cheers!)
   stee-nee-YAH-sou (singular)
   stee-nee-YAH-sass (plural)
   stee-nee-YAH-mas (us)
I don't understand
   THEN-kah-tah-lah-VEH-no

Please repeat it
   PEH-steh-toh PAH-lee,
   pah-rah-kah-LO
What time is it?
   TEE O-rah EE-neh?
How much is it
   PO-so-EH-ee? PO-so
   KAH-nee?
It's all right en-DAX-ee
It's not all right THEN
   EE-nai en-DAX-ee
I'm sorry li-PAH-mai
Men's room AN-thron
Ladies' room yee-NAI-kon
What? TEE?
Why? yah-TEE?
When? POH-teh?
How? POHSS?
How far? POH-soh
   mah-kree AH?
How long? POH-soh
   ke-ROH?
Good kah-LOH
Can you tell me
   boh-REE-teh nah-
   moo-PEE-tah?
I am lost EH-khah-sah
   tah-THROH-moh
I am sorry lee-POO-mee

TRAVEL EXPRESSIONS

I want to go to the airport.
   THEH-loh na PAH-oh stoh
   ah-eh-roh-THROH-mee-oh

**Am I going in the right
direction for . . . ?**
   pee-yeh-no kah-
   LAH YAH . . . ?

Please call a taxi for me.
  sass pah-rah-kah-LO
  fo-NAXT-eh EH-na
  ahf-toh-KEE-nee toh
Show me on the map.
  THEEK-steh-moo stoh
  KHAR-tee

**Please tell me where to get
off.** pah-rah-kah-LO
  PEH-steh-moo poo na
  VGOH

SHOPPING

I'm just looking.
  ah-PLOSS kee-TAH-zo
May I try this one?
  boh-ROH na toh
  thoh-kee-MAH-so?
It doesn't fit me
  then moo YEE-neh-teh
Will this fade (shrink)?
  thah kseh-VAH-psee
  (mah-ZET-see)?

**Will you please wrap
this?** moo toh
  tee-LEE-yeh-teh
  pah-rah-kah-LO
Where do I pay? POO
  thah-plee-ROH-soh?
**My (mailing) address
is . . .** ee (tah-khee-throh-
  mee-KEE) thee-EF-theen-
  see-moo EE-neh' . . .

TELEPHONE

Where can I telephone?
  POO boh-ROH
  nah-tee-lee-fo-NEE-so?
Will you telephone for me?
  tee-lee-fo-NEE-teh ya
  MEH-nah?
**Give me the long-distance
operator.** THOH-steh-
  moh tohn
  tee-lee-fo-nee-TEE
  mah-KRASS ah-poh
  STAH-seh-oss

Hello ehm-BROHSS
May I speak to . . .
  boh-ROH nah-mee-LEE-
  stoh . . .
Please speak more slowly
  pah-rah-kah-LO mee-
  LAH-teh PYOH ar-
  GHAH

CALENDAR OF EVENTS

The following is only a sample of the hundreds of special events—
folkloric, religious, festive, cultural—that take place throughout
the year all over Greece. For a complete list, contact the National
Tourist Organization of Greece.

JANUARY: Feast of St. Basil—a general celebration with traditional New Year's cake and national costumes (1st).

Epiphany—the "Blessing of the Waters" ceremony throughout Greece. The most spectacular spot to visit is Piraeus (6th).

FEBRUARY: In mid-February it's carnival time throughout Greece.

MARCH: Greek National Holiday, honoring the War of Independence, with military parades throughout the country (25th).

APRIL: Sound-and-Light performances in Athens, Corfu, and Rhodes (through October).

Anniversaries dedicated to St. Spyridon, patron saint of Corfu (mid-month).

Easter Sunday in the Greek Orthodox church, a public holiday and the most important religious holiday in the Greek calendar (movable).

MAY: Labor Day and Flower Festival, a public holiday (1st).

The anniversary of the union of the Ionian islands with Greece, celebrated mostly on Corfu (21st).

"Hadjipetria" Festival in Trikkali, in the province of Thessaly (end of month).

JUNE: Wine Festivals at Daphni (11 km, or 6½ miles, from Athens), Rhodes, and other locations—wine-tasting, tavernas, dancing.

JULY: Wine Festival at Alexandroupolis (mid-month).

Athens Festival—drama, concerts, opera, ballet at Herod Aticus Theater (through September).

Epidaurus Festival—performances of ancient Greek drama in open-air theater (through August).

Northern Greece National Theater performances of ancient Greek drama in the open-air theaters at Philippi and on the island of Thassos.

"Dionysia" Wine Festival on island of Naxos (mid-month).

AUGUST: Ancient Greek dramas performed in the open-air theater at Diou, near Mount Olympus (mid-month).

Art exhibition on Skyros island (first week of month).

Holiday honoring the Virgin Mary, celebrated on the island of Tinos (15th).

SEPTEMBER: Thessaloniki International Trade Fair.
Film Festival and Festival of Light Music, Thessaloniki.

OCTOBER: Demetrius Festival—music, opera, ballet—in Thessaloniki.
National Anniversary (28th).

NOVEMBER: St. Andrew's Day, celebrating the patron saint of Patras (30th).

THE ALPHABET

A α	álfa	N ν	ní
B β	víta	Ξ ξ	xí
Γ γ	gáma	O o	ómikron
Δ δ	thèlta	Π π	pí
E ε	èpsilón	P ρ	ró
Z ζ	zíta	Σ σ	sígma
H η	íta	T τ	táf
Θ θ	thíta	Y υ	ipsilón
I ι	yóta	Φ φ	fí
K κ	kápa	X χ	hí
Λ λ	làmtha	Ψ ψ	psí
M μ	mí	Ω ω	oméga

LAST WORD: As I said earlier, every care has been taken to check and cross-check prices, dates, opening hours, and other facts in this guide. Inevitably, some of them may change before you sit down to plan your trip; there's little the author or publisher can do about such variations, which are the responsibility of governments, economies, oil sheiks, and other quirky factors. Nevertheless, the prices should not be off by more than 15% to 20%, except in unprecedented circumstances; use the figures in these pages as a basic guide, and if precise dollar-and-cents calculations are a critical matter, check out the detailed prices with your travel agent before you leave home.

Index

Note: Unless otherwise specified, all references are to Athens

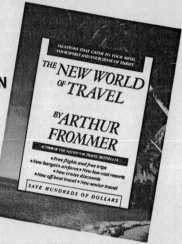

NOW, SAVE MONEY ON ALL YOUR TRAVELS!
Join Frommer's™ Dollarwise® Travel Club

Saving money while traveling is never a simple matter, which is why, over 27 years ago, the **Dollarwise Travel Club** was formed. Actually, the idea came from readers of the Frommer publications who felt that such an organization could bring financial benefits, continuing travel information, and a sense of community to economy-minded travelers all over the world.

In keeping with the money-saving concept, the annual membership fee is low—$18 (U.S. residents) or $20 U.S. (Canadian, Mexican, and foreign residents)—and is immediately exceeded by the value of your benefits which include:

1. The latest edition of any TWO of the books listed on the following pages.

2. A copy of any Frommer City Guide.

3. An annual subscription to an 8-page quarterly newspaper *The Dollarwise Traveler* which keeps you up-to-date on fastbreaking developments in good-value travel in all parts of the world—bringing you the kind of information you'd have to pay over $35 a year to obtain elsewhere. This consumer-conscious publication also includes the following columns:

> **Hospitality Exchange**—members all over the world who are willing to provide hospitality to other members as they pass through their home cities.
>
> **Share-a-Trip**—requests from members for travel companions who can share costs and help avoid the burdensome single supplement.
>
> **Readers Ask . . . Readers Reply**—travel questions from members to which other members reply with authentic firsthand information.

4. Your personal membership card which entitles you to purchase through the club all Frommer publications for a third to a half off their regular retail prices during the term of your membership.

So why not join this hardy band of international Dollarwise travelers now and participate in its exchange of information and hospitality? Simply send $18 (U.S. residents) or $20 U.S. (Canadian, Mexican, and other foreign residents) along with your name and address to: Frommer's Dollarwise Travel Club, Inc., Gulf + Western Building, One Gulf + Western Plaza, New York, NY 10023. Remember to specify which *two* of the books in section (1) and which *one* in section (2) above you wish to receive in your initial package of member's benefits. Or tear out the next page, check off your choices, and send the page to us with your membership fee.

FROMMER BOOKS
Date_____

PRENTICE HALL PRESS
ONE GULF + WESTERN PLAZA
NEW YORK, NY 10023

Friends:
Please send me the books checked below:

FROMMER'S™ $-A-DAY® GUIDES
(In-depth guides to sightseeing and low-cost tourist accommodations and facilities.)

☐ Europe on $30 a Day	$14.95	☐ New Zealand on $40 a Day	$12.95
☐ Australia on $30 a Day	$12.95	☐ New York on $50 a Day	$12.95
☐ Eastern Europe on $25 a Day	$12.95	☐ Scandinavia on $50 a Day	$12.95
☐ England on $40 a Day	$12.95	☐ Scotland and Wales on $40 a Day	$12.95
☐ Greece on $30 a Day	$12.95	☐ South America on $30 a Day	$12.95
☐ Hawaii on $50 a Day	$13.95	☐ Spain and Morocco (plus the Canary Is.)	
☐ India on $25 a Day	$12.95	on $40 a Day	$13.95
☐ Ireland on $30 a Day	$12.95	☐ Turkey on $25 a Day	$12.95
☐ Israel on $30 & $35 a Day	$12.95	☐ Washington, D.C., & Historic Va. on	
☐ Mexico (plus Belize & Guatemala)		$40 a Day	$12.95
on $25 a Day	$13.95		

FROMMER'S™ DOLLARWISE® GUIDES
(Guides to sightseeing and tourist accommodations and facilities from budget to deluxe, with emphasis on the medium-priced.)

☐ Alaska	$13.95	☐ Cruises (incl. Alask, Carib, Mex, Hawaii,	
☐ Austria & Hungary	$14.95	Panama, Canada, & US)	$14.95
☐ Belgium, Holland, Luxembourg	$13.95	☐ California & Las Vegas	$14.95
☐ Brazil	$14.95	☐ Florida	$13.95
☐ Egypt	$13.95	☐ Mid-Atlantic States	$13.95
☐ France	$14.95	☐ New England	$13.95
☐ England & Scotland	$14.95	☐ New York State	$13.95
☐ Germany	$13.95	☐ Northwest	$13.95
☐ Italy	$14.95	☐ Skiing in Europe	$14.95
☐ Japan & Hong Kong	$13.95	☐ Skiing USA—East	$13.95
☐ Portugal, Madeira, & the Azores	$13.95	☐ Skiing USA—West	$13.95
☐ South Pacific	$13.95	☐ Southeast & New Orleans	$13.95
☐ Switzerland & Liechtenstein	$13.95	☐ Southwest	$14.95
☐ Bermuda & The Bahamas	$13.95	☐ Texas	$13.95
☐ Canada	$13.95	☐ USA (avail. Feb. 1989)	$15.95
☐ Caribbean	$13.95		

FROMMER'S™ TOURING GUIDES
(Color illustrated guides that include walking tours, cultural & historic sites, and other vital travel information.)

☐ Australia	$9.95	☐ Paris	$8.95
☐ Egypt	$8.95	☐ Thailand	$9.95
☐ Florence	$8.95	☐ Venice	$8.95
☐ London	$8.95		

TURN PAGE FOR ADDITIONAL BOOKS AND ORDER FORM.

FROMMER'S™ CITY GUIDES

(Pocket-size guides to sightseeing and tourist accommodations and facilities in all price ranges.)

☐ Amsterdam/Holland $5.95	☐ Montreal/Quebec City. $5.95
☐ Athens. $5.95	☐ New Orleans. $5.95
☐ Atlantic City/Cape May $5.95	☐ New York. $5.95
☐ Boston. $5.95	☐ Orlando/Disney World/EPCOT $5.95
☐ Cancún/Cozumel/Yucatán. $5.95	☐ Paris $5.95
☐ Dublin/Ireland $5.95	☐ Philadelphia $5.95
☐ Hawaii. $5.95	☐ Rio (avail. Nov. 1988). $5.95
☐ Las Vegas. $5.95	☐ Rome. $5.95
☐ Lisbon/Madrid/Costa del Sol $5.95	☐ San Francisco $5.95
☐ London $5.95	☐ Santa Fe/Taos (avail. Mar. 1989) $5.95
☐ Los Angeles $5.95	☐ Sydney. $5.95
☐ Mexico City/Acapulco. $5.95	☐ Washington, D.C. $5.95
☐ Minneapolis/St. Paul $5.95	

SPECIAL EDITIONS

☐ A Shopper's Guide to the Caribbean. . $12.95	☐ Motorist's Phrase Book (Fr/Ger/Sp). . . $4.95
☐ Beat the High Cost of Travel $6.95	☐ Paris Rendez-Vous $10.95
☐ Bed & Breakfast—N. America $8.95	☐ Swap and Go (Home Exchanging). . . $10.95
☐ Guide to Honeymoon Destinations	☐ The Candy Apple (NY for Kids). $11.95
(US, Canada, Mexico, & Carib). $12.95	☐ Travel Diary and Record Book $5.95
☐ Manhattan's Outdoor Sculpture $15.95	☐ Where to Stay USA (Lodging from $3
	to $30 a night) $10.95

☐ Marilyn Wood's Wonderful Weekends (NY, Conn, Mass, RI, Vt, NH, NJ, Del, Pa) $11.95
☐ The New World of Travel (Annual sourcebook by Arthur Frommer previewing: new travel trends, new modes of travel, and the latest cost-cutting strategies for savvy travelers). $12.95

SERIOUS SHOPPER'S GUIDES

(Illustrated guides listing hundreds of stores, conveniently organized alphabetically by category)

☐ Italy. $15.95	☐ Los Angeles $14.95
☐ London $15.95	☐ Paris $15.95

GAULT MILLAU

(The only guides that distinguish the truly superlative from the merely overrated.)

☐ The Best of Chicago (avail. Feb. 1989) $15.95	☐ The Best of New England (avail. Feb.
☐ The Best of France (avail. Feb. 1989). . $15.95	1989) $15.95
☐ The Best of Italy (avail. Feb. 1989) . . . $15.95	☐ The Best of New York. $15.95
☐ The Best of Los Angeles $15.95	☐ The Best of San Francisco $15.95
	☐ The Best of Washington, D.C. $15.95

ORDER NOW!

In U.S. include $1.50 shipping UPS for 1st book; 50¢ ea. add'l book. Outside U.S. $2 and 50¢, respectively. Allow four to six weeks for delivery in U.S., longer outside U.S.

Enclosed is my check or money order for $_____

NAME _____

ADDRESS _____

CITY _____ STATE _____ ZIP _____